AN ALTERNATIVE PHILOSOPHY OF DEVELOPMENT

While development has been the foremost agenda before successive governments in India, it has been viewed narrowly – from the perspective of economic development and particularly in terms of gross domestic product (GDP). This book questions such an approach. It breaks from the conventional wisdom of GDP growth as being a definitive measure of the success of a country's policies and offers an alternative development philosophy.

The author contends that people's economic and social welfare, life satisfaction, self-fulfilment and happiness should be treated as indicators of real development. The book underlines that in a successful model of development, the country's economic policies will have to synergize with its cultural ethos and that the objective of development should be gross national happiness and well-being of the people.

This book will be useful to scholars and researchers of development studies, economics, public policy and administration, governance, political science and sociology, as well as to policymakers.

Birendra Prasad Mathur is a former civil servant and member of the Indian Audit and Accounts Service with extensive experience of working with the government. He has served as Deputy Comptroller and Auditor General and Additional Secretary, Government of India; and Director, National Institute of Financial Management, India. He holds a PhD and DLitt in Economics from the University of Allahabad, India, and has been a visiting faculty member at Panjab University, Chandigarh; Bajaj Institute of Management, Mumbai; Indian Institute of Public Administration, New Delhi, and many other national-level institutes. He is presently engaged as a spiritual seeker, author and social activist with spiritual interests. He is Vice-President, Common Cause. He has authored several books on governance, finance and economics, besides two novels in Hindi, and is the recipient of the Paul Appleby Award for services rendered for public administration.

'The author brings the light of vast experience and deep reflection in critiquing the prevailing economic narrative based on the neo-liberal free market capitalist model that has failed in solving human problems of poverty, injustice and inequality. He offers an alternate model of wholesome development that ensures sustainable progress, universal justice and peaceful coexistence. In this effort he pits the Gandhian economics premised on freedom from greed, possession and violence against the Adam Smith and Darwin-inspired economics of private property, mindless competition and free trade, and convincingly shows the superiority of the Gandhian model in ensuring gross human happiness. A seminal work in understanding contemporary economic and social woes and finding alternate ways of effective problem solving.'

Swami Bodhananda, Vedanta exponent and chairman, Sambodh Foundation India and Sambodh Society, USA

'This book gets back to the foundations of India's religion based on the concept of universal humanism (*vishwa kutumb*) rather than viewing religion as a political instrument. It is both provocative and practical, and blends India's culture with the international literature on "happiness". It is also very readable in its practical discussion of India's economy.'

Y. K. Alagh, Chancellor, Central University of Gujarat and Former Minister for Power, Planning and Science and Technology, Government of India

AN ALTERNATIVE PHILOSOPHY OF DEVELOPMENT

From economism to human well-being

Birendra Prasad Mathur

Routledge
Taylor & Francis Group

LONDON AND NEW YORK

First published 2017 by Routledge

2 Park Square, Milton Park, Abingdon, Oxfordshire OX14 4RN

52 Vanderbilt Avenue, New York, NY 10017

Routledge is an imprint of the Taylor & Francis Group, an informa business

First issued in paperback 2019

British Library Cataloguing in Publication Data
A catalogue record for this book is available from the British Library

Library of Congress Cataloging in Publication Data
A catalog record for this book has been requested

ISBN: 978-1-138-69312-8 (hbk)
ISBN: 978-0-367-27967-7 (pbk)

Typeset in Sabon
by Apex CoVantage, LLC

CONTENTS

CONTENTS

ILLUSTRATIONS

Tables

Boxes

PREFACE

This book is the outcome of my realization about the depth and charm of our ancient culture and civilization and the relevance of the wisdom contained therein, for our social and economic policymaking. India's ancient wisdom as expressed in the Bhagavad Gita, Upanishad and other scriptures gives meaning and purpose to human beings' existence on this planet earth and how to lead a happy and fulfilling life. It was this philosophy which inspired Swami Vivekananda, Rabindranath Tagore, Mahatma Gandhi and countless other noble men and women to usher in an Indian renaissance, with a view to not only give it political freedom but also liberate its suppressed soul. Indian philosophy has inspired some of the best minds in the West in the past two to three centuries, and today it exercises a defining influence in America, the land of riches, with a large section of the population practising yoga and meditation and moving away from a materialistic orientation of life.

Today as I look around, seven decades after independence, India is not a very hospitable place to live in. There is growing intolerance and violence in society. Our educational system is in disarray, and medical services are non-existent, except for the rich. The cities are crumbling, streets choked, slums mushrooming and garbage piled all over. A new class of super-rich has come up, leading a life of opulence and luxury with poverty all around. It is all a case of private affluence and public squalor. Much of our problems is due to the model of development we have adopted, which considers material progress or economic growth as the sole measure of people's welfare. We are blindly imitating the current ruling economic ideology of the West, without understanding the strength of those societies. The success of Western countries is largely due to their value system. Protestant ethics, which shaped these societies in the past two centuries, emphasized honesty, hard work, discipline and thrift. The Enlightenment movement brought the age of reason, scientific spirit, rule of law and democracy.

Successful development can take place only when it is built on the foundation of a country's cultural values. Indian culture is ethico-spiritual and believes in 'simple living and high thinking'. According to Indian thought, the spirit pervades the whole universe, and the material world is merely a manifestation of that spirit. Human beings have not only physical and biological dimensions but also psychological and spiritual dimensions. It is the spiritual dimension of human beings that gives rise to noble values such as truth, honesty, love, sharing, community spirit and service. On the other hand, materialistic values give rise to baser motives such as selfishness, corruption and greed.

In this book I have tried to present a philosophy of development whose foundation should rest on India's cultural ethos, which is 'spiritual' as distinct from 'materialistic'. This is best expressed in one of our famous prayers – *sarve bhavantu sukhina, sarvesantu niramayah* (may all be happy, may all be healthy). We need to resist the temptation of becoming a consumerist society with materialist values, where money becomes the prime motivator of human endeavour. All the religions of the world are deeply concerned with the problem of 'corrupting influence of money', which inter alia creates a vast economic inequality in society. The foundation of socialist philosophy is also built on the doctrine of equality, and our policies should pursue this goal. Mahatma Gandhi had emphasized that economics cannot be divorced from ethics and viewed development against the broader domain of human dignity, employment and elimination of poverty and deprivation. Therefore, public policy should promote egalitarian policies, which means a system of management in which life chances are not allocated by structural inequalities in social, economic and political power.

I worked in civil service for almost four decades, in Government of India ministries, audit department and public enterprise, and have first-hand experience of government's economic and financial policymaking and its implementation. I found the ideas of economists, who dominate policymaking in India, have often no relation to ground reality and are damaging our national interest (e.g. the doctrine of free trade, dismantling public enterprises in core sectors of the economy, privatization of higher education and health). This is largely because a vast majority of them are under intellectual influence of Western academic thought. Our leaders had warned us against blind imitation of Western ideas and values and becoming their intellectual slaves. We need to liberate our thinking and produce a philosophy of development indigenous to our native wisdom.

I present this study in all humility as a 'work in progress' and hope it throws some ideas for more research and exploration of the subject. I feel the philosophy of development should be rooted in our cultural and civilizational ethos, which lays emphasis on nurturing a humane and socially conscious individual. That will help us to create a peaceful, happy and prosperous India. According to me, India has a great future if only it adheres to its ancient cultural and spiritual values and is not overwhelmed by the forces of so-called modernization, which, in effect, means the materialist consumerist culture of the Western world and the brutality of its commercial civilization.

ACKNOWLEDGEMENTS

Swami Bodhananda, chairman of Sambodh Foundation, introduced me to Vedantic philosophy and made me understand its relevance for modern-day management. It is only through the inspiration given by him that I could take up the task of writing this book. I had also the privilege of receiving the blessings of Swami Jnanananda Giri of Barlowganj Mussourie/ Dehradun, who explained to me India's unique message of love, renunciation and unity of all beings and the importance of transcending this material world to attain peace and happiness. Swami Ji attained *mahasmadhi* (left for heavenly abode) in November 2015, but his legacy continues.

During my long professional carrier, as well as post-retirement, I received support and guidance from a large number of officers of civil services, Indian Audit and Accounts Service, Indian Administrative Service and others, besides defence service officers – the list of my benefactors is so large that I do not find it possible to enumerate them individually. In my academic forays, I greatly benefitted from my interaction with several distinguished professors and scholars of my alma mater, University of Allahabad; Panjab University, Chandigarh; Indian Institute of Public Administration, New Delhi; and National Institute of Financial Management, Faridabad, and I owe a debt of gratitude to them.

My family members provided me full support and encouragement which helped me in pursuing my academic interest. My wife Abha has been a pillar of strength and provided me a serene and congenial atmosphere at home which enabled me to complete the task of writing this book.

The publication of this book has been possible due to support given by the editorial team of Routledge, who are committed to promote works of scholarship and carry forward the flame of knowledge. I am deeply beholden to Dr Shashank Sinha who took special interest to see this publication through.

Besides students of development, this study is meant for general readers. Issues relating to employment, education, health, food and agricultural produce, industrial products, public expenditure, taxation, export–import matrix affect everyone in society, and therefore, the common man should have a right to express his views on them. Experts who make policies often hide behind esoteric theories, making their ideas unintelligible to common man. Einstein had cautioned that we should be on our guard against experts and their scientific methods, when it is a case of human problem. I have tried to demystify some of the development issues, which are of interest to ordinary citizens, and digressed from 'conventional wisdom' on the subject. I trust the readers will find the study interesting and stimulating.

May 2016

1

INDIA'S CULTURAL AND CIVILIZATIONAL ETHOS AND CHALLENGE OF DEVELOPMENT

> I love India not because I cultivate the idolatry of geography, not because I have had the chance to be born on her soil but because she has saved, through tumultuous ages, the living words that have issued from the illumined consciousness of her great sons – *Satyam Jnanam Anantam Brahma*: Brahma is Truth, Brahma is wisdom, Brahma is infinite; *Santam Sivam Advaitam*: Peace is in Brahma, goodness is in Brahma, and the unity of all beings.
>
> Rabindranath Tagore[1]

India attained independence on 15 August 1947 with great hope and aspiration. Pandit Jawaharlal Nehru, the first prime minister of India, proclaimed that 'India is waking up to life and freedom' and 'the soul of nation will find utterance'. But the promised dawn is nowhere in sight. The vision of a happy and prosperous society has been eluding us, even seven decades after independence. There is widespread poverty, unemployment, illiteracy and malnutrition in the country. Corruption has seeped every aspect of the society. Criminal elements rule the society, and women are not safe on the streets. India is at the bottom of Human Development Index prepared by the United Nations Development Programme (UNDP). The disenchantment of people led to the overthrow of the United Progressive Alliance government in May 2014, led by Congress which had ruled the country for most of the years since independence. A Bharatiya Janata Party–led National Democratic Alliance government with Narendra Modi as prime minister has come to power on the plank of 'development' agenda. However, the initial euphoria is slowly dying down, and the promise of a better life for people is nowhere in sight. The national mood continues to be one of helplessness, frustration and anger.

We need to realize that nation building cannot be done without high idealism, imbibing positive values and dedicated work. There are no quick-fix solutions. There is need to reflect and make a sobering appraisal as to why the country has come to its current situation. Not to compare with Western countries which enjoy a high standard of living, East Asian countries such as

Singapore, South Korea, Taiwan and China, which were at a similar stage of economic development as India in the 1950s and 1960s, have leapfrogged as developed or middle-income countries, leaving India far behind. What has gone wrong with the nation? How is it that a country possessing such great cultural heritage and rich economic resources reeling under the burden of poverty, unemployment and deprivation and has become a violent and intolerant society?

Our problems are largely due to two reasons: poor governance and wrong economic policies. The political leaders' sole aim is to ingratiate themselves into power. Once in power they manipulate every instrument at their disposal, to keep themselves in 'perpetual power', with scant regard to people's welfare. This results in stunting development and people remaining trapped in poverty, ignorance and backwardness. Tragically we are proving true Winston Churchill's diatribe pronounced at the time we were being given independence, 'Power will go into the hands of rascals, rogues and freebooters. . . . They will fight among themselves and India will be lost in squabbles.'

Good governance holds key to prosperity and well-being of the country. B. P. Mathur has written two books, *Ethics in Governance* and *Governance Reform for Vision India*,[2] discussing various aspects of this issue and outlining measures to put in place an ethical and value-based governance structure (see Chapter 14). However, good governance cannot be given in a vacuum. It is the economy which directly effects the economic well-being of people. In this book we address the issue of 'economic well-being' of people and how it can be secured by following 'the right economic policies', which is central to people's leading a decent and satisfying life.

Problem with current economic model

The economic development model that we have currently adopted is a blind imitation of Western ideas and ideology. The model is the product of our academic elite trained in the West, who are dazzled by the West's economic opulence and do not realize its unworkability in Indian conditions. There is total disconnect of this model with India's civilizational and cultural ethos; as a result, we are unable to solve the problems people face in their day-to-day living.

The current economic thinking in the West, driven by the US, is of *economism* – which believes that people are primarily 'economic men', driven solely by the desire of material goods and work to fulfil them, ignoring values such as quality of life, social justice, community feeling, love and sharing. Under economism, earning money and making profit becomes the summum bonum of life. Americans called the 20th century as the century of business. American president Calvin Coolidge said, 'The chief business of American people is business.' Henry Luce, founder of *Time* magazine, announced (1937), 'Make money, be proud of it, make more money, be prouder of it,' and Wall Street's nickname Gordon Gekko announced, 'Greed is good, greed is right, Greed works.'[3] America with its belief in capitalist philosophy of free enterprise no doubt became the most prosperous and powerful economy of the world. This ideology, practised with no holds barred, found its full expression in the neoliberal model of economic development, whose intellectual support came from Nobel Prize–winning economist Milton Friedman and his Chicago school and had the backing of powerful institutions such as the World Bank, International Monetary Fund and World Trade Organization. The philosophy believes in free play of market forces and emphasizes deregulation, liberalization, privatization and globalization. This model is based on a continuous growth of production and consumption of goods and services, irrespective of its social and economic utility. The corporates' and businesses' vested interest dictates this model. They are driven solely by profit motive. So long as production and sales are increasing, the gross domestic product (GDP) number would grow and keep the corporate and business sectors happy.

The economic downturn faced by the US and Western European countries from 2008 onwards, the aftermath of which they are unable to recover, shows the hollowness of free market ideology. This model creates serious socio-economic problems in society, such as rising inequality, consumerist culture and high level of unemployment, and is detrimental to ecology. Nobel Prize–winning economist Joseph Stiglitz observes that what has gone on can be described as 'moral deprivation', 'something has happened to our sense of values, when the end of making more money justifies the means, which in the US sub-prime crisis meant exploiting the poor and least-educated among us'.[4] Elaborating further he says that financial crisis has made us realize that economic system is not only inefficient and unstable but also fundamentally unfair. 'Capitalism is failing to produce what was promised, but is delivering on what was not promised – inequality, pollution, unemployment, and, most important of all, the degradation of values to the point where everything is acceptable and no one is accountable.'[5] Analysing the reason for the downturn of American economy, Jeffrey Sachs, another distinguished economist, comments,

> Our greatest national illusion is that a healthy society can be organized around the single-minded pursuit of wealth. The ferocity of the quest for wealth throughout society has left Americans exhausted and deprived of the benefits of social trust, honesty and compassion.[6]

Private splendour and public squalor

Making a break from the past, India has embraced a new liberalized economic policy from 1991, reposing full faith in market economy, kowtowing West's economic ideology. This has no doubt helped faster economic growth and created an ambitious upward mobile middle class. However, the sole aim of this class is to attain personal and material success, in terms of acquisition of money, power and prestige. A culture has been created in society which encourages the single-minded pursuit of economic success and believes that a good life is one in which a person has unrestricted enjoyment of sensuous pleasures and indulges in unabashed consumerism. In the past two decades a new class of billionaires has emerged. According to studies by experts, India has today more than 100 billionaires, with their combined wealth equivalent to almost one-fourth of the country's GDP. However, the growth in the economy is taking place at great socio-economic cost with vast increase in income inequalities in the society. According to the National Commission for the Enterprises in the Unorganised Sector (2009), chaired by Arjun Sengupta, the benefit of growth is being cornered by upper 20 per cent of the population.[7] The commission found that 84 crore Indians are poor and vulnerable, living on less than Rs 20 per day and experience hardly any improvement in living standards since the early 1990s. Even according to official estimates, which are conservative, 30 per cent of the population is living below poverty line. Another 50 per cent is living on the margin and barely eke out a living. Experts point out that squeezing labour has become the driving force of India's high growth rate, and the profits do not trickle down but are siphoned off to higher echelons in the chain of economic activity. In cities, India's affluent retreat into gated communities and high-rise apartments to a world of privatized education, health care and security and what we see all around: oases of private splendour in an ocean of public squalor.

Values, culture and human progress

The history of Western countries, from the time of the Industrial Revolution of the 18th century onwards, shows that they have achieved spectacular progress and prosperity on the foundation of a strong value system. Max Weber in his seminal work *Protestant Ethics and Spirit of Capitalism* has stressed on the cultural origin of capitalism. Protestantism, particularly its Calvinism version, defined and sanctioned an ethics of everyday behaviour that was conducive to economic success. It emphasized the virtues of hard work, dedication, honesty and thrift and produced a new kind of individual who lived and worked in a certain way. Weber emphasized that a good Calvinist did not aim at riches; it was the way that mattered, and riches were at best a by-product. Tom Peters and Robert Waterman in their well-known book, *In Search of Excellence*, explain that excellent companies have a sound set of values and it is this basic philosophy and spirit which has far more to do with their achievement than do technological or organizational resources and organizational structure. Excellent companies have a deeply ingrained philosophy of respecting human resource, rather than treating them as factors of production and cog in the industrial machine.

The success of Japan as a modern industrialized nation has been largely due to its work ethics, which was profoundly influenced by Buddhism. According to Buddhism, the function of work is to enable an individual to develop himself, help and assist others and produce goods and services needed for meaningful existence. This is best reflected by the Matsushita philosophy, a leading Japanese company, which gives meaning beyond the products it produces and emphasizes nationalism and spiritual values. The Matsushita values are national service through industry, fairness, harmony and cooperation, struggle for betterment, courtesy and humility, adjustment and assimilation and gratitude. The rise of East Asian countries, such as Singapore, South Korea and Taiwan, described as Asian Tigers, is attributed to Confucian values such as hard work, thrift, devotion to family and group loyalty. Confucianism emphasized virtuous human character in terms of generosity, righteousness, wisdom and trust.

The Indian philosophy towards work is most eloquently expressed in Bhagawad Gita's doctrine of *karmayog* (doing one's duty): *Karmanayevadhikaraste ma phalesu kadachana* – your right is only to action, never to the fruit thereof (47/II), and *Yogah karmasu kausalam* – excellence in action is Yoga (50/II). You should do your work with utmost dedication and *move* beyond desire-prompted selfish action. Life will be enriched by the accomplishment of right action, rather than outward success or failure. Honest work is the very insignia of life, and therefore, one should put one's heart and soul in it, and pursue excellence, and that will be service to society as well as give self-fulfilment to an individual. Gita extols the spirit of *yagna*; while performing one's duty, one should dedicate it to higher altar and do it in a spirit of service to society.

While our scripture and ancient wisdom set noble ideals towards work and duty, the whole country suffers from poor work culture and all-pervading inefficiency and sloth. This is largely due to the fact that our leadership is unable to inspire people to be disciplined and do hard work and dedicate themselves towards national development. The political leadership has created an environment and societal values that have created an anti-work culture in the country. All work organizations are instruments of national development in two specific ways: first, they create wealth through high productivity, efficiency and surplus generation; and second, they promote social justice through equitable distribution of wealth and employment opportunities. Somehow, aspects relating to social justice have taken precedence to one's relating to wealth generation, whereas employment provision has become an end itself. Public servants in particular view government as an unlimited supply of resources and benefits which are not contingent on their hard work. The politicians in order to win elections promise numerous 'entitlements' and create 'right-consciousness' in society without accompaniment of 'duty-consciousness'. While individuals zealously fight for their rights through human rights bodies and other similar institutions, they consider duty and responsibility to society, even those given as fundamental duties in the Constitution, an unnecessary burden and a cosmetic appendage.

History of civilization tells us that no society has progressed without hard and dedicated work. During my visit to Germany, the US and other European countries, I have found that people in relation to their work and duty, particularly the elite, practise the philosophy of *karmayog*. The general public in Western societies are highly disciplined and law abiding and perform their duties in the spirit of 'work is worship'.

David Landes, a Harvard scholar, who examines the question of the rise of Western civilization, says that in the final analysis it boils down to attitudes and culture. Protestant countries stressed on literacy for both boys and girls – a by-product of Bible reading – and accorded great importance to time – most clockmakers were Protestants. Protestant Reformation 'gave big boost to literacy, spawned dissents and heresies, and promoted skepticism and refusal of authority that is at the heart of scientific endeavour'.[8] If we learn anything from the history of economic development, it is that culture makes all the difference. Landes observes: 'The most successful cure for poverty comes from within. . . . what counts is work, thrift, honesty, patience, tenacity. . . . No empowerment is so effective as self-empowerment. . . . You want high productivity? Then you should live to work and get happiness as a by-product.'[9]

Contemporary historian Niall Ferguson[10] says that six ideas and institutions were responsible for the ascendency of the West over the rest. They are as follows: (1) competition – decentralization of both political and economic life, which created the launch pad for both nation-states and capitalism; (2) science – a way of studying, understanding and ultimately changing the natural world, which also gave the West military advantage; (3) property rights – these included rule of law which helped form stable representative governments; (4) medicine – helped improve health and life expectancy; (5) consumer society – production and trading of goods which helped sustain the Industrial Revolution; and (6) work ethic – a moral framework derivable from Protestant Christianity.

The prosperity of the Western countries is rooted in their cultural and civilizational ethos and not in some quick-fix economic ideology. From the 17th century onwards began an age of enlightenment, reason and scientific spirit, which profoundly shaped European societies. This gave birth to democratic ideals of equality, freedom and liberty, rule of law and application of science and technology, which helped launching of the Industrial Revolution. Today these features of Western culture, which are based on objective reality and universal human nature, are open to everyone, transcending geography and race. Over time they have become humanity's culture. These values are reflected in the charter of the United Nations, which aims at everyone living in peace and harmony, and the Declaration of Human Rights (1948), which recognizes inherent dignity and inalienable rights of everyone to freedom, justice and peace, as well as economic, social, political and cultural rights. India has embraced these values in its Constitution. Thus, democratic values of freedom, liberty, equality and social and economic justice are an article of faith with it.

Kishore Mahbubani,[11] a Singaporean diplomat and academic, argues that the recent rise of Asian countries is largely due to the fact that they have discovered and absorbed some of the key pillars of Western wisdom, which underpinned the Western progress. 'They are rising now because through a very slow and painful process they have finally discovered the pillars of western wisdom that underpinned Western progress and enabled West to outperform Asian societies for past two centuries.'[12] First, it was Japan in the late 19th and early 20th centuries, later it was Singapore, South Korea and Taiwan and now it is China, with India following behind. These seven pillars are free market economies; science and technology; meritocracy; pragmatism – no ideological perceptions and blinkers and taking the best practices; culture of peace and understanding; rule of law – protecting individual citizen from arbitrary use of power by government; and education – making education accessible to everyone and developing great centres of learning.

It needs to be appreciated that beyond certain values which are now universally accepted, there are significant differences in the cultural tradition of every society and civilization, and they have to set their development goals keeping those values in view. Lee Kuan Yew, former Singapore head of state, and Mahathir Mohamad, prime minister of Malaysia, talked about Asian values. These included respect for authority, hard work, thrift community being more important than individual and their Confucian underpinnings. They discounted certain aspects of human rights, to the discomfort of the Western liberals, on the ground that community is more important than individual.

Indian and Western cultural values

Attitudes, values, ideas, beliefs and social forms, which are passed on from one generation to another in a society, are generally referred to as culture. They play an important role in human behaviour and progress. A development model to be successful should be rooted in cultural values of the society. In Western cultural tradition earning wealth has become summum bonum of life. On the other hand, India's philosophy, while it recognized money and wealth as important, never regarded it as the ultimate aim of life. A famous Upanishadic saying is *tena tyaktena bhunjeethaah maa gridhah kasya chit dhanam* (enjoy wealth but in a detached manner and do not covet it). While earning wealth and prosperity is desirable, the enjoyment of such wealth for limitless personal wants and without sharing it with others is something to be frowned upon. India's ancient wisdom recognizes *trivarga* (three goals of life), which are *artha, kama* and *dharma* (wealth, pleasure and righteous action). While the desire for *artha* and *kama* is perfectly legitimate activity, they must remain within the bounds of *dharma*. *Dharma* is that which sustains and ensures progress and welfare of everyone in this world and embraces every type of righteous conduct essential for the sustenance and welfare of the individual and society.

The foundation of Indian culture rests on an ethico-spiritual view of life. The salient features of Indian culture can be described as tolerance and accommodation of everyone, oneness and solidarity of universe and all life, essential divinity of human being and family as basic unit of social system. Throughout history India has assimilated various religions and cultures with which it has come in contact. All faiths, races, languages, customs and traditions overlap in the salad bowl of India. This is reflected in the statement *vasudhaiva kutumbakam* (the world is one family).

Indian culture is distinct from Western culture. What distinguishes Indian culture from Western culture is the approach towards life.[13] Indian culture is predominantly a 'spiritual culture', which requires control over one's passions and senses and development of qualities of sympathy, empathy, comradeship and brotherhood. Indian culture supports humanistic values such as freedom of thought, compassion and service to fellow human beings. The orientation of spiritually dominated culture is that of 'welfare', 'social good' or the 'good of the greatest numbers'.

On the other hand, Western culture is predominantly 'materialistic'. A materialistic culture is guided by 'economic orientation', and its approach is the 'bottom line approach'. Western societies have certain values like independence, initiative, achievement, objectivity and impartiality. They also respect values such as 'individualism', 'competition', 'survival of the fittest' and 'self-centredness'. These values have grown in an environment where adults shun family protection and fend for themselves.

Economic orientation of Western values

While many of the values, originally nurtured by the West such as democracy, freedom, liberty, meritocracy and application of science and technology to production process, have become universal values and have been embraced by every country of the world, there is a serious problem with values such as individualism, competition and survival of the fittest. They give materialistic orientation to life and treat money and profit making as an ultimate value. Such an attitude leads to fierce competition, finding markets for goods and domination over other people. Historian K. M. Pannicker in his book *Asia and Western Dominance* pointed out that it was promotion of Britain's trading and commercial interests which provided the impulse to colonize India and subjugate it to the British political will.

Economic theory as it developed over the years has given predominance to materialistic aspects of life. Adam Smith had famously said in his *Wealth of Nations* (1776) that it is 'self-interest' that motivates people and the market beautifully harnesses the energy of selfish individuals. Thus, self-interest promotes competition, competition promotes markets and markets promote provisioning of goods and services and creation of wealth. Markets in this theory are supposed to provide automatic corrective to human failings. The economic downturn of Western countries from 2008 onwards has shown the fallacy of this theory. Jeffrey Sachs says,

> The US now stands at the extreme of the high income world in a consistent pattern of allowing market forces to penetrate or even dominate all facets of society. Health care, basic education, and child care are all commercialized in the US, as are military forces, arms manufacturing, and media access for election campaigns.[14]

Harvard political philosopher Michael Sanders[15] expresses serious worry for American society where everything is for sale. 'These uses of markets to allocate health, education, public safety, national security, criminal justice, environmental protection, recreation, procreation, and other social goods were most part unheard of thirty years ago.' The commodification of everything has sharpened the sting of inequality, 'as money comes to buy more and more – political influence, good medical care, a home in a safe neighbourhood rather than crime ridden one, access to elite school rather than failing ones – the distribution of income looms larger and larger'. Markets have corrosive influence and 'putting a price on good things in life can corrupt them'.

An ideology which separates ethics from economics and glorifies self-interest and Mammon worship, and making money by whatever means possible, has been responsible for most of the current problems in the world economy, as well as in India. It leads to greed, corruption and debasement of human beings. Scholar and poet Santikumar Ghosh comments,

> A tide of world-weariness has come upon the Western world. Most of the cultured men and women there are already weary of competition, the struggle, the brutality of their commercial civilization – the materialist consumer culture. . . . In the midst of the technological triumphs of high industrialism, man finds himself afflicted with a sense of alienation and inner loneliness which increasingly gives rise to frightful psychological maladies and weaken the will to live and let live. . . . Westerners have become richer, they haven't on average become happier. Gross National Happiness – encompassing material satisfaction and spiritual fulfillment – is more important than gross National Product.[16]

An economic system based on the assumption that people are not moral agents is fundamentally flawed. The world would not have survived if the bulk of people have no respect for moral values. India's cultural foundation is built on the foundation that people are manifestation of divine and ethical and are motivated by honesty, altruism and service to fellow human beings. Swami Vivekananda said, 'Each soul is potentially divine. The goal is to manifest this divinity within by controlling nature, external and internal.'[17] Ethics helps in mitigating the misery of the poor in a world of intense competition with the Darwinian principles of the survival of the fittest. Philosopher Immanuel Kant expressed this in picturesque words, 'Two things fill the mind with admiration and awe, the heavens with stars above, and the moral law within.'[18]

A humanistic approach

Humanism concerns with the well-being of people. It means showing concern, kindness and compassion towards fellow human beings and developing a harmonious relationship among one another. Taking a holistic view, Mahatma Gandhi had rejected a pure economic man. He felt that economics cannot be divorced from ethics:

> True economics never militates against the highest ethical stand-ards, just as all true ethics to be worth its name must be at the same time be also good economics. An economics that inculcates Mammon worship, and enables the strong to amass the wealth at the expense of the weak, is a false and dismal science. It spells death. True economics on the other hand promotes social justice, it promotes the good of all equally, including the weakest, and is indispensable for decent life.[19]

It may be noted that Mahatma Gandhi was not against development but perceived it against the broader domain of human dignity, full employ-ment and elimination of poverty, hunger and deprivation. Gandhian perspective did not view development in a narrow perspective of GDP growth, but essentially in terms of human development.

Taking a broader view of the development process, United Nations Development Programme (UNDP) has been bringing out the Human Development Report since 1990, recognizing that 'people are the real wealth of a nation'. Pioneered by Pakistani economist Mahbub ul Haq and supported by Nobel laureate Amartya Sen and other like-minded academicians, it recognizes that a country's success and an individual's well-being cannot be measured by money alone, and we must evaluate whether people are leading healthy lives, are educated and have the oppor-tunity to shape their own destinies. According to UNDP the core principle of development should be creation of an enabling environment for people to enjoy long, healthy and creative lives and its foundation should rest on the principle of equity, sustainability and empowerment.[20]

For the past almost seven decades India has experimented with an eco-nomic development model based on Western ideas and ideology, but it has not solved any of its problems and we continue to be trapped in poverty, illiteracy and deprivation. We need to realize that an economic system based on GDP growth and relentless consumerism is fundamen-tally flawed and is responsible for current global crisis and ecological devastation as well as social problems of inequality and unemployment, and it cannot be a model for us. The leaders of Indian renaissance such as Swami Vivekananda, Rabindranath Tagore, Sri Aurbindo and Mahatma Gandhi had warned us the dangers of imitating Western values, ideas and ideology, which are alien to India's time-tested culture and civilization and have withstood the ravages of 5,000 years of history.

Celebrated historian Arnold Toynbee in his classic *A Study of History* observes that the transportation of foreign cultural values on another civilization could have a disconcerting effect,

> [We] shall find that a culture-element which has been harm-less or beneficial in the body social in which it is at home is

apt to produce novel and devastating effects into an alien body in which it has intruded – a law which is summarized in the proverb: one man's meat is another man's poison. . . . The attempt to introduce one element of culture, while excluding the rest, is doomed to failure.[21]

Michel Danino, a contemporary French scholar and spiritual seeker, who has made India his home, makes a forceful point that 'the only way to build India on sound foundation – not the transient one's of today's economic boom' is to reconquer the political battlefield, on the strength of its 'culture' and manifest its human substance, as it has a divine essence. If like an old banyan tree today the Indian civilization is weighed down by some dead branches and overgrown thorns, they should be chopped off and the tree be given a new youth. In the past, Indian civilization has been prodigiously creative; it left footprints in numerous countries abroad in the fields of spirituality, religion, philosophy, language, literature, art, mathematics, astronomy and medicine. This outflow in colonial times impacted Western literature and philosophies and in our time has led to widespread practices of yoga and meditation. 'For in the world of ideal . . . India is more than a piece of land; she is a continent of humanity's inner geography: a quest for the true, the beautiful, the lovable.'[22]

The following chapters analyse the huge socio-economic problems facing the country and call for an alternative model of development, which should be humane and focus on overall economic and social well-being of people. Only a model rooted in India's cultural and civilizational ethos, which takes into account not only material but also psychological and spiritual dimensions of human beings, can provide a satisfied, fulfilling and happy life to people.

Notes

1 Rabindranath Tagore, 'A Vision of India's History', in S. Jeyaseela Stephen (ed.), *The Sky of Indian History Themes and Thoughts of Rabindranath Tagore*, New Delhi: UBSPD, 2010, pp. 100–101.

2 B. P. Mathur, *Ethics in Governance: Reinventing Public Services*, New Delhi: Routledge, 2014; *Governance Reform for Vision India*, New Delhi: Macmillan, 2005.

3 'Time 100 Series, Builders & Titans', *Time* Magazine, 7 December 1998, p. 24.

4 Joseph E. Stiglitz, *The Price of Inequality*, London: Allen Lane, 2012, p. xvii.

5 Ibid., pp. xiv, xviii.

6 Jeffrey Sachs, *The Price of Civilization: Economics and Ethics after the Fall*, London: The Bodley Head, 2011, p. 9.

7 National Commission for the Enterprises in the Unorganised Sector (NCEUS), *The Challenge of Unemployment in India: An Informal Economy Perspective*, April 2009, available at http://nceuis.nic.in/The_Challenge_of_Employ ment_in_India.pdf.

8 David Landes, *The Wealth and Poverty of Nations: Why Some Are So Rich and Some So Poor*, London: W. W. Norton & Co., 1998, pp. 178–179; also

see David Landes, 'Culture Makes All the Difference', in Lawrence E. Harrison and Samuel P. Huntington (eds), *Culture Matters*, New York: Basic Books, 2000, pp. 2–13.

9 Ibid., pp. 516, 523.

10 Niall Ferguson, *Civilization: The West and the Rest*, London: Allen Lane, 2011, pp. 12–13.

11 Kishore Mahbubani, *The New Asian Hemisphere: The Irresistible Shift of the Global Power to the East*, New York: Public Affairs, 2008, Chapter 2, pp. 51–99.

12 Ibid., p. 52.

13 G. D. Sharma, *Management and the Indian Ethos*, New Delhi: Rupa, 2001, pp. 1–43.

14 Jefferey Sachs, *The Price of Civilization*, London: Bodley Head, 2011, pp. xii, xiii.

15 Michael Sanders, *What Money Can't Buy: The Moral Limits of Markets*, London: Penguin Books, 2012, pp. 8–9.

16 Santikumar Ghosh, *Universal Values*, Kolkata: The Ramakrishna Institute of Culture, 2004, pp. 109–111.

17 *The Complete Works of Swami Vivekananda*, Vol. 1, Calcutta: Advaita Ashram, 1965, p, 257.

18 Kant, *Critique of Pure Reason*, excerpt given in *Immortal Words, An Anthology*, Bombay: Bhartiya Vidya Bhavan, 1990, pp. 148–149.

19 M. K. Gandhi, *India of My Dreams*, compiled by R. K. Prabhu, Ahmedabad: Navjivan Press, 2011, p. 71; *Harijan*, 9 October 1937.

20 UNDP, *Human Development Report 2010: The Real Wealth of Nations: Pathways to Human Development*, New York: United Nations Development Programme, 2010, pp. 1–9.

21 Arnold Toynbee, *A Study of History, Abridgement of Volumes VII–X by D. C. Somervell*, London: Readers Union, Oxford University Press, 1960, pp. 222, 388.

22 Michel Danino, *Indian Culture and India's Future*, New Delhi: D. K. Printworld, 2015, especially refer pp. 16, 21, 42, 215.

Part I

THE CURRENT
SOCIO-ECONOMIC SETTING

2

SEARCH FOR ECONOMIC WELL-BEING

The GDP measures everything except that, which makes life worth living.

Robert Kennedy (1968); *Newsweek* (2010)[1]

The significant problems we face cannot be solved, at the same level of thinking we were at, when we created them.

Albert Einstein[2]

After India attained independence, our policymakers sought to transform a backward peasant economy into a modern industrialized country by recourse to economic planning. Ambitious five-year plans were launched in the 1950s under the leadership of Pandit Jawaharlal Nehru. The Indian planning was deeply influenced by the Soviet economic planning and the growth models constructed by Western economists. The state was to provide main impetus for economic growth, with the public sector occupying commanding heights of the economy. However, from the 1970s onwards Indira Gandhi government shifted emphasis to populist slogans such as *garibi hatao* (remove poverty) and a licence permit raj was created, in the name of socialism. These policies resulted in slow growth and stagnation of the economy. During the first four decades of planning, the overall performance of the economy was dismal, and the gross domestic product (GDP) grew by only 4 per cent annually. One of the main reasons for poor performance of the economy was that the private sector was not accorded its rightful place in the development strategy.

The situation came to a boil in 1990 when the country faced severe foreign exchange crisis and the Reserve Bank of India had to pledge its gold reserve to a Swiss bank. The severe economic crisis which the nation faced forced the policymakers to rethink about the direction of economic development, and a new liberalized economic policy was launched in 1991. There was deregulation of the economy, most controls on setting of new industrial units were removed, import tariffs were reduced and a policy of encouraging foreign investment was initiated. The impetus to adopt a new policy was also given by change in global economic environment. The Soviet Union collapsed around 1990, and it became clear that the socialist command system with all decision making concentrated in government cannot sustain itself in the long run and is a recipe for disaster. The countries which had free market system, not only Western countries but also Asian tigers such as Singapore, South Korea, Hong Kong and Taiwan, had leapfrogged in economic development. Newly emerging countries which made rapid economic progress made a sobering realization that there is need for a balanced view about the state and the markets. The two should have cooperative relationship and work in tandem for optimum outcomes. Some problems can be tackled better by liberalization and privative initiative, but many others require state action.

The impact of New Economic Policy was positive in terms of GDP growth. The economy picked up with a GDP growth of 6.5 per cent per annum during 1992–2002 and 7.6 per cent during the Tenth Five-Year Plan (2002–7). During the 11th Five-Year Plan (2007–12), the average annual growth of GDP was 7.9 per cent against a target of 9 per cent. However, from 2011 to 2012 the economy slowed down but has again picked up. Growth rate was 5.6 per cent for 2012–13, 6.6 per cent for 2013–14 and 7.2 per cent for 2014–15, and estimated at 7.6 per cent for 2015–16 (at 2011–12 prices) Indian policymakers claim robust GDP growth as a success of their economic policies. However, as we will see in this chapter, it is a highly unsatisfactory measure to judge the performance of the economy.

Much of the problem that we face in India today is due to blind imitation of Western, more particularly Anglo-Saxon, free economy model. In Western economies, progress is judged by economic growth, that is growth of GDP or gross national product. This in effect means continuous increase in production and consumption of goods and services, irrespective of its social and economic utility. Following the Western pattern, Indian planners continuously harp on GDP growth as a success of its policy. The Tenth Five-Year Plan[3] (2002–7) observed, 'It must also be recognised that the growth rate of the economy is probably the most important summary measure of the degree of success of the development strategy and macroeconomic management.' The 11th Five-Year Plan (2007–12)[4] states, 'Rapid growth of the economy is an essential requirement to achieve this outcome (reduction in poverty and expansion of economic opportunities for all) since this is an instrument for a steady increase in employment and incomes for large number of our people.' The 12th Five-Year Plan[5] (2012–17) makes similar assertion, and while it recognizes improvement of economic and social conditions of people as an objective, it says, 'Rapid growth of GDP is an essential requirement for achieving this objective.' It advances two reasons for it. First, 'rapid growth of GDP produces a large expansion in total income and production which, if growth process is sufficiently inclusive, will directly raise living standard of our people by providing them with employment and other income enhancing activities'. Second, it helps financing inclusiveness. The 12th Five-Year Plan had fixed a target of 8.2 per cent growth, with 9 per cent for the last year of the plan. In their budget speeches every year, finance ministers have been emphasizing time and again GDP growth as a measure of the country's economic development. In his maiden budget speech (July 2014), delivered immediately after the installation of the NDA (National Democratic Alliance) government, Finance Minister Arun Jaitley announced that his target is to achieve a sustained growth of 7 to 8 per cent within the next three to four years. In his speech at the time of presentation of 2016–17 budget (February 2016), he claimed, 'Let us look at our achievements compared to the last three years of the previous government when the growth decelerated to 6.3 per cent. The growth of GDP has now accelerated to 7.6 per cent.'[6] He cited the International Monetary Fund (IMF) and World Economic Forum hailing India's growth performance.

Fallacy of GDP growth

The fetish with GDP growth as a main indicator of the success of economic policies can have disastrous consequences for the common person, as it ignores its impact on the individual's economic and social well-being. The time has come to question conventional wisdom that economic growth will make people better off. The GDP is basically a measure of a country's overall economic output – the market value of all final goods and services made within the borders of a country in a year. The GDP ignores the environment, home production for self-use and domestic work. The current system of measuring GDP counts armament production, wars and cigarette advertising as contributors to economic growth, while child rearing, housekeeping and volunteer work are ignored. The economic value of health care is a classic example of GDP as a wrong index of progress – it may rise if many people are sick and receive expensive treatment. But is it not a symptom of poor health of a nation and cause for anxiety? A country may achieve temporarily a high GDP by overexploiting natural resources or misallocating investment. Economies experiencing an economic bubble, like stock-market bubble or low private saving rate, tend to appear to grow faster due to higher consumption and mortgaging future growth for the present. GDP does not take into account the black market, where the money spent is not registered. GDP does not measure non-monetary economy, where no money comes into play at all, resulting in inaccurate or abnormally low GDP figures. Economic growth at the expense of environmental degradation can have serious consequences for future generations. The GDP does not measure the sustainability of growth nor the quality of life. American senator Robert Kennedy put it succinctly far back in 1968:

> Too much and too long, we seem to have surrendered community excellence and community values in the mere accumulation of material things . . . [that] gross national product counts air pollution and cigarette advertising, and ambulances to clear our highways of carnage. It counts special locks for our doors and the

jails for those who break them. It counts the destruction of our redwoods and the loss of our natural wonder in chaotic sprawl. It counts napalm and the cost of a nuclear warhead, and armored cars for police who fight riots in our streets. It counts Whitman's rifle and Speck's knife, and the television programs which glorify violence in order to sell toys to our children. Yet the gross national product does not allow for the health of our children, the quality of their education, or the joy of their play. It does not include the beauty of our poetry or the strength of our marriages; the intelligence of our public debate or the integrity of our public officials. It measures neither our wit nor our courage; neither our wisdom nor our learning; neither our compassion nor our devotion to our country; it measures everything, in short, except that which makes life worthwhile. And it tells us everything about America except why we are proud that we are Americans.[7]

Stiglitz report

Severe dissatisfaction with GDP as an indicator of economic and social progress has been expressed by the Commission on the Measurement of Economic Performance and Social Progress[8] chaired by Nobel Prize–winning economist Joseph Stiglitz, which included Amartya Sen as a member, besides many eminent academicians, and was set up at the initiative of French president Nicholas Sarkozy (November 2009). The commission observed the following: when evaluating material well-being, look at income and consumption rather than production. GDP only measures market production in money units. Production may expand, while income may decrease. Give prominence to distribution of income, consumption and wealth. The commission recommended broadening income measures to non-market activities. Service received from family members is now purchased on the market which may result in rise in income as measured in national account and give a false impression of an increase in living standard. The commission observed that 'well-being' is multidimensional and should include (1) material living standards – income, consumption and wealth; (2) health; (3) education; (4) personal activities including work; (5) political voice including governance; (6) social connections and relationships; (7) environment; and (8) insecurity, economic as well as physical. Quality of life depends on the objective conditions and opportunities available to people. The commission emphasized importance of sustainable development and measuring environment cost and proposed a new set of indices to measure it. The commission has recommended a shift from measuring economic production to measuring people's well-being and sustainability.

A report published by British Sustainable Development Commission[9] (March 2009) titled *Prosperity without Growth* concluded that pursuit of economic growth is one of the root causes of the financial crisis, as well as environmental crisis and undermining well-being of developed countries. The report notes that reliance on debt to finance the cycle of growth has created a deeply unstable system, which has made individual families and communities inherently vulnerable to cycles of boom and bust, while increasing consumption does not make people happier. Tim Jackson, economic commissioner at the commission, observed 'that allegiance to growth is the most dominant feature of an economic and political system that has led us to the brink of disaster'. The report says that growth imperative has shaped the architecture of modern economy. The market was not undone by rouge individuals or turning a blind eye by incompetent regulators. It was undone by growth itself.

In a survey by *Newsweek*[10] (2010) about the 'Best Countries in the World', which was conducted by some of the top subject experts, five categories of national well-being were selected: education, health, quality of life, economic competitiveness and political environment. Metrics were compiled across 100 nations. It rated Finland, Switzerland and Sweden as the top three, India occupying the 78th place. Environmentalists have been pleading against global fixation of GDP growth, which implied that all consumption was good, even if it meant dooming future generations to a decline in quality of life – or no life at all.

Problem with current ruling economic ideology

In post–Second World War world 'economic development' has come to occupy an important place in national and international dialogues. A large number of developing countries attained political independence from their erstwhile colonial masters and wanted to raise their standard of living. They were faced with two conflicting models of economic development: the centralized planned socialist economy model led by the Soviet Union and the free market ideology championed by the US and Western countries. They represented two opposing economic philosophies: distributive justice produced by the government versus efficient production based on privative initiative. With the collapse of command economy of the Soviet Union type, it was thought that free market economy system has triumphed. The original inspiration of this philosophy came from Adam Smith with the publication of *Wealth of Nations* (1776), but its most recent supporters have been the Chicago school, under the leadership of Nobel Prize–winning economist Milton Friedman, and it has advocates in influential institutions such as the World Bank, IMF and World Trade Organization. The ideology known as neoliberal model emphasized deregulation, liberalization, privatization and globalization. Francis Fukuyama wrote a treatise, *The End of History and the Last Man* (1992), lauding free market as the only economic system to create a prosperous society.

The severe recession facing the US and Western European countries, from 2008 onwards, from which they have not been able to recover yet, shows the hollowness of free market ideology. In order to boost economic growth, governments in these countries turned Keynesian and have poured billions of dollars in the economy. The deregulation of the banking sector led to financial engineering, with big banks trading worthless securities, under all kinds of innovative products, making huge profits and their executives cornering astronomical salaries and bonuses, until the bubble burst, and many banks and financial institutions collapsed. It was a catastrophic failure of the market economy, which nailed the lie that free and unregulated markets can deliver the best outcome. While governmental intervention helped in the revival of the economy to some extent, it has created a new set of problems. The developed countries are burdened with heavy public debt, which they find it difficult to service. In recent years, most euro-zone countries have reversed their economic policies and adopted severe austerity measures and cut down public expenditure. Countries such as Italy, Greece, Spain and Portugal are facing serious economic crisis, with high unemployment rate particularly of educated youth, creating social unrest.

While India has adopted free market economic ideology since 1991, during ten years of UPA (United Progressive Alliance) rule (2004–14), it went all out for neoliberal model of economic development, with the Planning Commission headed by Montek Singh Ahluwalia and C. Chidambaram, finance minister, strongly supporting this strategy. There was a mix with a populist 'inclusive growth' policy, and huge public money was poured in numerous poverty alleviation and employment generation programmes, as well as rural and urban missions. The real intent was to catch vote of the gullible section of the masses. This cocktail of economic policy, which was neither free market nor socialist, landed the economy in a real mess.

What is development?

It is with great hope and aspiration that people have voted NDA to power. Its major electoral plank was 'development'. The key issue is, what is development and what path of development the country is going to follow? Kamal Jaswal, director of Common Cause,[11] a leading public advocacy organization, in its editorial comments,

> Development will mean different things to the promoters of a major industrial project sited in a forest area and to the forest dwelling communities liable to be displaced. RWAs (Resident Welfare Society) of tony South Delhi colonies do not have the same idea of development as their counterparts in the neigbouring shanty towns. Development means one thing to the leaders of caste panchayat in rural Haryana and something else to young women in its fiefdom who are struggling to break free of the multiple social structures which deny them their autonomy.

> Essentially development is about creating an environment where all Indians are free to realize their full potential; where barriers to knowledge, skills, public resources and opportunities, which perpetuate

20

poverty, deprivation, and exploitation are systematically brought down; where fundamental rights and freedom promised in the Constitution becomes a living reality. In such a development paradigm, there is no place for exclusion, discrimination, or intimidation on the basis of identity. In this development model, the imperatives of efficiency in provisioning of public goods and services, expeditious approval of investment proposals and timely execution of prestigious projects are balanced by considerations of access, environment impact, protection of livelihoods and rehabilitation.

Business as usual

The new NDA government is pursuing the same economic model as the previous UPA government, with some nuances. Great emphasis is being given to foreign capital and technology and wooing of foreign investors. Public–private partnership model will continue to be followed, with main reliance on private sector, for development and infrastructure projects. The share capital of profitable PSUs (public sector undertakings) in core sectors of the economy is to be disinvested and strategic sale route will be adopted to privatize some of the PSUs. Bullet train will be launched between major cities such as Ahmedabad and Mumbai. One hundred smart cities will be set up. The New Land Act 2014 was to be amended to facilitate land acquisition for industrial development and infrastructure, and an ordinance issued to that effect, but has been shelved for fear of political backlash.

It is apparent that the NDA government intends to follow a model of economic development, which is the 'conventional wisdom of the West', rather than chartering an independent course. The model is no different from the previous UPA government's economic policy. On the economic front, therefore, it will be business as usual. Keynes said famously,

> The difficulty lies not in the new ideas but in escaping from the old ones, which ramify for those brought up as most of us have been born into every corner of our mind.[12]

The NDA government has abolished the Planning Commission. We may not shed tears for this. Although we are a federal country, the Planning Commission had usurped the functions of the state governments, as it was doing meticulous planning and micro-management of every aspect of the state's economic activity in areas such as agriculture, health, education and roads, which fell within their jurisdiction, under the constitutional scheme. Under the Constitution, it is the responsibility of the Finance Commission to allocate funds to the states, but the Planning Commission had taken over this function for a substantial portion of central funds and had become an extra-constitutional body. Having said this, we do need a high-powered think tank or policy making institution to decide on the direction of economic and social policy. The NDA government has constituted Niti-Ayog, but as yet it is not clear what role it is going to play in policymaking.

There is little doubt that for long-term strategic planning in critical areas such as agriculture, industry, energy, transport and employment we need a policy think tank. We are all planners, individuals, corporates and nations and cannot do without it, call it by whatever name you like.

The challenge

India is currently facing huge challenges. Liberalization of imports has destroyed India's modest industrial base, built assiduously over the years. Prime Minster Modi has declared a policy of 'make in India', but as yet there are no visible concrete steps to implement it. The flood of imports without an export surge has created a huge export–import imbalance and placed severe pressure on the rupee, and the rupee has gone into tailspin against dollar. The huge public expenditure incurred by government over the years, financed by borrowing, has left mountains of debt, threatening financial bankruptcy. In the garb of market solutions, the government has abandoned its responsibility towards higher education and health. This has resulted in hundreds of engineering, medical and management colleges mushrooming all over the country, which charge exorbitant capitation fees and dish out degrees, without imparting any knowledge, and produce third-rate graduates who are unemployable. Quality-affordable health services are non-existent, except private hospitals in metropolitan cities, which only the rich can afford and common man has nowhere to go.

The success of economic policy should be judged by its impact on the life of common man in India. The most critical factor for economic well-being is income level of people in general – is there a policy of raising everyone above the threshold poverty, which can be secured only through gainful employment? Decent employment is possible only if we have robust industry and agriculture, supported by good infrastructure such as electricity and road network. A population can be productive only if it is educated and has access to minimum health care services and other essential public goods. Unfortunately, all the parameters of socio-economic well-being of our people are negative, and majority of people are living in miserable conditions, as discussed in the following chapters. This puts a serious question mark on our economic policies and direction of economic development. There is need for a paradigm shift in our thinking and putting in place a new perspective of development so that we can move towards creating a happy, healthy and prosperous society.

Notes

1 Robert Kennedy quoted by Jeffry Sachs, *Price of Civilization*, London: The Bodley Head, 2011, pp. 205–206; 'The Best Countries in the World', *Newsweek*, 23, 30 August 2010, p. 41.

2 Albert Einstein, famous quotes, available at http://www.quotes.net/quote/9226 (accessed 6 April 2016).
3 Government of India, Planning Commission, *Tenth Five Year Plan, 2002–2007*, Vol. I, New Delhi: Government of India, 2002, p. 23.
4 Government of India, Planning Commission, *Eleventh Five Year Plan (2007–12)*, Vol. I, New Delhi: Oxford University Press, 2008, p. 2.
5 Government of India, Planning Commission, *Twelfth Five Year Plan (2012–17)*, Vol. I, New Delhi: Sage Publication, 2013, p. 3.
6 Government of India, Budget 2016–17, Speech of Arun Jaitley, Minister of Finance, 29 February 2016, p. 1.
7 Robert Kennedy quoted by Jeffry Sachs, *Price of Civilization*, pp. 205–206.
8 Joseph Stiglitz, Chairman; Amartya Sen, Adviser; and Fitoussi, Coordinator, 'Commission on the Measurement of Economic and Social Progress', November 2009, available at http://www.stiglitz-sen-fitoussi.fr/documents/rapport_anglais.pdf (accessed 6 April 2016).
9 Sustainable Development Commission, *Prosperity without Growth*, November 2009, available at http://www.sd-commission.org.uk/data/files/publications/prosperity_without_growth_report.pdf (accessed 6 April 2016); also published as a book, *Prosperity without Growth: Economics for a Finite Planet*, London: Earthscan, 2009.
10 'The Best Countries in the World', *Newsweek*, 23, 30 August 2010, pp. 32–41.
11 Kamal Kant Jaswal, 'For a New Development Paradigm', Common Cause, April–June 2014, Vol. XXXIII, No. 2, pp. 1–2.
12 J. M. Keynes, *The General Theory of Employment, Interest and Money*, available at Classic Quotes, http://www.quotationspage.com/quote/38205.html.

3

EDUCATION AND HEALTH
Key to nation's prosperity

A nation is advanced in proportion as education and intelligence spread among the masses. . . . If we have to rise again we shall have to do it in the same way (Western countries), i.e. by spreading education among the masses. . . . Education, education, education alone! Traveling through many cities of Europe and observing in them the comforts and the education of even the poor people, there was brought to my mind the state of our own people, and I used to shed tears. What made the difference? Education was the answer I got. Through education comes faith in one's own self.

Swami Vivekananda[1]

School education in India is in a terrible state, and given the wide ranging individual and social roles of education, this failure has played no small part in whole gamut of problems – from lack of participatory growth and poor health achievements to problems of public accountability, social inequality and democratic practice.

Jean Dreze and Amartya Sen[2]

The problem of health is the most vital problem in life. Everything depends on health: the inner peace and happiness of man, his attitude and behavior towards others, his accomplishment in life; above all, life itself depends on health.

Maharishi Mahesh Yogi[3]

Education is fundamental to a civilized society. Proper education alone builds the character of an individual and awakens the consciousness in him or her to serve the society. Education should aim at producing young men and women of knowledge, character and cultural values so that they

24

are prepared to face life and become responsible citizens. The leaders of Indian renaissance such as Swami Vivekananda, Rabindranath Tagore and Mahatma Gandhi, as well as Western educationalists and statesmen, have all emphasized its importance time and again.

Part I: primary education and literacy

Literacy is essential to survival and development in modern society, but India's educational development record since independence is deplorable. India's literacy level is around 74 per cent (2011), but a large percentage of those classified as 'literate' can hardly do basic reading, writing and arithmetic and are as good as 'illiterate'. Post-independence, the Indian government and policymakers have failed to realize the importance of literacy and education in social transformation, obsessed as they have been with gross domestic product (GDP) growth as a panacea for all ills – particularly post-1991 liberalization of the economy. State action was behind the spread of literacy and education in Europe and America in the 19th century, followed by rapid expansion of schooling under communist rule in the Soviet Union, Cuba and elsewhere. Japanese realized the importance of education during the Meiji era (1868–1912), and by 1910 Japan was almost completely literate. Later South Korea, Taiwan, Singapore, Hong Kong and China followed similar route and transformed their countries.

The Indian government has, however, belatedly realized the importance of literacy and education in development and taken legislative measures, launched several schemes and poured huge sums of money. Public spending on education which was 3.3 per cent of GDP in 2004–5 increased to over 4 per cent by 2011–12, and about Rs 1,244,000 crore was spent during the 11th Five-Year Plan (2007–12). About 43 per cent of public expenditure on education was incurred on elementary education, 25 per cent on secondary education and 32 per cent on higher education.[4] But quality of education remains abysmally poor. This is largely due to poor governance, bureaucratic apathy and absence of any 'genuine commitment' on the part of political leadership to make the nation literate and educated.

Today, India has a gigantic primary school infrastructure,[5] with an enrolment of 13.71 crore children in lower primary classes I–V and 6.19 crore in upper primary classes VI–VIII (of whom 9.16 crore and 3.77 crore [65 per cent], respectively, children are in government-funded schools), which makes an overall enrolment of 19.90 crore (2011–12). These children are enrolled in 14.12 lakh schools, out of which 10.78 lakh (76 per cent) schools are publicly funded. These schools employ 66.87 lakh teachers, of whom 42.89 lakh (64 per cent) are paid through state coffers. In addition, there is an enrolment of 3.2 crore children in 1.284 lakh high schools (classes IX and X) and 1.94 crore in 71,800 intermediate/higher secondary schools (classes XI and XII).

Periodic surveys conducted by NGO Pratham known as Annual Status of Education Report (ASER) present an alarming picture of primary education, particularly in rural areas. The survey for 2012[6] notes that while the overall enrolment level in 6- to 14-year age group remained high at 96 per cent, more than half the children of standard V are at least three grades behind of where they should be. In standard V, 58 per cent children could not read class II textbook, 46 per cent children could not do simple two-digit subtraction with borrowing and more than 75 per cent were unable to do division. The survey notes that the overall learning knowledge deteriorated over the past two years. Primary schooling is characterized by high drop-out rates, as children have no incentive to study. The drop-out rate in classes I–V was 27 per cent, in classes I–VIII the rate was 40 per cent and in classes I–X the rate was as high as 50 per cent. Over the years the quality of teaching in government primary schools has not improved. ASER 2014 notes that the situation with basic readings has not changed and arithmetic continues to be a cause of serious concern.[7]

The standard of government/municipal schools even in urban capital cities such as Delhi, Dehradun and Lucknow is so pathetic that most lower-income-bracket parents prefer to send their children to B and C category private schools, although they fleece them by charging exorbitant fees and follow unethical practices. ASER survey notes that private school enrolment is steadily increasing all over the country. It was 28 per cent overall in 2012, but in states such as Jammu and Kashmir, Punjab, Haryana, Rajasthan, Uttar Pradesh, Madhya Pradesh and Meghalaya, 40 per cent children in the 6- to 14-year age group go to private schools.

In 2002 a constitutional amendment was made, granting fundamental right to free and compulsory education for children in the age group of 6–14 years. A 'Right of Children to Free and Compulsory Education Act, 2009', was enacted, which came into effect from 1 April 2010. The act legalizes right to education of every child and places responsibility on the governments and authorities to provide schools to the children. However, the act has not helped the improvement in quality of education. It has an 'extraordinary provision' that no child can be detained in a class for failure to qualify minimum benchmark. This has spelled disaster for learning. ACER 2012 survey notes that learning outcomes were low but steady in the years leading to 2010, but across the country children's ability to read simple text and do basic arithmetic has declined since then and most children in school today are at least three grade levels behind where they should be. Similar concern is voiced by Jean Dreze and Amartya Sen, 'Abolishing standardized tests of any kind and in a system where pupil achievements are so low and teacher supervision is so scanty can hardly be a sound idea.'[8]

The biggest problem in primary education is absence of 'good teaching facility', which can motivate and inspire a child to study. The schooling systems suffer because of poorly qualified and ill-trained teachers. There are contrasting service conditions for teachers in private and public schools. Barring some good private schools in metropolitan cities, teachers in private schools are paid very low salaries, have no job security and are exploited by management. In government schools teachers are paid reasonably well, but there is no accountability. Due to political interference, there is large-scale corruption in teachers' recruitment, and underqualified teachers who have no interest in teaching get recruited. Many of these teachers absent themselves at will and shirk work, as there is hardly any fear of punishment. In addition, most schools suffer from problems such as the following: one/two/three teachers have to handle a large number of students, large number of vacancies of teachers, teachers engaged in non-teaching jobs such as election and census work and inadequate school infrastructure and teaching aids. A number of incentive schemes under Sarva Shiksha Abhiyan, Mid-day Meal and Mahila Samakhya, and Teacher Education, free uniforms and textbooks have been introduced at a huge cost to exchequer, to improve learning, but they have not made any significant dent.

It needs to be realized that education is not simply an issue of passing legislation and provisioning of funds. Providing quality education so that every child becomes 'truly literate' needs a great deal of commitment and dedication on the part of the teaching community, as well as educational administrators. The most important reason for the pathetic state of education is lack of will on the part of political leadership, which treats the poor in India as a vote bank and manipulates them with various catchy schemes but have no genuine interest in their learning and becoming dignified members of the community.

Secondary education

Secondary education suffers from the same ills as primary education. Barring central schools run by Kendriya Vidyala Sansthan, most public-funded high schools and higher secondary schools, particularly in BIMARU states (an acronym from the first letters of the names of the Indian states of Bihar, Madhya Pradesh, Rajasthan and Uttar Pradesh suffer from the same fate. It has a resemblance to a Hindi word *Bimar* which means 'sick'), suffer from abysmally low standards of teaching and learning. While there are some excellent schools run by private societies like DPS, DAV and Christian missions, they are mostly in metropolitan cities and state capitals and cater to the need of elite and influential sections of the society. High-quality secondary education within the reach of every student is essential to raise the standard of living of the masses.

In our educational system there is very little emphasis on vocational education and skill development, which is job oriented. There is huge requirement of technical manpower for industry, agriculture and services. There is a mismatch between the manpower which our educational institutions produce and what the market needs. We can learn a great deal from the German vocational training system with its combination of classroom and business, theory and practice, where learning and working is recognized as a highly effective model for vocational training.

An essential characteristic of the German dual system is the cooperation between largely private companies, on the one hand, and public vocational schools, on the other. The federal government is responsible for vocational training in the companies and the federal states (Länder [states or provinces in Germany]) for the vocational schools. Thus, the German dual system of vocational training combines theory and practice, knowledge and skills and learning and working in a particularly efficient manner. In Germany, there are currently some 350 officially recognized occupational standards. More than 50 per cent of all students who were college-bound in high school but decide against university go for vocational training. Companies provide training voluntarily, and often at their own expense, because they believe that this is the best way to meet their own need for skilled staff. The main benefit for trainees is receiving market-relevant training that improves their chances in the labour market while simultaneously improving social skills and developing personality.

We should learn from Germany and reorient our educational system towards vocational and job-oriented courses, and discourage our young men and women from mindlessly joining colleges and universities in courses which offer no prospect of gainful employment. Only students with scholastic bent of mind should be allowed to join universities for higher education.

Higher education

University is the place which nurtures and trains young people in different professions – science, industry, business and administration – and provides leadership to enable the country to progress and attain freedom from want, disease and ignorance. Several high-powered bodies such as Radhakrishnan Commission (1949), Kothari Commission (1966) and National Education Policy (1986) had envisaged noble vision for education, relating it to the needs of the society, improving its quality and developing vocational skill in the students. Radhakrishnan Commission had observed that universities are the organs of civilization.

> If India is to confront the confusion of our time, she must turn for guidance, not to those who are lost in the mere exigencies of the passing hour, but to her men of letters, and men of science, to her poets and artists, to her discoverers and inventors. These intellectual pioneers of civilization are to be found and trained in the universities, which are the sanctuaries of the inner light of the nation.[9]

The noble vision of education has remained a pipe dream. The bulk of students coming out of colleges are unemployable, unable to stand on their own feet and out of tune with the realities of life. There has been haphazard expansion of education with no consideration of quality. Higher education is fragmented and scattered and is offered in thousands of institutions called affiliated colleges, which are small sized with no infrastructure and have poor-quality and inadequate teachers. These institutions of higher learning perform only classroom teaching and prepare students for examinations like tutorial colleges. All over the world higher education takes place in big clusters of learning which are built over long years of patience through hard and dedicated effort of teachers and students. They have big libraries, modern research labs, motivated students and a highly qualified and dedicated teaching community in an atmosphere that encourages research, creativity and innovation. Massachusetts Institute of Technology (MIT) USA, one of the world's premier centre of learning, has 3,000 faculty members and 30,000 students.

According to government policy as envisaged in the 11th and 12th Five-Year Plans, the main objective of higher education is quantitative expansion and inclusive education. In pursuance of this policy a large number of new central universities have been opened (one for each state), and eight IITs (Indian Institutes of Technology) and six IIMs (Indian Institute of Management) in addition to the existing ones. There is no physical infrastructure and worthwhile teaching facility in these new institutions of higher learning. The policy of indiscriminate expansion is seriously flawed, as it would result in lowering the standard of some existing premier institutions in the country. Not a single Indian university features among the first 250 universities ranked by Times World University Rankings (2014–15) (only four universities feature in the top 400 universities ranked by it – Indian Institute of Science, Bangalore, Panjab University, IIT Bombay and IIT Roorkee. Over the years the rank of IIT Bombay and some other IITs is slipping down, showing deterioration of standard). Our universities and institutes of higher learning today do not have an environment for extending frontiers of knowledge and innovation, a prerequisite for moving the society forward. All the four Indian post-independent Nobel Prize winners, for scholastic achievement, Hargobind Khorana, S. Chandrashekhar, Amartya Sen and Venkatraman Ramakrishna did all their work abroad (other than Peace). It took several centuries of nurturing for Oxford and Cambridge to become the world's prime centres of knowledge creation and scholastic excellence, inspiring scholars all over the world. To develop world-class centres of learning, we should have nurtured old and established universities which are presently languishing for want of funds and lack of autonomy. The existing IITs and IIMs should have been developed as centres of excellence of technical and management education, instead of converting them into factories for mass production of students whose sole ambition is to look for cushy, white-collared, high-salaried corporate jobs.

Prof. S. L. Sharma, B. S. Ghuman and Shital Prakash analyse that poor quality of education is due to

> system of affiliating universities with huge number of colleges; poor, inadequate and deficient infrastructure and equipment; lack of regular and qualified faculty; outdated, inflexible and irrelevant curriculum; monologue and boring pedagogy; deficient testing procedures; lack of quality research and innovation; bureaucratic controls and lack of professional and financial autonomy; and lack of internal quality control and assessment.[10]

Commercialization of education

The government today views the objective of the education system to produce manpower for the market as its mandate, instead of recognizing that the aim of education is quest for knowledge and producing enlightened citizens. This has paved the way for the policy of free entry of private players, making education a tradable and marketable commodity. In the process an exploitive band of private players, mostly belonging to political or business class, with no background in education and commitment to serve the society, have entered in the domain of education. They exploit the new-found aspiration of the rising middle class, who consider a professional degree, howsoever earned, as a passport to success. Hundreds of capitation-fee engineering, management and medical colleges have sprung up all over the country. They have poor infrastructure and lack qualified teaching faculty. An *Indian Express* report found out that in Maharashtra, 21 former ministers, half of cabinet strength of Congress-National Congress Party government, or their immediate relatives run educational institutions across the state, many of which are embroiled in controversy. Acknowledging its disastrous impact, Prithviraj Chavan, when he was chief minister, admitted, 'Too much privatization of education has reduced the role of government to an agency that releases grants. Improvement and development of education cannot be done through privatization of education, which is rapidly mushrooming.'[11]

The most alarming situation relates to medical education. There has been an alarming expansion of private medical colleges from 1996 onwards. Presently, out of 422 medical colleges 224 are private, accounting for more than 50 per cent of MBBS (Bachelor of Medicine and Bachelor of Surgery) seats. Most of these colleges are substandard, but they manage to get recognition due to corruption in approving bodies, as well as political influence. While on paper there is merit-based system for admission, in practice exorbitant sums are charged. A *Times of India* (2016) report says that the rate for an MBBS seat ranges from Rs 25 lakh to Rs 1 crore, and for a Doctor of Medicine seat it may be even Rs 3 crore in some disciplines.[12] It estimates black money generation in medical admission of the order of Rs 12,000 crore annually. With no hospital infrastructure and a handful of semi-qualified medical professionals on the rolls for teaching, these colleges produce half-baked doctors, who are in no position to treat patients, even for simple ailments, and can even pose serious health hazard to them.

Most of the regulatory agencies such as the Medical Council of India, All India Council for Technical Education and University Grants Commission are riddled with corruption and manned by mediocre staff. Some of their officers have been facing enquiry by the Central Bureau of Investigation. They are unable to enforce even the minimum quality standards. S. L. Sharma *et al.* observe,

> Many of the private institutions are known to indulge in all kind of malpractices including corruption, fleecing, duping, cheating,

playing games, flouting norms and compromising with standards. They indulge in corruption in seeking approvals and accreditations; in fleecing, duping and cheating students and their parents by showing them rosy dreams; in playing games with regulatory bodies for flouting norms of infrastructure, admissions, faculty recruitment and payment and professional standards.[13]

The privatization of higher education is serving the very opposite of the professed objective of inclusive education as it restricts the access of the deprived section to education. Only the rich and wealthy have finances to obtain a seat in private colleges. Education has become a commodity available to the highest bidder.

The overall story of private participation in higher education is sordid incompetence, corruption, nepotism and abysmally low standards. One can imagine the quality and competence of young boys and girls who come out from these colleges and on whose shoulder rests the future of the country. There is an urgent need to correct the misdirection of higher education and restore its ennobling mission. Education is meant to ignite the mind for a lifelong search for knowledge and enlarge mental horizon. It is training of the will which enables an individual to make use of knowledge to benefit not only himself or herself but also the society. The aim of education should be building character and producing responsible members who serve the society.

Part II: medical and health services

Public health services in India are in a poor and pathetic state. Health centres in rural areas are not able to attract qualified doctors and nurses, and lack equipment and medicines even to provide rudimentary medical services. In urban centres, government hospitals and dispensaries suffer from chronic mismanagement; they are overcrowded and filthy, lack basic medical equipment and perpetually remain short of medicine; the medical staff is indifferent to patients' need. The result is that members of the public bypass government medical services and go to private doctors and hospitals, even if they have to pay exorbitant charges for the service.

The government's indifference coupled with poor governance is the main reason for poor health services. Ever since India became independent, health has not been a priority for public funding, both by central and by state governments, forcing people to spend their own money on private medical treatment, which often lands vulnerable sections into penury due to its huge cost. Health spending in India is estimated to be 4 per cent of GDP, out of which public health spending has been around 1 per cent of GDP, though it has risen marginally in recent years. Public spending in India is very low as compared to other countries.[14] It is 2 to 3 per cent of GDP in newly emerging economies such as Malaysia, China and Thailand and 8 per cent in countries of the European Union, with a world average of 6.5 per cent. The neglect of health services by government would be evident from the fact that public spending as compared to total expenditure on health is a little over 25 per cent, compared to 50 per cent in East Asia, Middle East and Latin America, and 75 per cent in the European Union, with world average of over 60 per cent. Government has announced a goal of increasing public expenditure on health to 2 to 3 per cent of GDP, but this objective is nowhere near fulfilment.

Persistence underfunding is the most important reason for India's pathetic health services, as health care has not been a priority issue for both central and state governments. Naresh Dayal, former health secretary, Government of India, says that if we analyse data of expenditure on health care, this become evident. He laments,

> That [persistent underfunding] gave a weak public health system, forcing the poor to spend their hard earned money for expensive care. Millions of poor have fallen below the poverty line because of high out of pocket expenditure in health calamities and this is seen as one of the most important causes of impoverishment in India.[15]

The National Rural Health Mission (NRHM), a major programme of health care in rural area, was launched in 2004–5, which caters to the needs of the population through primary health centres (PHCs) and community health centres to district hospital. However, there is persistent underfunding of NRHM, and in the seven years of its functioning from 2005 to 2012 against an approved outlay of Rs 151,000 crore, only Rs 66,500 crore (44 per cent) was released by the central government, averaging Rs 9,500 crore per year. The health centres under NRHM suffer from serious problems such as shortage of doctors, doctors and nursing staff absenting themselves at will and inadequacy of basic infrastructure, particularly in northern states. But at least in rural areas there is a structured public health system which can be improved upon. However, in urban areas with a population of 38 crore spread over 430 cities, there is practically no public health coverage for the common man. While the Ministry of Health has been proposing coverage of urban population for a long time, the Planning Commission had opposed it, due to its misguided policy that urban population be covered by health insurance and public–private partnership mode.

In a belated move from 2013–14, government has decided to cover urban population also under the National Health Mission, with provision of PHC and emphasis on slum dwellers and vulnerable sections of the population, and modest funding is being provided to states. However, its impact is not yet visible in urban areas.

The government's policy of private players as the main channel to provide medical services in urban areas is based on the philosophy of neoliberal economics, which advocates withdrawal of state from as many activities as possible. Such an approach is contrary to practice in advanced countries of Europe as well as countries in East Asia, Middle East and elsewhere, with the possible exception of the US, as medical and health services are considered an essential public good, with the state taking full responsibility for its provision.

The availability of poor medical services reflects in overall health of the nation and is alarming when measured in terms of some critical health indicators such as infant and maternal mortality rates (MMR), life expectancy and nutrition along with incidence of communicable and non-communicable diseases. The goals relating to health indicators fixed by the end of the 11th Five-Year Plan (March 2012) were as follows: reducing MMR to 100 per 100,000 live births, reducing infant mortality rate (IMR) to 28 per 1,000 live births, reducing total fertility rate (TFR) to 2.1, reducing malnutrition among children (0–3 age group) to half from the level of 40 per cent and reducing anaemia among women (15–49) to half from the level of 55 per cent. None of the targets were achieved. At the beginning of the 12th Five-Year Plan, MMR was 212, IMR 44 and fertility rate 2.5, with practically no change in malnutrition in children and anaemia among women. This has forced the 12th Five-Year Plan to fix almost same targets as for the 11th Five-Year Plan. It may be mentioned that there has been wide divergence in performance among states. The southern states such as Kerala and Tamil Nadu have fulfilled most of the targets, while in the northern states, particularly in the Hindi belt, the health indicators are pathetic. Jean Dreze[16] observes that during the past 20 years India has fallen behind even Bangladesh in a wide range of basic indicators such as life expectancy, child survival and fertility rates.

India also faces the formidable challenge of communicable diseases such as tuberculosis, leprosy and filariasis and non-communicable diseases such as diabetes, cardiovascular diseases and cancer. Without a universal health scheme, which is able to provide affordable treatment to everyone, it is difficult to see how the gigantic problem of treating these diseases can be solved. It may be worth mentioning that the country has the capacity to meet major health challenges when concerted efforts are made. India has eradicated small pox some years back, and polio lately, and there has been considerable reduction in the incidence of AIDS.

One of the major problems faced by the Indian health system is shortage of doctors, nurses and other paramedical staff. The present ratio of doctors is 45 per 100,000 persons, against a desirable ratio of 85 per 100,000. With a view to meet the shortage of doctors, private medical colleges are allowed to function. However, this has created a whole set of new problems. As most of them have been opened on commercial consideration, they charge heavy capitation fees, which only the rich can afford. Thus, many meritorious boys and girls are deprived of medical education, making medical education a commodity available to the highest bidder, while severely lowering the standard of education. Dr K. K. Talwar and Meenu Singh caution against chasing number and emphasize the need for a pragmatic, holistic and multi-pronged approach to meet the shortage of doctors and specialists.[17]

The private health sector, which is the main channel through which health services are available, is known for exploitative pricing, over-medication and unnecessary surgeries and many other malpractices. Only the rich and persons whose cost is borne by their employer (government and corporate) can access them. The cost of treatment in private hospitals and clinics is well beyond the reach of the ordinary individual, and he or she has no place to go in case of severe illness or disease. Dr Shoaib Mohammad, who has two postgraduate degrees and worked in a reputed hospital in London, describes his experience in one of the corporate hospitals in New Delhi, where he was advised to have 'market value', even if it meant following unethical practices, and was forced to quit. He asserts,

> The terms normally used on boardrooms – market, market value, business model – should not creep into our day to-day clinical practice because it may further dehumanize our profession, our individual thought process, and we could end up losing the all-important 'human touch'.[18]

The government's policy in health sector which relies on private sector as the main provider of health services, backed by medical insurance, is deeply flawed. Indian policymakers virtually want to adopt the US model, which President Obama has been trying to remedy – although he has faced huge resistance.[19] The US health care system is one of the most costly and ineffective systems in the industrialized world: per capita expenditure is twice as high as that in Europe, but health outcomes are poorer. The system is also inequitable, which had left behind 20 per cent (almost 50 million) uninsured of the most vulnerable population group, before Obama's new health policy. A New York–based Commonwealth Fund[20] conducted surveys of health care system in nine developed countries and found the US system worst and the UK system the best. The survey ranked the nation's health system on five parameters – quality of care, access to care, efficiency, equity and health lives, which included three indicators: mortality amenable to medical care, infant mortality and healthy life expectancy at age 60. While the US has a privatized system, the UK has a substantial public-funded National Health Scheme. The survey noted that the US spends $8,500 per capita annually on health, while the UK spends less than half at $3,600 per person. The US spends 17.7 per cent of its GDP on health care, with 7.15 per cent of that spending on administrative costs, while the UK spends 9.4 per cent GDP on health care, with 3.4 per cent on administrative cost. The US system is in the hands of powerful drug companies and private insurance players, who have a vested interest in keeping the cost of treatment expensive and manipulate the medical fraternity and exploit the patients. Jean Dreze and Amartya Sen after making a detailed analysis warn,

> [Stop] believing, against all empirical evidence, that India's transition from poor health to good health could be easily achieved through private health care and insurance.[21]

For becoming a healthy nation, the government should step in to provide primary and secondary health services to the general population. A universal health coverage means that each individual would have assured access to a defined essential range of medicines and treatment at an affordable price, with poor sections of the population having it for free or nominal payment. There would be major resource problem in instituting such a system, as it would be largely tax-funded. But its long-term benefit to society will outweigh the short-term financial burden. However, a portion of the cost can be recovered from the users, depending on paying capacity on Central Government Health Scheme pattern.

Advocacy of the aforesaid view does not mean that private health providers do not have an important role and are not doing a good job. In fact, during past ten years some excellent private hospitals have come up in metropolitan cities and are providing medical services of international standards. For advanced treatment and critical surgeries, they have to play an important role in the country's health system. However, it is imperative that private hospitals do not follow the 'business model' but run on 'no profit–no loss basis'. India has a great tradition of charitable societies and religious organizations, particularly Christian missions, running some excellent hospitals. Government policy should encourage such institutions to set up more hospitals and medical outfits by giving them suitable incentive and facilities.

We need to realize that primary and secondary medical treatment accessible to every citizen, at affordable price, can be provided only with public funding. Government should not shirk from this responsibility. For improving the health of the nation, a universal health care system should be put in place at the earliest. We need to emulate the example of the UK, France and other progressive countries, which have provided their citizens this essential component of social security. The fact that existing public health services are inefficient and that we should discard them and rely on private health care is like throwing the baby with bath water. We should resolve governance problems in efficient delivery of medical services in the existing governmental and public-funded hospitals and medical outfits and fix the system with determined effort.

The population burden

India is facing a huge burden of population, which puts severe pressure on its overstretched resources. The population of the country was around 35 crore during independence, increased to 44 crore in 1961, almost doubled in 30 years to 85 crore by 1991, jumped to 100.02 crore in 2001 and presently stands at 1.21 crore (2011 census).

During the past 60 years, life expectancy has risen from 33 to 64 years and IMR has fallen from 148 to 58 per 1,000. Although TFR has been falling, it was 6 in the early 1950s and has presently declined to 2.5 (2010); it is still not close to the replacement level goal of 2.1, fixed a decade earlier. The population growth is uneven across the states. There is visible decline in population growth rates in several states, and nine states have reached a replacement level of 2.1. But seven states, namely Bihar, Uttar Pradesh, Madhya Pradesh, Rajasthan, Jharkhand, Chhattisgarh and Orissa, accounting for nearly 40 per cent of the population of the country, continue to have high rate of population growth. Most poor families have four to five children, whom they cannot support. This leads to their increasing impoverishment and substandard condition of living. The government is not making any serious effort to promote family planning among these vast swathes of impoverished population. After the Indira Gandhi government's election debacle (one reason being the forced sterilization programme), post-Emergency in 1979, family planning has gone off the government's radar. People should be persuaded to voluntarily take to family planning and adopt small family norms, by launching massive educational programmes and providing good medical services. Population explosion is the single biggest reason holding back the country's economic development.

India has a very young population, and our leaders often talk of demographic dividend. However, demographic dividend will kick in only if the population is healthy and educated. Unfortunately, northern states mostly in the Hindi belt have the highest growth rate of population, have the worst health indicators and malnutrition and are backward in education. In contrast, states like Kerala and Tamil Nadu have already reached TFR of 1.7, well below the replacement rate of 2.1. If we have to take advantage of demographic dividend, the backward states in particular should substantially improve their education and health services.

Summing up

All the countries of the world which are in the league of developed countries have done so on the strength of full literacy, high-quality education and universal health care. A survey by *Newsweek*[22] (2010) of the Best Countries in the World found education and health as key component of national well-being, and the main factor behind their outperforming other countries. In 1960, South Korea's national wealth was on par with Afghanistan; today it is one of the world's richest nation, thanks to its focus on education. If India is to progress, it needs to ensure that every child becomes truly literate, by resolving the serious issue of governance deficit. Secondary education should have strong vocational content so that majority of boys and girls who pass out of schools get meaningful jobs and become productive members of the society. Higher education is meant only for the meritorious and the brilliant. The commercialization of higher education, making it a commodity available to the highest bidder, should stop. The state must take full responsibility for its provisioning. The aim of education should be building character of young boys and girls, and developing in them a spirit of service to society.

Good health of the general population is important for national prosperity. This is possible only through public-funded Universal Health Coverage so that every citizen can have access to primary and secondary health care. The present policy of insurance-based health care, through private providers, copying US model, is costly and inefficient, and should not be made the main channel for health care for the general population.

We should adopt international best practice and look at the UK, France and other progressive countries as models so that affordable health care is available to everyone. History tells us that nations which provide high-quality education to their citizens and look after the health of their citizenry are at the forefront of economic development.

Notes

1 Swami Kamalananda, *Education, Total Development of Personality*, Mysore: Ramakrishna Institute of Moral and Spiritual Education, 2003, pp. 5–6; *The Complete Works of Swami Vivekananda*, Vol. IV, pp. 482–485.

2 Jean Dreze and Amartya Sen, *An Uncertain Glory: India and Its Contradictions*, London: Allen Lane, 2013, p. 139.

3 Maharishi Mahesh Yogi, *The Science of Being and the Art of Living*, London: International SRM Publication, 1966, p. 188.

4 Government of India, Planning Commission, *12th Five Year Plan 2012–17*, Vol. III, New Delhi: Sage, 2013, p. 47.

5 National University of Educational Planning in India, *Elementary Education in India: Progress towards UEE, DISE 2011–12*, May 2013, available at http://www.dise.in/Downloads/Publications/Publications%202011-12/Flash%202011-12.pdf (accessed 22 September 2014); also see Government of India, Ministry of Human Resource Development, Bureau of Planning, Monitoring and Statistics, *Statistics at a Glance*, 2014.

6 *Annual Status of Education Report (Rural)*, January 2013, available at http://img.asercentre.org/docs/Publications/ASER%20Reports/ASER_2012/nationalfinding.pdf (accessed 22 September 2014).

7 *ASER Report 2014*, available at http://img.asercentre.org/docs/Publications/ASER%20Reports/ASER%202014/nationalfindings.pdf (accessed 22 September 2014).

8 Dreze and Sen, *An Uncertain Glory*, p. 138.

9 Ministry of Education, Government of India, *Report of the University Education Commission*, Vol. I, 1950, reprint 1962, p. 29, available at http://www.academics-india.com/Radhakrishnan%20Commission%20Report%20of%201948-49.pdf (accessed 7 April 2016).

10 S. L. Sharma, B. S. Ghuman and Shital Prakash, *Higher Education in India*, Jaipur: Rawat Publication, 2014, p. 4.

11 'Campus Cabinet – 21 former ministers . . . run schools, colleges and universities', *The Indian Express*, 17 October 2014, p. 8.

12 'Black Money quota: MBBS, PG seats go for Rs 12,000 cr. yr', *Times of India*, 30 January 2016; and 'What spurred Rs. 12 K cr med ed black market', *Times of India*, 11 February 2016.

13 S. L. Sharma *et al.*, *Higher Education in India*, p. 13.

14 For details regarding neglect of health care, see Dreze and Sen, *An Uncertain Glory*, pp. 145–181.

15 Naresh Dayal, 'Key Issues in Health Care Governance', *The Journal of Governance*, July 2013, Vol. 7, pp. 3–14.

16 Jean Dreze and Amartya Sen, 'Putting Growth in Its Place', *Outlook*, 14 November 2011, pp. 50–59; and 'Putting Growth in Its Place', *Yojna*, January 2012.

17 K. K. Talwar and Meenu Singh, 'More Doctor for Health Care Services', *Journal of Governance*, July 2013, Vol. 7, pp. 158–167.

18 Shoaib Mohammad, 'My Market Value', *Economic and Political Weekly*, 7 November 2015, Vol. L, No. 45, pp. 26–28.
19 'How to fix Obamacare', *The Economist*, 20–26 September 2014, pp. 12, 35–37.
20 'US worst in developed world healthcare', *Times of India*, 30 June 2014, p. 10.
21 Dreze and Sen, *An Uncertain Glory*, p. 178.
22 'The Best Countries of the World', *Newsweek*, 23, 30 August 2010, pp. 32–49.

4

AGRICULTURE, RURAL DISTRESS AND POVERTY

We town-dwellers have believed that India is to be found in its towns and the villages were created to minister to our needs. . . . I have found that the town-dweller has generally exploited the villager, in fact he has lived on the poor villager's subsistence.

Mahatma Gandhi[1]

The political influence of urban consumers and industry enables them to extract cheap food at the expense of the vast number of poor rural people . . . Policy is designed to give top priority to industry, which includes keeping food grains cheap.

Theodore Schultz, Nobel Laureate, Economics[2]

Agriculture is more revolutionary than industry. In twenty-five years Israel increased its agriculture yields seventeen times. This is amazing. People don't realise this. Agriculture is ninety-five per cent science, five per cent work.

Shimon Peres, President of Israel[3]

The problem of poverty and unemployment in the country has its roots in agriculture becoming a totally unremunerative occupation, causing huge rural distress. While more than half the workforce in the country is engaged in agriculture and allied activities, its contribution to GDP is only around 15 per cent. (Agriculture and allied activities include horticulture, dairying, fishing and forestry.) Agriculture's contribution to gross domestic product (GDP) was half at the time of independence, but its share in national wealth is declining over years largely due to the development strategy we have adopted. The GDP from agriculture had increased fourfold between 1950–51 and 2006–7, while the increase per worker in real terms is only

75 per cent, while there is fourfold increase in overall per capita GDP.[4] This shows terms of trade moving adversely against agriculture and huge transfer of income from rural to urban population. Nobel Prize–winning economist Theodore Schultz had observed that production has suffered in many low-income countries as policymakers deliberately underprice agricultural products and in doing so they have 'by political means created an indentured agriculture to supply cheap food for urban people'.[5]

The Indian farmer and the Indian agriculture has shown tremendous response to a sensible policy regime. The Green Revolution ushered in the late 1960s resulted in spectacular growth in food grain production, and the country attained self-sufficiency, from chronic shortage and imports, which characterized the economy for three decades from the 1940s to the 1960s, when India was totally dependent on PL 480 imports from the US and had to go round the world with a begging bowl. The production of food grains which was 51 mt (million tonne) in 1950–51 increased to 108 mt in 1970–71, 176 mt in 1990–91, 218 mt in 2000–2001, 245 mt in 2010–11 and was an all-time high 265 mt in 2013–14 and 253 mt in 2014–15. There were several reasons for the success of Green Revolution: land reforms, increase in net sown area, irrigation facilities and, most important, technological innovation due to introduction of high-yielding varieties of wheat and rice seeds and pragmatic price policy based on minimum support prices (MSPs).

Unfortunately, post-economic liberalization, the agriculture sector has lost dynamism. While during 1981–82 to 1990–91 agriculture GDP grew at 3.5 per cent per year (against the national average of 5.40 per cent), from the Ninth Five-Year Plan onwards it has decelerated – growth rate was 2.5 per cent in the Ninth Five-Year Plan (1997–2002) (against the national average of 5.50 per cent) and 2.4 per cent in the Tenth Five-Year Plan (2002–7) (against the national average of 7.8 per cent). However, agricultural growth rate picked up during the 11th Five-Year Plan (2007–12) and was 3.7 per cent against a target of 4 per cent. The growth rate declined again and was only 1.5 per cent on average during the first four years of the 12th Five-Year Plan (2012–16), against a target of 4 per cent.

The average yield of crop in India is very low compared to other countries. For example, in paddy the Indian yield is 3,500 kilogram per hectare, as compared to world average of 4,400 kilogram per hectare, China 6,600 kilogram per hectare and the US 7,900 kilogram per hectare; in wheat, Indian yield is 3,000 kilogram per hectare, China 4,700 kilogram per hectare and the UK 8,800 kilogram per hectare; in maize, Indian yield is 2,300 kilogram per hectare, world average 5,100 kilogram per hectare and the US 8,800 kilogram per hectare. Application of modern science and technology is required to improve yield.

Problems facing agriculture

Indian agriculture faces serious problems, whose most visible symbol is the spate of suicides committed by farmers across the country during the past ten years – a very tragic and disturbing phenomenon. Land is the prime natural resource, but over the years net prime sown area is showing a declining trend. Since 1990–91 net sown area has come down from 143 million hectares to 140 million hectares, largely due to urban use, government's policies and speculative purchase by unscrupulous elements in society. A major challenge in farming is the small size of land-holdings. Average size of a farm is 1.23 hectare, with farms less than 2 hectares constituting 83 per cent of land-holdings and 43 per cent of area.

Irrigation is critical for agriculture. At present only 46 per cent of net cultivated land is covered with irrigation. In the budget of 2016–17, some positive steps for increasing irrigation potential have been announced. 'Pradhan Mantri Krishi Sinchai Yojna' will be implemented in mission mould and projects languishing under Accelerated Irrigation Benefit Programmes will be fast-tracked. A dedicated irrigation fund under the National Bank for Agriculture and Rural Development will be created. Another welcome step is a new crop insurance scheme under which farmers will pay a small premium (2 per cent for all kharif crops and 1.5 per cent for rabi and 5 per cent for commercial/horticulture), but full value of crop will be insured, the government picking up the gap between actuarial premium and what the farmers will pay. Only time will tell how well these schemes are implemented to make an impact on farmers' lives.

There are a large number of structural and social factors because of which agriculture has become an unrewarding occupation: changed pattern of land-holdings, changed cropping patterns due to shift from light crops to cash crops, growing cost of cultivation due to heavy dependence on high-cost inputs, volatility of crop output and lack of remunerative prices. The biggest problem is shortage of water, and much of agriculture continues to be rain dependent.

Agriculture scientist and former vice-chancellor of Agriculture University, Pantnagar, Suresh C. Modgal observes:

> Complacency on the part of policymakers and administrative machinery, collapse of extension wing of public agencies, wrong and inadequate use of modern production technology, breaking of input supply chain, irrational use of natural resources capped with a degradation of environmental components, are jointly responsible for the deceleration in agriculture productivity and its growth rate.[6]

Declining investment

One of the most disquieting features of the farm sector for the past several decades is declining public investment in agriculture. During the Tenth Five-Year Plan (2002–7), while gross capital formation (GCF) was 14 per cent of agriculture GDP, the contribution of the public sector was only 3 per cent, the balance coming from the private sector. During the 11th Five-Year Plan (2007–12 – first four years), there was an increase in gross capital formation to around 19 per cent of agriculture GDP, but most of it came from the private sector, which accounted for 15.5 per cent as compared to 3.5 per cent by the public sector.[7] In recent years GCF in agriculture is again showing a declining trend; it was 18.3 per cent in 2011–12 and came down to 15.8 per cent in 2014–15. This is mainly due to decline in public sector investment. Its share in GCF was 20 per cent in 2004–5 but came down to 16.8 per cent in 2013–14.

Over the years public investment in agriculture is getting reduced, while most of the public resources are going towards subsidies. Public subsidy to agriculture, which averaged 4.1 per cent of agriculture GDP in the Tenth Five-Year Plan (excluding food subsidy which is a consumer subsidy) increased to 8.2 per cent during the 11th Five-Year Plan (this does not include subsidy given to utilities for electricity and subsidy for water). The 12th Five-Year Plan documents as well as other experts point out that giving subsidy for fertilizers like urea and other inputs is inimical to the long-term health of agricultural productivity, as it encourages excessive use of fertilizers and power and results in harmful mining of soil nutrients and groundwater, leading to loss of quality of both soil and groundwater.

The planners have been neglecting the agriculture and irrigation sector in budgetary allocation in successive plans. During the Tenth Five-Year Plan (2002–7) this sector was allocated 6.22 per cent of overall plan outlay (its allied sector rural development and Panchayati Raj was given 10.70 per cent).[8] In the 11th Five-Year Plan (2007–12), agriculture and irrigation accounted for 7.33 per cent of plan expenditure – Rs 1.17 lakh crore was allotted out of a total plan outlay of Rs 15.9 lakh crore.[9] (Rural development was allocated 25 per cent of plan outlay, but much of this money was for poverty alleviation programmes and does not add to agricultural productivity.) The same trend is being continued in the 12th Five-Year Plan (2012–17) as agriculture and water resource sector has been allocated only 7.96 per cent of overall budgetary outlay of the plan.

Studies of rural expenditure done by G. Gangadhar Rao, Praveen Jha and Nilachala Acharya[10] (2011) for the 60-year period 1950–2010 show highly discriminatory treatment given to rural India in allocation of public funds. The study finds that *rural expenditure* combining (fertilizer subsidy, cooperation, agriculture and allied activities, rural development and irrigation) both central and state governments is totally mismatched with the population. Rural expenditure ranged on an average between 9.5 and 12 per cent of total public expenditure, while 69 to 82 per cent of India's population lived in rural areas, as per periodic ten-year census. During 1950–51 to 1960–61, while 82 per cent of the population was living in rural areas, rural expenditure to total expenditure was only 11.4 per cent – of which expenditure on irrigation was 7.8 per cent. During 2000–2001 to 2010–11, while the rural population was 69 per cent, rural expenditure to total public expenditure was 9.70 per cent, with a meagre 0.60 per cent expenditure on irrigation. One of the biggest problems in agriculture is declining public investment, particularly in irrigation – which is the backbone of agriculture. There could not be a more telling commentary on government's apathy towards agriculture and rural economy.

Prices of agricultural products

Agriculture must be remunerative for farmers in sustaining their interest in its cultivation and production. B. P. Mathur[11] had done a study of impact of American PL 480 Assistance on India's food grains economy, published in his book *Foreign Money in India*, and had come to the conclusion that American wheat imports in the 1950s and 1960s had severely repressed price of wheat, and farmers lost interest in its production. India was forced to depend on imported food grains in what was known as 'ship to mouth existence'. This had serious consequences for national security, as well loss of national self-respect. The US stopped supply of food grains, following Indo-Pak war of 1965, and thanks to Prime Minister Lal Bahadur Shastri's leadership ably supported by C. Subramaniam, the then agriculture minister, India launched a policy of national self-sufficiency with the call of 'Jai Jawan Jai Kisan' (salute the soldier, salute the farmer). A Committee on Food Prices (1965), chaired by L. K. Jha, was appointed, which recommended MSP (minimum support price) for wheat and rice. By the implementation of the committee's recommendation, together with the application of high-yielding varieties of wheat and rice, developed by the ingenuity of Noble laureate Norman Borlaugh and his team, India attained self-sufficiency in food grains production and brought the Green Revolution.

Today, 24 agricultural commodities are under MSP regime, which is fixed on the basis of recommendations of the Committee on Agriculture Cost and Prices. Although wheat and rice are the main commodities procured by government, it includes pulses, oilseeds, cotton and sugarcane. The MSP more or less serves as a ruling price for public sector agencies engaged in procurement. While this helps farmers in preventing distress sale, the price support mechanism hardly gives a decent income to farmers, as MSP is very conservatively fixed.

There is severe distortion in pricing of agricultural commodities due to governmental interference. In the name of affordable food prices for the poor, government has created a vast Public Distribution System (PDS), for which grain is procured by the Food Corporation of India and distributed through the state governments. There is huge leakage and corruption in PDS. Subsidized distribution of grain makes sense if it is given to really poor people, those who are below the official poverty line. However, certain states, particularly in the south, started a policy of extending the benefit of giving cheap rice and wheat to majority of its population, as an election gimmick, with a view to secure votes. The contagion caught the previous UPA II (United Progressive Alliance) government, which enacted a National Food Security Act in September 2013. The act covers 75 per cent of rural and 50 per cent of urban population, who will be entitled to get rice at Rs 3 per kg and wheat at Rs 2 per kg. The policy of giving subsidized food grains to large sections of the population imposes heavy burden on governments finances, which is already under severe strain. During 2013–14 food subsidy bill was Rs 89,800 crore and in 2014–15 it was Rs 113,200 crore.

Does food subsidy help the poor and vulnerable sections of the population? According to Key Indicators of Consumer Expenditure 2011–12, conducted by National Sample Survey Office, total consumption expenditure on cereals was 12 per cent in rural areas and 7.3 per cent in urban areas.[12] Talk to the maidservant, mali or chowkidar (gardener or watchman) working in or around your household and you will find out that such subsidized food grain makes no significant difference to their living. (If they are given freebies, they will of course take it. Who would not?) They would much like to provide milk, fruits and vegetables to their children, are more concerned with their education and timely medical help in case of illness and possess the same incentive system as the better-off class. Imagine the economic benefit to the rural population if the money spent on food, fertilizer and other subsidies was utilized in providing irrigation and upgrading agricultural infrastructure and improving productivity. It would have transformed the face of rural India.

Nobel Prize–winner economist Theodore Schultz points out that intervention by governments is the major cause of lack of optimum economic incentives to agriculture.[13] Governments' intervention in sugarcane farming has a devastating impact on farmers in cane-growing states. In Uttar Pradesh, a state whose economy is critically dependent on this crop, sugar mills have not paid hundreds of crores of dues to farmers for cane supplied to them. For three consecutive seasons from 2012–13 to 2014–15, the administered price at which cane was to be lifted by sugar mills has not been raised, despite the rising cost of inputs. In 2014 (March–June) the mills did not lift sugarcane, on the ground that at current pricing, the commercial production of sugar is unviable. Many farmers were forced to burn their standing crop, as they had to clear their land for the next crop. Greedy mill owners, perverse pricing policy, excessive control reminiscent of pre-1991 licence raj, capricious import/export policy and pampering the urban consumers play havoc with the lives of farmers who grow sugarcane and reduce them to a life of penury and misery.

Consumers of food grains, vegetables and fruits who live mostly in urban centres want them at low prices and raise a huge hue and cry when prices rise. High price of onions hits newspaper headlines and becomes an election issue, but nobody tries to find out that shortage was due to drought conditions or crop failure. Government responds by banning export or importing onions, jeopardizing the interest of growers.

There has been a fantastic increase in potato production in the country, currently at 45mt, accounting for 12 per cent of global production, India being the second-largest producer after China. Prices often slump due to bumper harvest; the farmer is forced to throw away his crop due to unviability of bringing it to the market – no safety net is available to the farmer. India has performed wonders in milk production, which has transformed the lives of millions of milkmen in villages, and supplies crucial nutrients to the country's burgeoning population. Thanks to Operation Flood, pioneered by Dr Verghese Kurien, India is now the largest producer of milk in the world – 146 mt in 2014–15 and 138 mt in 2013–14, a steep rise from 17 mt in 1950–51. (India's per capita milk production today is 302 grams per day well above the minimum recommended by the World Health Organization.) The cooperative movement organized throughout the country, under the auspices of National Dairy Development Board, has replicated the Anand pattern and handles the entire gamut of milk production from collecting and processing to marketing and conserving seasonal surpluses. The Mother Dairy, as it is known in Delhi, has full autonomy in fixing price of milk and its products and keeps the incentive of milkmen, spread across thousands of villages, in its production.

Low prices of agricultural products, due to a number of factors, are the biggest cause of rural distress. When there is a bumper crop, prices slump; when there is fall in production due to vagaries from which agriculture suffers, farmers are not able to take advantage of market forces as the government intervenes to check prices – often resorting to imports, in the interest of consumers and other interest groups. Nobel Prize–winning economist Theodore Schultz observes in his Nobel Prize lecture:

> The 'reason' why governments tend to introduce distortions that discriminate against agriculture is that internal politics generally favor the urban population at the expense of rural people, despite the much greater size of the rural population. The political influence of urban consumers and industry enables them to extract cheap food at the expense of the vast number of poor rural people. . . . The lowly cultivator is viewed as indifferent to economic incentives because it is presumed that he is strongly committed to his traditional ways of cultivation. Rapid industrialization is viewed as the key to economic progress. . . . Policy is designed to give top priority to industry, which includes keeping food grains cheap.[14]

Eminent agriculture scientist M. S. Swaminathan, who had chaired the National Commission on Farmers, notes that under the existing policy farmers hardly get 15 per cent margin between cost of production and purchase price. The MSP should be at least 50 per cent more than the weighted average cost of production.

> Agriculture reform should start with the improvement of economics of farming through appropriate pricing and marketing policies. Public procurement at remunerative price will be the greatest stimulant to farmers for improving agriculture productivity.[15]

Analysing the causes of suicide by farmers, agriculture economist K. C. Suri says political leaders are not sensitive to people's suffering, most bureaucrats and think tanks have neither stakes nor empathy for farmers and

> businessmen, traders, industrialists, professionals etc are all interested in extraction of 'surplus' from agriculture, as their profits

and earnings are inversely related to net retainable incomes of those engaged in agriculture. Farmers do not have the where-withal to lobby in the corridors of power.[16]

There is huge agrarian distress due to declining productivity and higher costs of input. Government policy intervention is limited to giving input subsidy on some products and MSP for some categories of food grains and agricultural products. The liberalization of the economy has compounded the problem and has prematurely pushed Indian agricul-ture into global markets without a level-playing field. The farmers are getting squeezed on both sides, due to high cost of seeds and pesticides imported by foreign companies and heavily subsidized agricultural prod-ucts dumped by Western and other countries in the Indian market.

People have a wrong notion that agriculture cannot be a source of pros-perity for the country. We have to learn from Israel, a world leader in agri-cultural research and development, which has led to dramatic increases in the quantity and quality of the country's crops. Israel increased agriculture production 17 times in 25 years, despite largely an arid land. Agriculture can be revolutionized by application of science and technology and giving appropriate incentive and support to farmers. Farmers should be given remunerative prices as low prices of agriculture products are the biggest cause of rural distress. There is need for massive public investment in agricultural infrastructure such as irrigation, farm machinery and equip-ment, seeds, post-harvesting handling and processing and research and development to make agriculture dynamic and mainstay of the economy.

Poverty

India has 35 crore people below the poverty line, and the absolute num-ber is not declining despite several decades of planning, due to the fact that while there has been some decline in the percentage of people living below the poverty line, it is being offset by rising population. As per the estimates made by the 12th Five-Year Plan (2012–17), in 2009–10, there were 35 crore people below the poverty line (29.8 per cent of the population), based on Tendulkar formula. At the time of formulation of the 11th Five-Year Plan (2007–12), the absolute number of poor esti-mated was 30 crore (22 crore in rural areas and 8 crore in urban areas), on the assumption that 27 per cent of the people are living below the poverty line. This was based on the then prevailing formula of calorie intake (2,100 in urban areas and 2,400 in rural areas, fixed in 1993 on the recommendations of Lakdawala Committee). Subsequently, a com-mittee appointed by the Planning Commission, chaired by economist Suresh Tendulkar[17] (November 2009), came out with the finding that the number of people who are below the poverty line is 37 per cent, tak-ing 2004–5 as the base year, if we take the norm of consumption of basic goods and services as a basis for determining poverty. The Tendulkar Committee had taken the household consumption of goods and services, which includes food, education and health, as the norm to determine the poverty line, instead of calorie intake. People whose consumption expenditure was less than Rs 447 per month in rural areas (Rs 15 per day) and Rs 579 (Rs 19 per day) in urban areas were categorized as poor. On the basis of the new norm, the number below the poverty line in rural area worked out to 42 per cent and not 28 per cent as was estimated earlier, though there was not much change in earlier poverty line estimates of the urban area at 26 per cent. More than half the population that was below the poverty line were in two states: Orissa (57 per cent) and Bihar (54 per cent). In the following states between 40 and 50 per cent of the population was below the poverty line: Chhattisgarh (49.4 per cent), Madhya Pradesh (48.6 per cent), Jharkhand (45.3 per cent), Uttar Pradesh (40.9 per cent) and Tripura (40.6 per cent).

Subsequently, the Planning Commission updated the 2004–5 prices taken by Tendulkar Committee for 2009–10 and worked out Rs 26 per day for rural areas and Rs 32 for urban areas as the basis for poverty line. According to the 12th Five-Year Plan, poverty has been declining over the years; it declined by 0.74 per cent every year in the period 1993–94 and by 1.5 per cent during 2004–5 to 2009–10. On this basis the number of people below the poverty line for 2010–11 was more than 34 crore (28.3 per cent of 121 crore as per 2011 census). Thus, the absolute number of about 35 crore poor people has not changed substantially over years of planning.

A new committee headed by C. Rangrajan[18] has revisited the poverty line (July 2014) and suggested that persons spending Rs 47 per day in cities (Rs 1,407 per month) and Rs 32 in villages (Rs 972 per month) should be considered poor at 2011–12 prices. The committee felt that a better way to look at the poverty line is to look at the monthly consumption expenditure of a household of five persons. On this basis the committee has pegged the poverty line at Rs 7,035 in urban areas and Rs 4,860 in rural areas. The number of persons below the poverty line goes up as per the new formula when compared with Tendulkar norm from 35.47 crore to 45.46 crore in 2009–10 and from 26.98 crore to 36.3 crore in 2011–12.

Working out the poverty line and fine-tuning it is simply a statistical jugglery. It gives no relief to the poor or those who are at the margin. In 2011, there was a countrywide controversy regarding the unrealistic basis for fixing poverty line, based on Tendulkar formula, and a writ petition was filed in Supreme Court challenging it. Government has adopted money-metric poverty line due its practicability, as well as the need to cap the welfare entitlements.[19] It has been argued by some experts that there should be a 'capability-based' approach, and elimination of poverty should be reflected in achievement of functioning parameters such as freedom from hunger, literacy level and state of health.

Irrespective of the manner in which poverty line is determined, it is a fact that a vast population – almost 30 to 35 per cent population – lives in abject poverty and another 40 to 45 per cent lives at margin. The fact that such a vast population lives in poverty and misery, almost seven decades after independence, is a severe indictment of the Indian state, our governance and economic policies.

Unemployment

The main reason for India's poverty is widespread unemployment and underemployment. The 12th Five-Year Plan (2012–17), using the data of the National Sample Survey's (NSS) 66th round for 2009–10, notes that the total workforce was 46.88 crore (34.19 crore in rural areas and 12.69 crore in urban areas), of whom 45.9 crore (33.64 crore in rural areas and 12.26 crore in urban areas) were employed, with an unemployment rate of 2.1 per cent and only 98 lakh persons unemployed. The subsequent NSS survey for 2011–12 estimates a labour force of 48.48 crore, of whom 47.42 crore are employed, with an unemployment rate of 2.2 per cent and 1.06 crore persons unemployed.[20] These figures present a misleading picture of unemployment in the country.

According to the Census 2011[21] data released in September 2014, 11.3 crore persons are 'seeking or are available for work', that is unemployed, which is around 15 per cent of working-age population of 74.8 crore in the 15–60 age group. They are distributed over 7 crore households, constituting 28 per cent of households in the country. This is an all-time high; as in the previous Census 2001, 23 per cent of households had members who were unemployed. The figures reveal that in the past few years there has been no growth in employment.

The employment situation in the country is grim. According to the 12th Five-Year Plan (based on NSS 2009–10 data), there was total employment of 46.02 crore persons, out of which organized sector employment was 7.29 crore, with 3.08 crore persons employed in the formal sector (remaining 4.21 crore were in the informal sector). Thus, more than 93 per cent of the workforce is employed in the unorganized/informal sector of the economy, mostly working in non-skilled jobs at whatever wages they can get, instead of sitting idle at home, which is captured as 'employment' by government statisticians. A disquieting feature of employment situation in the country is decline in employment in the manufacturing sector, where employment is of higher quality with better-paid jobs.

The workforce employed in manufacturing in 2004–5 was 5.58 crore, but declined to 5.07 crore by 2009–10; thus, more than 51 lakh jobs were lost (12th Five-Year Plan, citing NSS survey 2009–10). The National Commission for the Enterprises in the Unorganised Sector[22] (2009), chaired by Arjun Sengupta, had found that 83.6 crore Indians are poor and vulnerable, living on less than Rs 20 per day, and experienced hardly any improvement in living standards since the early 1990s. The commission had noted that 39.49 crore workers, which constitutes 86 per cent of the working population, are in the unorganized sector from agriculture to micro-industries to self-employment. They work under utterly deplorable conditions and have few livelihood options with no job or social security.

Dutch sociologist Jan Bremen,[23] who has done an in-depth study of India's informal economy, faults the dualism of 'formal' and 'informal' economy – while 'capital' is treated as formal, 'labour' is regarded as informal, 'capital owners often resort to informalization of their business in order to avoid the appropriation of the surplus value generated by labour through taxation by the state'. Bremen points out that India is a case of unregulated capitalism, which has dire consequences for the labour. The workforce in the informal economy contributes roughly half of the national output. 'Squeezing labour has become the driving force of India's high growth rate. And the profits made do not trickle down but are siphoned off to higher echelons in the chain of economic activity.'

The employment situation is worst for the educated youth. According to NSS survey,[24] for the year 2011–12 for the age group up to 29 years, the unemployment situation (including male, female and both urban and rural) was as follows: graduate and above, 22.1 per cent; diploma/certificate, 18.9 per cent; higher secondary, 11.7 per cent; secondary, 8.45 per cent. The data revealed that chances of getting employment for young men and women once they acquire vocational skill or college degree become less. Broadly, one in four youth with a graduate degree or vocational skill is unemployed. What an irony of our educational system!

The employment data compiled by NSS is completely flawed. The unemployment rate is determined on the basis of surveys of a select sample done only periodically and does not systematically capture job creation in the organized sector, where employment is of high quality, employing skilled and educated force, giving them some kind of job security and social security benefits. Employment data also does not capture employment of educated youths, particularly those with graduate degrees and technical qualification, so that we understand the mismatch between education system and job market. In its absence, the voluminous statistics compiled by NSS become a meaningless jumble of incoherent data. In the US and Western countries, employment rate is tracked every month, and high unemployment becomes a major issue of national concern.

In India, the policymakers are indifferent to severe unemployment problem. The real test of good economic policy is to create employment opportunities in the organized sector with job security and social security benefits and employment of educated youths coming out from colleges and universities. The government has completely failed on this front.

Poverty alleviation schemes – are they helping?

Over the years the government's effort to fight poverty and improve living standards is mainly through centrally sponsored schemes (CSSs), which are implemented through state governments. The most important programme is Mahatma Gandhi National Rural Employment Guarantee Act under an act of the same name (MGNREGA). There are other schemes such as the National Rural Livelihood Mission/Ajeevika; National Social Programme to provide pension to the elderly, widows and disabled persons; Pradhan Mantri Awas Yojna to provide dwelling to the poor in rural areas and scheduled castes/scheduled tribes; and Pradhan Mantri Gram Sadak Yojana (PMGSY) to provide rural connectivity. In addition, there are schemes to impart education and improve health such as Sarva Shiksha Abhiyan, Mid-Day Meals and National Health Mission. There are altogether 66 CSSs, out of which 17 are major schemes, termed 'flagship programmes'.

The UPA government had launched a very ambitious programme of poverty alleviation MGNREGA, which is being continued by the present NDA government, more or less in its original format. A sum of around Rs 314,000 crore has been spent during its ten years' existence from February 2006 to March 2016; Rs 38,500 crore has been allocated for FY 2016–17. The objective of MGNERGA is to enhance the livelihood security of people in rural areas by guaranteeing 100 days of wage employment in a financial year to a rural household whose members volunteer to do unskilled work. While MGNREGA has been able to make some difference to the really poor in rural areas, the issue is whether the best value for money for the huge money spent has been realized. MGNREGA has reduced distress migration to cities and has helped improvement in bargaining power of agriculture labour leading to higher wages, but it has created a sidespin effect. It has caused shortage of labour for agricultural farming during the sowing and harvesting seasons. It also encourages 'idleness' among labourers, as they get wages by simply signing on the muster role being in the nature of dole. N. C. Saxena,[25] a distinguished civil servant and expert on the subject, points out that the programme has been badly designed with poor monitoring mechanism. It has been reduced to creating short-term unproductive employment with no focus on asset creation or soil or water conservation. States with a large number of 'below-the-poverty-line' population such as Bihar, Uttar Pradesh and Maharashtra have not benefitted, as money is not allocated in proportion to the number of poor in the state, while states such as Kerala and Tamil Nadu have been able to corner most of the funds despite low incidence of poverty. He contrasts this programme with PMGSY, which is better designed and has helped in improving rural road connectivity in backward states, where it was lacking. This is due to its better designing as money is released as per predetermined gaps in infrastructure and has an effective monitoring mechanism for project implementation and maintenance.

It needs to be appreciated that MGNREGA is not a long-term solution to rural poverty. But politicians favour it due to its immediate benefit in terms of electoral gains. Many experts feel that instead of doling out huge money, investment should have been made in increasing rural productivity by investing in durable assets such as irrigation canals, farm equipment and warehouses, which would have created employment opportunities and more income for the rural population.

Most anti-poverty programmes suffer from a fundamental flaw, as they do not upgrade capability of people through provision of better education, health and skill to become employable and make a dignified living.

There is an old parable: give a person a fish, he makes a living for a day; give him a fishing rod and he makes a living for life time. It is doubtful if Mahatma Gandhi would have approved such programmes, as they are not based on economic self-reliance and individual dignity.

Transforming rural India – the PURA model

How do we transform the face of rural India? Experts agree that rural–urban divide is the main reason for rural impoverishment, and the gap should be bridged for the country to progress. Former president and eminent scientist A. P. J. Abdul Kalam[26] championed PURA (Providing Urban Amenities in Rural Area) model, for rejuvenation of rural India. PURA stands for integrated development, starting at the village level, with employment generation as its focus, driven by providing good habitation, health care and education, and by developing skills through physical and electronic connectivity and marketing. PURA, apart from concentrating on agriculture, emphasizes agro-processing, developing local crafts, dairy farming, fishing, and so on, so that non-farm revenue is enhanced, based on core competency of the region. Its economy will be driven by sources of renewable energy, sun, wind and biofuels. PURA involves physical connectivity, electronic connectivity and knowledge connectivity. The villages must be connected with each other and with the main towns and cities by good networked roads. There must be other amenities such as schools, colleges, hospitals, irrigation networks and electricity. Knowledge connectivity implies that there should be vocational training, land and crop management, water management, forest management and so on.

India has great agriculture potential as nature has richly endowed its climate and soil. It has 52 per cent cultivable land as compared to world average of 11 per cent; all 15 major climatic regions are present in India; it has 46 out of 60 soil types; it has 20 agro-climatic zones and 10 bio-diversity regions and gets plenty of sunshine for round-the-year cultivation.[27] India ranks first in production of milk and fruits and second in production of wheat, paddy, sugarcane, tea, groundnut and vegetables (although its yields per unit are low).

There have been some half-hearted attempts by the Ministry of Rural Development to implement PURA. In the 10th Five-Year Plan, seven pilot projects were implemented under PPP (public–private partnership) mode. During the 11th Five-Year Plan a modified scheme was formalized, with government's funding limited to 35 per cent of project cost, with a cap on total liability, to be operated by private developers.[28] The scheme has not made much headway. The designing of the scheme under PPP mode is flawed and goes against the very concept of PURA, for which government should take full responsibility, including its funding.

India has around 6.4 lakh villages, in which 83 crore people – 70 per cent of population – live. Some 7,000–8,000 PURA clusters would be needed to cover the whole country, one cluster providing all the amenities to an average of 1 lakh persons. It should be the responsibility of the government to provide basic human amenities such as education, health care, sanitation, road and electricity among each cluster of villages grouped under a PURA, as they are essential public goods. PURA can be extended to the whole country in a period of say ten years, if we operate it under a mission mould, by a dedicated team of professionals, by taking 70–80 clusters every year. For its success, the local community's full involvement and participation is essential.

Moving forward

Eminent economist J. K. Galbraith explains in *The Affluent Society* that it is the failure to invest in people, which is the real cause of poverty. Writing six decades back in 1958 he was prescient,

> The first and strategic attack on poverty is to see that it is no longer self-perpetuating. . . . Poverty is self perpetuating because the poorest communities are poorest in the services which would eliminate it. It is there that high quality schools, strong health services, special provision for nutrition and recreation are most needed to compensate for the low investment which families are able to make in their own offspring. The effect of education and related investment in individuals is to enable them either to contend more effectively with their environment, or to escape it and take life elsewhere on more or less equal terms with others.[29]

Eminent journalist P. Sainath in his book *Everybody Loves a Good Drought*[30] castigates the elite, including the mainstream media, for their indifference to the problem of rural people and says that the existing 'development' approach is a strategy of evasion. Sainath says that millions of rural Indians have astonishing resilience. They want to live their life with dignity and have quest for self-reliance. They can achieve wonders if given the right opportunities, that is genuine land reform, education, health, shelter and work.

The degradation of living conditions of rural classes is largely due to economic and industrial development strategies that we have adopted, imitating the Western economic model. The place of agriculture in Western countries has declined in terms of both national income and employment due to rapid industrialization in the past two centuries. But in India, agricultural income has declined without a corresponding decline in population dependent on agriculture, as it has not been absorbed in manufacturing or services. Mahatma Gandhi supported decentralized rural-centric development, with agriculture and small-scale industries being given pride of place. (See Chapter 12 for discussion of Gandhian economic philosophy.) A time has come to radically rethink our economic development model, as without giving primacy to agriculture and rural upliftment, we cannot solve our country's gigantic problem of poverty and unemployment and become a prosperous society.

Notes

1 M. K. Gandhi, *India of My Dreams*, Ahmedabad: Navjeevan Press, 2011, p. 91; *Harijan*, 4 April 1936 (quoted by R.K. Prabu).
2 Theodore Schultz, 'The Economics of Being Poor', Nobel Prize Lecture, 8 December 1979, available at http://www.nobelprize.org/nobel_prizes/economic-sciences/laureates/1979/schultz-lecture.html (accessed 9 October 2014).
3 Quoted in Dan Senor and Saul Singer, *Start-Up Nation: The Story of Israel's Economic Miracle*, New York: Hachette Book Group, 2009, p. 226.
4 Planning Commission, Government of India, *Eleventh Five Year Plan*, Vol. III, New Delhi: Oxford, 2008, p. 3.
5 Theodore Schultz quoted by B. P. Mathur, *Foreign Money in India*, New Delhi: Macmillan, 1989, p. 150.
6 Suresh C. Modgal, *Food Security in India*, New Delhi: National Book Trust, 2014, p. 30.
7 Data in this section is from Planning Commission, *Twelfth Five Year Plan 2012–17*, Vol. II, New Delhi: Sage Publications, 2013, pp. 7–14.
8 Planning Commission, *Eleventh Five Year Plan (2007–12)*, Vol. I, p. 45.
9 Planning Commission, *Twelfth Five Year Plan (2012–17)*, Vol. I, p. 82.
10 G. Gangadhar Rao, 'Inevitability of Gandhian Village Reconstruction in Rural India', *Mainstream*, 4 October 2014, Vol. LII, No. 41; Praveen Jha and Nilachala Acharya, 'Expenditure on the Rural Economy in India's Budgets since the 1950s: An Assessment', *Review of Agrarian Studies*, Vol. 1, No. 2, pp. 134–156.
11 B. P. Mathur, 'American PL 480 Assistance and India's Food Economy (1954–1972)', in *Foreign Money in India*, New Delhi: Macmillan, 1989, pp. 109–158.
12 Government of India, *Economic Survey 2013–14*, New Delhi: Government of India, Ministry of Finance, 2014, p. 158.
13 Theodore Schultz, 'The Economics of Being Poor', Nobel Prize Lecture, 8 December 1979, http://www.nobelprize.org/nobel_prizes/economic-sciences/laureates/1979/schultz-lecture.html (assessed 9.10.2014).
14 Ibid. Also see Theodore Schultz, *Economic Impact, 1981–84*, Washington: International Communication Agency.
15 M. S. Swaminathan, 'Farm Policy: Let's Make Farming Profitable', *Down to Earth, State of India's Environment 2016*, New Delhi: Centre of Science and Environment, pp. 46–48.
16 K. C. Suri, 'Political Economy of Agrarian Distress', *Economic and Political Weekly*, 22–28 April 2006, Vol. XLI, No. 16, 1523–1529.
17 Government of India, Planning Commission, *Report of the Expert Group to Review the Methodology of Estimating Poverty*, November 2009, available at http://planningcommission.nic.in/reports/genrep/rep_pov.pdf (accessed 11 December 2013).
18 'New poverty line', *The Times of India*, 7 July 2014; 'Poverty count', *The Indian Express*, 8 July 2014.

19 S. Subramanian, *The Poverty Line*, New Delhi: Oxford University Press, 2012, pp. 138–139.
20 Santosh Mehrotra, Jajati Parida and Sharmistha Sinha, 'Explaining Employment Trends in the Indian Economy: 1993–94 to 2011–12', *Economic and Political Weekly*, 9 August 2014, Vol. XLIX, No. 12, 49–57.
21 'Army of jobless now 11 cr. strong', *Times of India*, 24 September2014, p. 13.
22 National Commission for the Enterprises in the Unorganised Sector, *The Challenge of Unemployment in India: An Informal Economy Perspective*, April 2009, available at http://dcmsme.gov.in/The_Challenge_of_Employ ment_in_India.pdf (accessed 8 November 2013).
23 Jan Bremen, *At Work in the Informal Economy of India*, New Delhi: Oxford University Press, 2013, pp. 22–23.
24 'Jobs report gloomy, prospects worst for graduates, shows all-India government data', *The Indian Express*, 1 April 2014.
25 N. C. Saxena, 'Why are some programmes doing better than others: PMSGY vs MGNREGS', A policy brief by Skoch Development Foundation, *The Indian Express*, 23 March 2016, p. 7.
26 A. P. J. Abdul Kalam and Srijan Pal Singh, *Target 3 Billion*, New Delhi: Penguin Books, 2011.
27 Ibid., p. 51.
28 Ministry of Rural Development, *Annual Report 2013–14*, New Delhi: Government of India, Ministry of Rural Development, pp. 75–77.
29 J. K. Galbraith, *The Affluent Society*, Great Britain: Penguin Books in association with Hamish Hamilton, 1963, pp. 266–267.
30 P. Sainath, *Everybody Loves a Good Drought*, New Delhi: Penguin Books, 2012 reprint, pp. 135, 421–437.

5

INDUSTRIAL DEVELOPMENT
Route to prosperity

In order to 'Make in India' and compete with better or cheaper goods from abroad, one must first 'invent in India' and in order to 'invent in India', one must 'discover in India'. I suggest the strategy: Discover, invent and make in India.

David J. Gross, Nobel Laureate, Physics[1]

It is through industrialization that Western countries have achieved the present level of prosperity. The history of Western countries shows that the growth of modern industry provided employment to an underutilized labour force bottled up in agriculture and lifted it out of stagnation. Industrialization radiated a stimulus throughout the economy, raised productivity of the labour force and increased national output and income. Industrialization is considered a manifestation of modernization and application of science and technology to productive activities.

Industrialization was built in the development strategy of India in early years of its planning. However, the planners erred in relying solely on the public sector to provide commanding heights of the economy and did not give a meaningful role to the private sector in industrial growth. This resulted in slow growth of the economy. Post-1991 economic liberalization, the policymakers have swung to the other extreme and have opened the economy to forces of global competition, without first building a strong domestic industrial base, which the existing industries are unable to withstand.

Two hundred years of world's economic history shows that Western countries built their industrial base on the foundation of a strong dose of state support and protection and embraced free trade philosophy, timing it strategically when they developed sufficient competitive strength. This has been the case with pioneering industrial power Britain, and later with Germany and the US in the 19th century and first few decades of the 20th century. Britain became a dominant industrial power by the mid-19th century and felt it advantageous to completely liberalize its trade and became an ardent champion of free trade doctrine. In 1860, it accounted for 20 per cent of world manufacturing output and by 1870,

46 per cent of world trade in manufactures. However, by 1880 countries such as Germany and the US caught up, and its relative position declined. Nevertheless, the dominance of manufacturing in the British economy continued for a long time. Until the 1970s, Britain had one of the world's largest share of manufacturing employment – around 35 per cent in total employment – and was a quintessential manufacturing economy. It was only from 1980 onwards that its share started shrinking. Before the liberalization and globalization wave, which began in the early 1980s, manufacturing accounted for more than one-fourth of developed countries' gross domestic product (GDP). In 1980, manufacturing accounted for 23 per cent share of GDP in France, 25 per cent in the UK, 27 per cent in Japan and 30 per cent in Germany. It is only in recent years that manufacturing share has come down, as these developed countries believe that they have entered post-industrial stage and knowledge-based services have become engines of economic growth. Currently, the share of manufacturing is 10 per cent in the UK and France and 13 per cent in the US, but in more dynamic economies such as Japan, it is 19 per cent and in Germany 22 per cent (2012).

The newly emerged Asian tigers such as Singapore, South Korea and Taiwan and the current industrial powerhouse China have adopted a route of economic development similar to that of Western countries. Manufacturing growth is behind the spectacular economic performance of these countries. The share of manufacturing in Singapore is 21 per cent of GDP, Malaysia 24 per cent, Thailand 34 per cent, South Korea 31 per cent, and China 32 per cent (2012).

In India we seem to have forgotten this lesson of economic history and have relegated industry, particularly manufacturing, to a backseat in the naïve belief that 'services' will bail out and leapfrog us as a developed economy. At least that has been the position of post-economic liberalization up to the tenure of UPA II (United Progressive Alliance) (2014). Currently, services account for 60 per cent of GDP, while agriculture accounts for 15 per cent and industry 25 per cent (industry group includes manufacturing, mining, electricity and construction). The manufacturing sector accounts for only 15 per cent share of GDP, and due to lack of dynamism of this sector, the country is unable to develop industrially. It may be noted that there are stages of economic growth through which every country has to pass through, and it is an error to think that the Indian economy can 'take off' to a developed stage directly through a predominantly services sector growth and skip through the stage of a dynamic manufacturing base. Cambridge economist Ha-Joon Chang says:

> As for developing countries, it is a fantasy to think that they can skip industrialization and build prosperity on the basis of service sector. Most services have slow productivity growth and most of those services that have high productivity growth are services that cannot be developed without a strong manufacturing sector. Low tradability of services means that a developing country specializing

in services will face a bigger balance of payment problem, which for a developing country means a reduction in ability to upgrade the economy. Post-industrial fantasies are bad enough for the rich countries, but they are positively dangerous for developing countries.[2]

The US, which had been the most industrially advanced and innovative country in the world, is facing serious economic problems and adverse balance of trade, largely due to declining share of manufacturing in national output. Seymour Melman,[3] a professor of industrial engineering, Columbia University, observes that post-1960, wrong economic ideology is behind the slow decline in US productivity. He finds fault with the theory propounded by American business schools and corporate executives, that America should become a 'post-industrial society' and the sole objective of business is to make profit, relegating efficient production to a secondary position. The consequence of investing power in the hands of corporate managers results in investment of money wherever return is highest, regardless of effects on industry, working people and the community. Melman argues that there has been a breakdown of social contract between management and rest of society, as there is deterioration of production systems, while management is making money, in the presence of a growing workless population. The economic meltdown of 2008 showed that it was 'money-making-spree' – basically greed – that was driving corporate managers to move production abroad, particularly to China, to take advantage of lower wages on the pretext that they would become competitive in the global economy. This played havoc with the US economy, as it transferred millions of jobs abroad, and America became virtually 'de-industrialized'. The real beneficiary has been China, which has today become the manufacturing hub of the world. Lately, America is having a rethink about its economic policy and trying to bring back manufacturing to revive the economy and provide more employment to its people.

David Upton[4] of Oxford University says that it is not possible to have a healthy economy without a manufacturing base, and the Western countries that have chosen to farm out production of home-developed technologies to emerging economies have created a skill and knowledge gap, which leaves them commercially vulnerable. An example is cited of light-emitting diode (LED) display technology, in which the West was once the leader, but now the Asian economies have mastered it and developed their own forms of LED lighting and new ways of manufacturing it, and now the West does not know how to manufacture it. Upton says there is a symbiotic relationship between research and development (R&D) and the manufacturing process, and the two are constantly evolving and have become intertwined – outsourcing may be cheaper in the short run, but in the long run you lose out.

Manufacturing in India

Manufacturing is the backbone of the economy in both rich countries and newly emerged Asian tigers. However, in India the manufacturing sector has been neglected right from the time we commenced planning in the 1950s. Manufacturing requires capability to acquire complex technology, management ability and highly skilled manpower, which we badly lack. A principal reason for the inability of the manufacturing sector to come up is lack of good infrastructure such as transportation and uninterrupted power supply. Manufacturing in India employs 50 million persons, which is around 10 per cent of total employment. This is very low as compared to 15 to 30 per cent in newly emerged Asian countries. A disturbing trend in recent years is decline in employment in the manufacturing sector, with the sector shedding 5 million jobs between 2004–5 and 2009–10, and employment decreasing from 55 to 50 million. The government had announced a National Manufacturing Policy (2011), which envisages manufacturing to grow to 25 per cent of GDP, with additional job creation of 100 million in a decade, but there is hardly any visible impact of this policy in terms of implementation.

Prime Minister Modi soon after taking over has given a call that India should become a manufacturing hub. But to implement this, there is need for a supportive policy environment. There are three main components of national industry – small and medium enterprises, public enterprises and large corporate sectors – each responding to different policy initiatives, and we should understand their inner dynamics in order to develop a vibrant industrial economy.

Small and medium enterprises

In India micro, small and medium enterprises (MSMEs) account for 45 per cent of the manufacturing sector's output and 40 per cent of its exports and contribute 8 per cent of the country's GDP. They provide employment to 60 million people in 26 million enterprises. MSMEs are the largest employers after agriculture and provide employment with low investment. They manufacture over 6,000 products ranging from handloom sarees and carpets to drugs and machine parts for large industrial products. The MSME sector in India is highly heterogeneous in terms of the size of the enterprises, variety of products and services produced and the levels of technology employed. While one end of the MSME spectrum contains highly innovative and high-growth enterprises, more than 94 per cent of MSMEs are unregistered, with a large number established in the informal or unorganized sector. The innovative sectors where MSMEs have made significant contribution to the economy include textiles and garments, drugs and pharmaceuticals, IT hardware, electronics and chemical products.

Some of the basic problems from which the SME sector suffers are non-availability of easy credit, marketing of products, non-availability of raw material at competitive prices, low technology and lack of skilled manpower. Another big problem is lack of electricity and transport infrastructure. Access to finance at reasonable cost is one of the biggest constraints. Small firms do not issue bonds or sell equity in the market; they rely on banks for borrowing. In India the lending rate to SMEs is 17 to

18 per cent, a rate at which no firm can be viable. In the European Union (EU), firms borrow between 3 and 6 per cent. Unless SMEs get credit at 4 to 5 per cent, they will find it very difficult to be profitable. The organized financial system is totally apathetic to their need. In 1990, 15 per cent of gross bank credit went to the unorganized manufacturing sector, but this fell to 3.6 per cent by 2005–6, according to NSS data.

A Prime Minister's Task Force for Micro, Medium and Small Industries[5] (January 2010) had given wide-ranging recommendations to deal with various problems with which this sector is bedevilled. The 12th Five-Year Plan (2012–17) has also recommended that a strategy for growth of this sector requires special attention to the problems of credit and finance, technology upgradation, improvement of infrastructure and skill development and training. An Inter-ministerial Committee for Accelerating Manufacturing in Micro, Small and Medium Enterprise Sector[6] (September 2013) noted that the existing regulatory mechanism and the bureaucracy of the local, state and central governments place huge demand on the time and resources of small entrepreneurs which they cannot cope with. The complex and unfriendly ecosystem pushes small entrepreneurs towards the informal and unregistered segment, which is growing faster than the organized segment by more than five times and accounts for over 95 per cent of all SMEs. It recommended overhaul of the ecosystem to assist entrepreneurs through the life cycle of creation, growth and closure of enterprises and encourages them to work in the organized sector. The committee has made over 60 recommendations regarding regulation, finance, infrastructure, technology and market through different stages of the life cycle of the enterprises.

Electronics: One of the major missed opportunities in the manufacturing sector is in the area of electronic manufacturing. While India has done well in IT software, the neglect of electronic systems and design manufacturing is proving dear in terms of both job creation and foreign exchange drain. In the hardware segment within IT and electronics, India remains way behind in electronics manufacturing compared to countries like China, Malaysia, Taiwan and South Korea. Electronics is today the largest industry in the world, but India is not a significant player in this market. According to a report by the India Electronic and Semiconductor Association (IESA),[7] the share of domestic production and services is $30 billion out of $68 billion market in 2012 and estimated at $42 billion out of $94 billion in 2015. The Indian Electronic System Design and Manufacturing (ESDM) industry is growing at a compound annual growth rate of 10 per cent, and demand is expected to be of the order of $400 billion by 2020. Currently, 65 per cent of demand for electronic products is met by imports in the country, and even the balance 35 per cent, which is manufactured in India, is mainly 'low-value-added manufacturing', mostly screwdriver technology. India is largely dependent on import of not only critical hardware but also the general-use consumer electronics such as mobile phones, flat panel television, notebooks, desktops, cameras and liquid crystal display monitors (accounting for 60 per cent of electronic consumption). This is an alarming situation for the country, and if domestic production is not increased, it will result in a major balance of payments crisis.

Despite these high-level committees, little action seems to have been taken on the ground. Rashmi Bagga,[8] a United Nations Conference on Trade and Development economist, observes that a worrisome trend in the manufacturing sector is its declining value-added growth, which is termed 'hollowing out'. Value added in total manufacturing output declined from around 25 per cent in the mid-1990s to 18 per cent in 2011–12. This is mainly due to intense competition this sector is facing, in both the domestic and external markets. The Trade Facilitation Agreement, which the World Trade Organization (WTO) is pressing India to sign, will further compound the problem.

Arun Maira,[9] former member of Planning Commission, argues that employment and job creation should have been the objective of planning, rather than GDP growth, which can be done through manufacturing via small and medium enterprises. Youths should be imparted skill by revamping the education system and providing vocational training. Small enterprises have lower capital-employment ratios than larger organized enterprises and therefore greater job creation potential. He cites the example of Germany and Sweden which has employers-trained apprentice system and low unemployment rate as compared to Britain and the US.

Learning from best international practices

Worldwide SMEs have been recognized as engines of economic growth. SMEs are defined as non-subsidiary independent firms which employ fewer than given number of employees. They account for 95 per cent of firms and 60 to 65 per cent employment in rich (Organization for Economic Cooperation and Development [OECD]) countries. In the US half the jobs are in small- and medium-sized firms (SMEs). In Europe they play a bigger role. In France SMEs employ 60 per cent workers, in Spain 67 per cent and in Italy 80 per cent.[10] An OECD[11] policy brief says that they are the source of all new job creation and play a major role in economic growth of member counties. In OECD countries, smaller firms are increasingly present in technology-intensive industries such as information and communication technology and biotechnology. A vibrant entrepreneurial culture is essential for such technology-driven industries. In OECD countries, SMEs also face problems such as lack of finance, difficulty accessing new technology and limited managerial capability. Forces of globalization have posed serious threat to their competitiveness. But governments make serious effort to promote them.

Germany is a typical country where SMEs, known as *Mittlestand*, provide the backbone of the economy.[12] Germany is the world leader in export of high-tech machinery and equipment. German firms are generally family owned, located in small towns and mostly sell their products such as specialized machinery and components to big businesses and do not have high visibility. Small firms offer two advantages. First, they prevent concentration of too much economic activity in a small number of giant firms and in a few megacities. Second, they offer youth employment. A large number of medium-sized companies with local roots and a strong apprentice system has helped Germany, finding employment for educated youths unlike other European countries, who are reeling under double-digit unemployment. Many countries such as South Korea and China are flocking to Germany to learn about their manufacturing success.

India should learn from best international practices. There is urgent need for the government to reorient its policies to give massive support to SMEs, by way of provision of credit and finance, technology upgradation, skill development and other measures as recommended by expert committees, to make them a dynamic sector of the economy. There is also the need to protect domestic industries from unfair foreign competition, particularly China.

Public enterprises

> Privatization therefore is not any better guide for public action than is socialism. In a good society there is in these matters one basic rule, decision must be made on the social and economic merits of a particular case. This is not any age of doctrine, it is the age of practical judgement.
>
> J. K. Galbraith[13]

Much of the debate regarding industrialization strategy centres around respective roles of public sector and private sector. Public enterprises were the edifice on which India's development strategy was built in the first three decades of planning, and they were supposed to occupy commanding heights of the economy.[14] However, with the launch of the New Economic Policy of 1991, privatization has become the new mantra, and attempts are being made to dismantle them. The policy of privatization is an essential component of neoliberal model of economic development, which emphasized deregulation, liberalization and globalization, and is backed by powerful international institutions such as the World Bank, International Monetary Fund and WTO. After the 1980s there had been a worldwide wave of privatization of state enterprises, with Britain under the leadership of Margret Thatcher taking the lead. However, the global economic meltdown of 2008 has exposed the hollowness of this model of development, with blind faith in the free and unfettered markets. However, the Indian policymakers continue to be prisoners of a defunct economic ideology, pursuing a policy of dismantling state enterprises and eroding the industrial base of the country built assiduously over the years.

Privatization and disinvestment in India has a chequered history. In the first phase 1991–99, disinvestment of shares of a large number of public sector enterprises (PSEs) was done, but majority control remained with the government. The sale in initial rounds created a great deal of controversy, as it was alleged that enterprises were undervalued and there was loss to exchequer. However, real privatization in the sense of passing ownership to private entrepreneurs took place during the NDA (National Democratic Alliance) regime (2000–2004), when Arun Shourie was disinvestment minister under Vajpayee government. Majority control of large number of enterprises such as Modern Foods (MFIL), BALCO, CMC, HTL, VSNL, PPL, ITDC, HCI, HZL and IPCL was passed on to private players. The methodology adopted by the NDA government for privatization was severely flawed as privatization was done through strategic sale route, which allowed management control to pass through private placement, enabling big industrial houses to acquire control over valuable national assets. Thus, Sterlite Group acquired BALCO and HZL; Tatas acquired VSNL and CMC (via TCS); and Reliance acquired IPCL, commanding 80 per cent share over the country's petrochemical market.

During the UPA regime (2004–14) there was a shift in policy in the sense that profit-making PSUs (public sector undertakings) were not privatized and majority shareholding remained in the government's hand. Nevertheless, the government started a policy of divesting portfolios of profit-making companies – and shares of most *navratnas* (valuable jewels) and *mini-ratnas* (jewel) companies have been disinvested. The Bharatiya Janata Party–led NDA government, which came to power in May 2014, has not only continued the policy of the previous government but also accelerated the pace. Over the years shares of India's most prized and profitable companies such as ONGC, SAIL, NALCO, NTPC and BHEL have been sold. There is no sound economic logic to sell shares of profitable PSUs in core sectors of the economy, while retaining status as government company. Selling shares to disparate shareholders contributes to destabilizing the management of PSEs. During 2014–15 the government earned Rs 32,600 crore from disinvestment of shares of profit-making PSUs and Rs 25,300 crore in 2015–16. In the budget of 2016–17, a provision of Rs 36,000 crore has been made as disinvestment proceeds and another Rs 20,500 crore from strategic sale, a total of Rs 56,500 crore. Altogether between 2001–2 and 2014–15, the government garnered Rs 177,130 crore as proceeds of disinvestment. This money has been frittered away by the government in meeting its burgeoning revenue expenditure and covering budgetary deficit. The money should have been used for capital investment of PSUs and in setting up new green-field high-tech projects such as chip manufacturing and solar energy. This violates all canons of prudent fiscal management and tantamount to selling family silver to pay for grocer's bill.

Apparently the main objective of disinvestment is to raise revenue to meet the budgetary deficit. It may be mentioned that PSUs as a group have been paying substantial dividends to central exchequer – Rs 30,000 crore in 2012–13, Rs 25,900 crore in 2013–14, Rs 31,700 crore in 2014–15 and Rs 44,000 crore (estimated) in 2015–16. This short-sighted policy has the effect of slowly killing the goose that lays the golden egg.

On the other hand, the government is stuck with a large number of sick and chronically loss-making enterprises, which are a huge drain on the economy. There are 63 sick enterprises, which are registered with Bureau of Industrial and Financial Reconstruction (BIFR). Out of this, there are 39 operating sick enterprises whose accumulated losses have run up to Rs 56,000 crore (March 2015). During 2014–15, out of 235 operating public enterprises, 77 companies incurred losses of the order of Rs 27,300 crore. A large number of these industries are takeover units from the private sector and incapable of revival. Similarly, several industries set up in the 1960s/1970s suffer from technological obsolescence and other infirmities, and cannot compete, and it is difficult to nurse them back to health. Sick industries should have been the first candidates for privatization, and if there are no takers, they should be liquidated after taking care of workers' interest.

With the commencement of liberalized economic policy and more particularly during UPA's ten-year regime, a policy environment was created under which PSEs, in vital sectors of the economy, have been squeezed, their assets have been stripped and they were being slowly bled to death. Merging of Air India with Indian Airlines, burdening it with huge purchase of aircraft and passing on its profitable routes to private airlines, both domestic and international, has spelled its death. The public–private partnership at Indira Gandhi Airport has resulted in a huge financial benefit to the private player, GMR Group, and virtual ouster of the Airport Authority of India from its operations. Several lucrative oil fields have been passed on to private players, particularly Reliance, for exploration and extraction, at highly disadvantageous terms, jeopardizing the interest of ONGC and the government of India. A number of coal blocks, where work had already begun by Coal India, were dereserved, for captive allocation to private parties, and a high-grade coal field allocated to NTPC was de-allocated and handed over to Reliance's Sasan Ultra Mega Power.

The situation that has emerged on the ground during the past two decades of privatization and disinvestment can be described as a typical case of 'privatization of profits, and nationalization of losses'.

International scenario

Worldwide emerging market countries are relying on state enterprises as the main vehicle of industrial development. Some of the most successful companies are state owned, such as Russia's Gazprom (natural gas), China Mobile, Saudi Basic Industries Corporation (chemical), Dubai Ports and Emirates Airlines. Thirteen biggest oil companies, which between them control three-fourths of the world's oil reserves, are all state owned. Despite the privatization wave of the 1980s, in rich countries club – OECD, state-owned enterprises have even today an important presence in the strategic sector such as telecom, electricity, gas, transportation and finance.[15] There are over 2,000 enterprises, employing 6 million people, accounting for 2.5 per cent employment. In Norway state-owned enterprises (SOEs) account for over 10 per cent employment and in France 6 per cent. Today China dominates the world in industrial production through its state-owned companies. China adopted a pragmatic policy of privatization with the philosophy of 'grasping the large and letting go the small'. While thousands of small enterprises were privatized, large firms whose ownership was retained by government were given special treatment and reforms were initiated which made them more efficient and big enough to have international presence. In China, companies in which the state is a majority shareholder account for 60 per cent of stock-market capitalization and in Russia and Brazil 30 to 40 per cent. A survey by *The Economist* concluded, 'State capitalism is successful in producing national champions that can compete globally.'[16]

James Meek,[17] an eminent British litterateur, in his perceptible book *Private Island – Why Britain Now Belongs to Someone Else* observes that mindless pursuit of the policy of privatization had done great damage to Britain and its society and destroyed its social compact. Privatization has failed to demonstrate that private companies are more competent and efficient than the state owned. It has failed to make firms compete and give customers choice and better services. Privatization has resulted in services such as water, rail transport and housing becoming costly. Today there is a backlash and a serious debate about 'reclaiming' the railways from the capricious private owners.

Two Harvard academicians Aldo Musacchio and Sergio Lazzarni in their new book *Reinventing State Capitalism* point out that following the privatization wave of the 1980s and 1990s, state-owned-enterprises have reinvented themselves and are thriving. They are listed in stock exchange, run by professional managers and given more financial autonomy and have overcome classic problems of state ownership. The Club of Rome commissioned a study by eminent experts, regarding experience of more than two decades of privatization, and has come to the following conclusion:

> Privatization is not an end in itself. Privatization should be treated as a means of increasing efficiency and not as a way of reducing or undermining the role of the state. Privatization may be the best option in some cases; but reforming the public sector, instead, may be a better choice in other cases. We advocate a healthy awareness of the limits of privatization, rather than unconditional approval or rejection. To achieve the best of both worlds, we need strong private enterprise and capable public agencies working together.[18]

We should understand that only a strong and vibrant public sector can meet India's vast infrastructure and capital-intensive high-tech industry needs and withstand competition with multinationals in a highly competitive globalized world. To make our public enterprises national champions, the government should create supportive policy environment and give them more autonomy, professionalize their management and free them from political and bureaucratic interference.

Corporate sector

Private corporate sector steals all the attention on any debate on industrial development of the country because of its political and economic clout. It has powerful lobbies to espouse its cause. It seeks tax concessions, labour law reform, acquisition of land by government at concessional rates and favourable foreign investment regime to collaborate with multinational corporations which possess technology, knowhow and capital. While the legitimate concerns of the corporate sector need to be addressed, it should not be at the cost of other stakeholders and neglecting the SMEs and public enterprises. It must be said to the credit of the corporate sector that freeing it from stifling regulatory regime, post-1991 liberalized economic policy, the organized manufacturing sector has come up and become competitive in several high-technology sectors such as automobile and automobile parts, drugs and pharmaceuticals, heavy machinery and equipment, steel and textiles. It has been able to meet domestic needs and not only is exporting products to developed countries but also has acquired/set up industrial units there.

One disturbing phenomenon of the organized manufacturing industry that has emerged recently is its inability to create new jobs. A study by K. P. Kannan and G. Raveendran[19] notes that there has been acceleration in capital intensification at the expense of creating employment.

> A good part of labour productivity was retained by the employers as the product wage did not increase in proportion to output growth. The workers as a class thus lost in terms of both additional employment and real wages in organised manufacturing industry.

Economist Amit Bhaduri[20] says that the existing model of corporate growth and industrialization has a depressing effect on employment generation and terms it 'a process of internal colonization'.

Arun Maira[21] cites a study commissioned by the Planning Commission, which revealed that total employee costs (including salary of management personnel) to total revenues did not exceed 10 per cent in any manufacturing enterprises. If these enterprises were to pay their contract workers the same as permanent employees doing the same work, their net profit will decline by less than 1 per cent. This shows that the large-scale practice of employing workers on a non-permanent basis has no sound basis and is done simply to extract maximum profit by management. According to Annual Survey of Industries, the share of wages to net value in Indian enterprises fell from 25.6 per cent in 1990–91 to 11.9 per cent in 2011–12. In 1990–91 workers' wages constituted 64 per cent of total emoluments; they fell to 46.5 per cent of total emoluments in 2011–12, with a much faster rise in management emoluments. Over the same period, the average rate of workers' wage increase was 7.5 per cent per annum, whereas the consumer price index for industrial workers rose by 7.3 per cent per annum, which means real earning per worker has barely increased. Maira calls for adoption of industrial practices of Germany, Sweden and Japan, where there is union–management collaboration and workers participate in quality and process improvement and are given respectable deal in terms of wages and service condition.

If the country is to industrialize, policy measures have to be designed for balanced growth of all three sectors: small and medium enterprises, public enterprises and corporate sector. The three sectors have to work in tandem and in harmony for the country to industrialize.

Import liberalization and bureaucratic hurdles – obstructing manufacturing

As a result of economic reforms in the 1990s, India has reduced tariffs with the idea of exposing domestic industries to international competition and enhancing efficiency. But this has severely damaged the domestic industry. A study by Sudip Chaudhuri[22] shows that during the period 2004–5 to 2010–11 import share went up substantially in capital goods industry such as machine tools, earth-moving and mining equipment, heavy electrical and power plant equipment, metallurgical machinery, textile machinery and engineering goods. Import share in some of these industries is as follows: textile machinery, 48 to 56 per cent (up from 46 per cent from 2004 to 2005); earth-moving and mining equipment, 51 to 54 per cent (up from 40 per cent); machine tools 67 to 75 per cent (up from 53 per cent); and metallurgical machinery, 87 per cent. Not only is import share in domestic market high, but the import content of domestic production is also very high in technology-intensive industries – 78 per cent in earth-moving and mining equipment, 40 per cent in machine tools, 37 per cent in electrical equipment, signifying low value addition. In another vital segment, electronics products, out of a total demand of $45 billion, imports accounted for two-thirds – $30 billion.

There are several reasons for heavy imports of industrial products. India has very low tariff rates – customs duty is only 10 per cent for most industrial products. Domestic producers face further disadvantage, as indirect taxes (excise, sales tax) paid by them on domestically produced goods are not fully neutralized by countervailing duty on imported goods. Chaudhuri points out that policymakers should have fixed duty up to the 'bound rate' permissible under WTO, and supported domestic manufacturers, instead of indiscriminately reducing it. India has voluntarily joined IT Agreement, which enjoins it to eliminate all duties on computers, semiconductors and telecom equipment. India has also entered several bilateral agreements, which are again voluntary, but they allow duty-free imports of power equipment and construction equipment for mega power projects and national highway development projects.

Policymakers consider foreign direct investment (FDI) will help economic growth, and accordingly, India has created a very favourable policy regime post-economic liberation. For most manufacturing, 100 per cent FDI is permitted, but it has not been able to attract it substantially. During 2000–2012, 60 per cent of the flows had gone to the service sector and only 30 per cent to manufacturing, mostly in sectors such as automobile and pharmaceuticals where the country already had a strong presence. Half of these flows in manufacturing went to acquire existing companies. Thus, FDI has not helped create much of fresh manufacturing capacities.

World over public procurement is a strong tool to encourage domestic manufacturing. Countries such as the US, China and Brazil and even the World Bank and Asian Development Bank (ADB) procurement procedures have provisions for preferential purchase of domestically manufactured goods. But our public procurement rules have no such provision. The government is a major purchaser, and a very substantial portion of government budget is spent on purchase of goods and services.

India imports huge quantities of medical equipment such as CT and MRI scanners and ventilators, dialysis machines, implants and stents for heart surgery. Medical equipment segment is estimated at Rs 35,000 crore annually, imports accounting for Rs 27,000 crore – 75 per cent of the market. Domestic manufacturers point out that often equipment of questionable quality and refurbished machines after use are dumped in the Indian market. The government has reduced duty on imported medical devices, and there are poor-quality regulations. This thwarts the efforts of domestic manufacturers to indigenize them.[23]

At the initiative of renowned cardiac surgeon Dr K. M. Cherian, Frontier Mediville company was set up in Chennai, for doing research in medical science and manufacture of life-saving heart valves.[24] In this state-of-the-art facility, bioprosthetic valves are to be developed in collaboration with the Georgia Institute of Technology in the US, and prototypes are to be developed at the Global Centre for Medical Innovation in the US. This indigenously developed bioprosthetic valve would make heart treatment accessible to thousands of patients. Presently an imported valve for porcine pulmonary artery costs Rs 4 lakh, while the locally developed valve will cost only Rs 50,000. Although the process to get approval from Drug Controller of India and Indian Council of Medical Research started in 2010, final clearance for its production has not yet been forthcoming and stuck in bureaucratic rigmarole (January 2016). Meanwhile, the country continues to spend huge foreign exchange to import valves from abroad, and persons with modest means are unable to access treatment.

Chinese imports – thwarting domestic manufacturing

China, a communist country with a non-democratic political system, has embraced capitalist market economy model and has confronted the world with a unique economic phenomenon. It is the second-largest economy after the US and has become a manufacturing hub of the world and an export powerhouse, and its competitive advantage has threatened industries all over the world – in the US, West Europe and India. Over the past two decades China has become legendary for its ability to undercut prices everywhere from consumer goods to industrial products. The China price has redrawn the global manufacturing, has put legions of people out of work around the world and has become an open wound in international trade.[25] Much of the huge trade deficit of the US and a good deal of its economic woe is on account of China's huge manufacturing exports. On account of its massive trade surplus, China has a huge foreign exchange reserve, a large part in US government bonds, and can hold US economy to ransom.

China has emerged as India's biggest trading partner, commanding huge trade surplus. China's annual import in India was $51 billion in 2013–14 and $60 billion in 2014–15, against India's exports of $15 billion and $12 billion, with a whopping trade deficit. On top of it, almost 80 per cent of China's imports in India are concentrated in the manufacturing sector, mainly machinery and mechanical appliances and chemicals. On the other hand, India's exports are mostly in the primary and resource-based sector, with minerals such as iron ore, accounting for 40 per cent of export. The trade pattern is typical colonial type, where colonies were exporting raw material for use of manufactured goods to their erstwhile imperial masters. Cheap Chinese imports have threatened the entire Indian manufacturing sector, both heavy industry and consumer durables, and many industrial units have closed down or been threatened with closure as they are unable to compete.

A report by *Nikkei, Asian Review* says that 'a flood of counterfeits and knockoffs from China, alongside legitimate goods, are drowning Indian industry'.[26] Chinese companies are ripping away chunks of India's low-end market, causing local disgruntlement and loss of job. Shanzhai cellphones, called 'China mobile' in India, have captured massive market share in the country, as Chinese manufacturers have a competitive advantage because they evade tax, regulatory fees and safety checks at home. Chinese companies have captured smartphone, electrical appliances and many other low-end product market. Gujarat's ceramic industry, which makes tiles and sanitaryware, local small and midsize players face a severe crisis as low-priced ceramic imports from China are growing at dizzy annual rates, pricing them out. Fuelled by cheap credit and aggressive marketing, Chinese power equipment manufacturers have captured a good part of India's vast power-generating equipment market, displacing efficient producers such as BHEL – a PSU, and Larsen & Toubro, who are crying foul. India's Chamber of Commerce has sounded a warning about the coming crisis for national industry if nothing is done to stop the China crisis.

Some unscrupulous Indian importers in league with Chinese companies are undervaluing goods to evade duty. The declared value of an MP3 player is Rs 1.83, when it sells in the market for Rs 230; of an LED torch is Rs 8, when it sells for Rs 150 to 200; and of an emergency light is Rs 16, when it sells for Rs 620. The Directorate of Revenue Intelligence found that for over 3,600 items brought from China, the importers declare 1 to 9 per cent of the value of goods – customs duty is 31 per cent of the declared value.[27] Undervalued manipulated invoices are produced before customs, to evade duty. Indian manufacturers have no chance of competing against such undervalued goods sold in the market and have to wind up their business.

Although China is now a member of WTO, it violates its norms with impunity. A large number of anti-dumping cases have been filed against it, one-fourth of all cases initiated in India. Out of 690 anti-dumping cases, China accounts for 166, with duty imposed on 134 cases[28] (June 2014). China gives huge export subsidy through internal administrative measures, which are not easy to identify. These include credit allocation, low interest loans, debt forgiveness and reduction of freight rates. China vigorously pursues a policy of national champions under which special concessions are given to national firms to become global players and exploit foreign markets.

If we want our manufacturing to come up, we must take strong tariff and non-tariff measures against the flood of imports from China and other countries, protect domestic industries and create a favourable regime for them to grow and thrive.

Electric power

> Communism is Soviet power plus electrification of the whole country.
>
> V. I. Lenin[29]

Electric power is one of the most important components of rapid industrialization and development strategy. The country is woefully short of power. The present generating capacity is about 258,000 MW (March 2015), with 70 per cent coming from fossil fuel (coal 60per cent, gas/oil 10per cent), 15 per cent from hydro sources, 2 per cent from nuclear sources and 13 per cent from renewable resources. There is an immediate need of additional power for both industrial and domestic needs, but this sector faces numerous challenges.

In the long run the country cannot solve the energy problem through conventional modes of production. Thermal plants suffer from major constraints due to coal supply bottleneck, and for gas- and oil-based power plants, there is heavy dependence on imports. The big hydro projects face serious rehabilitation and environmental issues, and nuclear power has problems of safety and environmental concerns. Extensive use of fossil fuel accelerates climate problem, due to emission of greenhouse gases, particularly carbon dioxide. We have therefore to change our methods of generating electricity and focus on green and non-emission process of electric generation. Decentralized renewable energy projects have another advantage: they can supply off-grid electricity and can transform the face of rural India. India has great potential for energy from renewables as it has plenty of sunshine, biofuels such as jatropha and bagasse, agriculture residue and a large sea coastline to harness wind energy. The Ministry of New and Renewable Energy estimates India's potential at 900 GW (900,000 MW) – wind 100 GW, small hydro 20 GW, bioenergy 25 GW and solar 750 GW.[30]

As on 31 March 2015 the installed capacity of non-renewable energy was 33,800 MW (wind 22,500 MW, small hydro 4,000 MW, bioenergy 4,200 MW, solar 3,100 MW). The Modi government has set a very ambitious target of renewable energy of 175,000 MW by March 2022, which includes 100,000 MW of solar power. The question is, can we fulfil these targets?[31] There are two major problems in increasing production of solar energy. First, the per unit cost of production is very high, though lately it is coming down. Second, it is largely dependent on imports. There is a very modest domestic manufacturing capacity of solar cells and modules. Domestic manufacturers face huge problems and are getting priced out due to cheap imports from China, the US and elsewhere. Solar panels worth $448 million (Rs 2,800 crore) were imported during 2014–15, and the import bill is going to grow up steeply unless we augment domestic production. The government needs to provide massive support, including price subsidy in initial years, for solar power industry to come up.

Developed countries such as the US, Great Britain, Germany and Sweden have developed technology to produce affordable electricity from renewable sources. Britain has perfected technology of off-shore wind farms and is a world leader. In California, US, a company Desert Sunlight Solar Farm has operationalized (February 2015) a solar plant which produces 550 MW of electricity, equal to the output of a conventional power plant.[32] It uses millions of panels covered by a thin film of glass, which absorbs sunlight using second-generation solar technology, taking advantage of round-the-year sunshine at its location. The EU has made a law to generate 30 per cent of its energy requirement from renewable resources by 2020, up from 13 percent in 2013. Sweden has invested heavily in search of alternative energy sources and produces 45 per cent of its energy from renewable sources, with a target of 50 per cent by 2020. In Germany 25 per cent of electricity is generated from renewable resources – solar panels, wind turbines and biogas plants. It has taken a policy decision to shut down nuclear power generation by 2022 and to get 80 per cent of its power from renewable energy by 2050. Germany has set a new global trend of producing electricity at home by installing solar panels in houses, schools, hospitals and industrial plants. Of the total electricity consumed, its share is 8 per cent. It is clean and cheaper, as there are no taxes on it.

There is no fundamental and applied research done in our universities and Council of Scientific and Industrial Research labs to harness cheap affordable power from solar, wind and biomass resources. We should invest heavily in R&D of energy production, as well as collaborate with foreign research institutes and corporates that have mastered technologies for production of electricity. Strategic rethinking to go in for renewable energy resources for future energy requirement, heavy investment in R&D and massive governmental support are needed to meet the country's long-term demand for power.

Discover and invent in India

If we look at the history of the world's great industrial countries, we find that they have done so on the strength of a strong scientific base, research institutions and quality technical education. Four Nobel laureates and a winner of Fields Medal, David Gross (physics), Serge Haroche (physics), Dan Shechtman (chemistry), John Gurdon (medicine) and Manjul Bhargava (Fields Medal, mathematics), attending the Indian Science Congress (January 2016), issued a statement that efforts to make high-technology products in India will not benefit the country in the long term, unless backed by sustained investment in basic science and fostering the spirit of curiosity. 'New inventions, technologies, products that can compete on the world stage are in the end based on new discoveries, new understanding of the working of nature – what we call basic science, which eventually translates into applied sciences and technologies.'[33] India spends only 0.9 per cent of GDP on R&D, which has remained unchanged for the past 15 years. The US spends 2.7 per cent and South Korea 4.4 per cent of GDP on research. Chinese investment in technology and science has doubled in the past 15 years to 2.1 per cent of GDP. David Gross[34] writing in *The Indian Express* emphasized that lack of necessary funds in science guarantees failure, but that alone is not enough. There is need for fundamental reform in India's structure of higher education and research institutions.

Dr A. P. J. Kalam, eminent scientist and former president, observed that for 'make in India', we have to do research, design, develop, produce and thus truly 'create in India'.[35] In an article written jointly with Srijan Pal Singh, he says there are five pillars of the strategy: human resource, capital and incubation, tech infusion, building the ecosystems and domestic consumer leverage. The quality issue in education should be addressed, and research should be promoted in a big way to create new skill set. Given right incentives, India has the capacity to develop technology indigenously. Dr Kalam cites a case in which the Indian Space Research Organisation needed beryllium diaphragm for a new device and approached a US firm, which agreed to supply it, but the US government blocked it due to strategic reasons (1975). Later, it was learnt that US diaphragm was made from beryllium rods produced in Japan for which beryllium was outsourced from India. Indian scientists were startled at this information but took up the challenge of making it in India, and in four months' time succeeded in producing it.

Summing up

Prime Minister Modi has been rightly emphasizing that India should become a manufacturing hub for the country to develop. The challenge is how to do it. To implement the idea, we have to create a favourable policy environment. There is need to invest heavily in science and basic and applied R&D and rely on time-tested principles of self-reliance and domestic resource endowment to promote the country's industrialization. There are four key components of manufacturing and industrialization strategy: (1) give massive support to small-scale and medium industries, which alone have the potential to provide employment to the country's vast population; (2) recognize importance of public enterprises in core, capital-intensive and high-tech sectors of the economy; (3) strictly restrict the flood of imports from foreign countries, particularly China; and (4) fully meet industry's/country's demand for electric power. We should target for the manufacturing share to become 25 to 30 per cent of GDP in the next ten years, which will inter alia create higher-quality jobs and break the poverty trap in which we are caught.

Notes

1 David J. Gross, 'Discover, invent in India', *The Indian Express*, 15 January 2016, p. 14. Expressing views during his visit to India to attend the Indian Science Congress at Mysore, January 2016.
2 Ha-Joon Chang, *Things They Don't Tell You about Capitalism*, New York: Bloomsbury Press, 2012, p. 101.
3 Seymour Melman, *Profits without Production*, New York: Alfred Knoff, 1983.
4 Ernst & Young, 'Why manufacturing matters', *Performance Preview*, January 2012, No. 3, pp. 10–11.
5 Government of India, *Report of the Prime Minister's Task Force on Micro, Small and Medium Industries*, January 2010, available at http://msme.gov.in/WriteReadData/DocumentFile/PM_MSME_Task_Force_Jan2010.pdf (accessed 26 February 2015).
6 Ministry of Micro, Small and Medium Industries, *Inter-ministerial Committee for Accelerating Manufacturing in Micro, Small and Medium Enterprise Sector*, September 2013, available at http://msme.gov.in/Accelerating%20Manufacturing%20in%20the%20MSME%20Sector.pdf (accessed 26 February 2015).
7 IESA, 'Indian Electronic System Design and Manufacturing (ESDM) Disability Identification Study', available at http://www.iesaonline.org/downloads/IESA-EY-Indian-ESDM-Disability-Identification-Report-Executive-Summary.pdf (accessed 26 February 2015); '65 percent of electronic items demand met by imports', *Business Standard*, 13 January 2014, available at http://www.business-standard.com/article/economy-policy/65-per-cent-of-electronic-items-demand-met-by-imports-report-114011300761_1.html (accessed 26 February 2015).
8 Rashmi Bagga, 'Trade Facilitation and Hollowing-out of Indian Manufacturing', *Economic and Political Weekly*, 4 October 2014, Vol. XLIX, No. 40, pp. 57–63.
9 Arun Maira, 'Jobs, Growth, and Industrial Policy', *Economic and Political Weekly*, 23 August 2014, Vol. XLIX, No. 34, pp. 35–39.
10 For data source, see 'Europe's credit crunch', *The Economist*, 4 May 2013, p. 11.
11 OECD Policy Brief, *Small, Medium-Sized Enterprises: Local Strength, Global Reach*, available at http://www.oecd.org/regional/leed/1918307.pdf (accessed 4December 2014).
12 'Schumpeter: German lessons', *The Economist*, 12 July 2014, p. 56.
13 J. K. Galbraith, *The Good Society*, Boston: Houghton Mifflin Co., 1996, p. 20.
14 For detailed discussion on the role of public enterprises and privatization debate, see B. P. Mathur, *Public Enterprise Management*, New Delhi: Macmillan, 1999.

15 OECD, *The Size and Sectoral Distribution of SOEs in OECD and Partner Countries*, available at http://www.keepeek.com/Digital-Asset-Management/oecd/finance-and-investment/the-size-and-sectoral-distribution-of-soes-in-oecd-and-partner-countries_9789264215610 (accessed 27 April 2015).
16 'Behind the mask, a survey of business in China', *The Economist*, 20 March 2004.
17 James Meek, *Private Island: Why Britain Now Belongs to Someone Else*, London: Verso, 2015.
18 Ernst Ulrich von Weizsacker, Oran R. Young and Matthias Finger (eds), *Limits to Privatization*, London: Earthscan, 2005, p. 360.
19 K. P. Kannan and G. Raveendran, 'Growth sans Employment', *Economic and Political Weekly*, 7–13 March 2009, Vol. XLIV, No. 10, pp. 80–91.
20 Amit Bhaduri, 'Alternatives in Industrialisation', *Economic and Political Weekly*, 5–11 May 2007, Vol. XLII, No. 18, pp. 1597–1600.
21 Maira, 'Jobs, Growth, and Industrial Policy', pp. 37–38.
22 Sudip Chaudhuri, 'Import Liberalisation and Premature Deindustrialisation in India', *Economic and Political Weekly*, 24 October 2015, Vol. L, No. 45, p. 6069.
23 'First world's medical device rejects flood Indian markets', *Times of India*, 26 March 2015, p. 13.
24 'Made-in-India heart valves tied in red tape', *Times of India*, 24 January 2016, p. 16.
25 Alexandra Harney, *The China Price*, London: The Penguin Press, 2008.
26 '"Shamsung" smartphones strain India–China relations', *Nikkei, Asian Review*, 27 November 2013, available at http://asia.nikkei.com/Business/Trends/Shamsung-smartphones-strain-IndiaChina-ties (accessed 1 November 2014).
27 'Duty evasion: MP3 player for Rs2, LED torch for Rs 8', *Times of India*, Thursday, 23 January 2014, p. 13.
28 See Director General of Anti Dumping, available at http://commerce.nic.in/traderemedies/Data_Anti_dumping_investigations.pdf?id=25 (accessed 1 November 2014).
29 V. I. Lenin, *Collected Works*, Moscow: Progress Publishers, 1964, Vol. XXXI, pp. 513–518, available at http://soviethistory.msu.edu/1921-2/electrification-campaign/communism-is-soviet-power-electrification-of-the-whole-country (accessed 17 April 2016).
30 Ministry of New and Renewable Energy, *Annual Report 2014–15*, available at http://mnre.gov.in/file-manager/annual-report/2014-2015/EN/Chapter%201/chapter_1.htm (accessed 13 April 2016).
31 For India's renewable energy capability, see Aruna Kumarankadath, 'Renewable energy: Can India achieve its ambitious targets?', *Down to Earth Annual, State of India's Environment*, 2016, pp. 89–94.
32 'Solar farm', *Time*, 9 March 2015, pp. 17–26.
33 'Nobel and Fields wisdom: For Make in India, first discover and invent in India', *The Indian Express*, 5 January 2016, p. 12.
34 Gross, 'Discover, invent in India'.
35 A. P. J. Abdul Kalam and Srijan Pal Singh, 'To Make in India, give a break to our tech and talent', *Sunday Times of India*, 18 January 2016, p. 12.

6

INDIA'S FOREIGN TRADE DEFICIT, DEPRECIATING RUPEE AND THE FRAUD OF MODERN ECONOMICS

[The] free-trade, free-market policies are policies that have rarely worked. Most of the rich countries did not use such policies when they were developing countries themselves, while these policies have slowed down growth and increased income inequality in developing countries in the last three decades. Few countries have become rich through free trade, free-market policies and few ever will.

Ha-Joon Chang, Cambridge Economist[1]

Despite almost seven decades of independence, the economic relations between India and the developed countries continue to be 'colonial', India a huge importer of manufactured and capital goods, while a large part of its export basket consists of agriculture and 'primary manufactures', in a shrinking global market. There is a French proverb, 'the more things change, the more they remain the same'. This has been never more true in the field of the current-day globalized economy, and unless India pursues a pragmatic policy, it will remain in economic backwaters, 'as hewers of wood and drawers of water'. It is necessary to look at economic history to draw lessons, as Churchill said, 'The farther back you can look, the farther forward you are likely to see.'

The economic history of Great Britain, Germany and the US in the 19th and early 20th centuries, Japan in the post-1950s and China currently shows that they built their economic strength through higher value-added manufacturing exports. Much of India's problem on the external front today is due to a weak manufacturing base, because of which it is unable to export value-added industrial products. This results in a huge trade deficit, which puts severe pressure on the rupee, resulting in continuous decline in the value of the rupee in relation to the dollar. The launching of the five-year plans in the 1950s resulted in a heavy demand for imported machinery and industrial goods, in order to build a self-reliant industrial base. But the country was unable to build an efficient industrial sector which could compete internationally, and exports lagged dynamism. The liberalization of the economy in the 1990s has compounded the problem as it has given further push to imports, which continue to grow exponentially, without corresponding rise in exports.

Table 6.1 gives the exports–imports for the past eight years. It shows a heavy adverse balance of trade; export earnings have been able to finance import, only to the extent of 60 to 70 per cent, putting severe pressure on the rupee, resulting in its declining value in relation to the dollar and other foreign currencies. Exports have remained stagnant for the past four years, and there has been a steep fall of 16 per cent to $261 billion in 2015–16, according to preliminary estimates. There has been a corresponding fall in imports as well, at the level of $380 billion, with a trade deficit of $119 billion for the year, but that is hardly a consolation. A dynamic IT (information technology) sector and NRI (non-resident Indian) remittances, which bring substantial foreign exchange for the country; as indicated in the table, there has been a measure of stability in our foreign exchange front.

Our policymakers are indifferent to the burgeoning trade deficit, and there is no serious effort to restrict imports, considering that we are unable to boost exports due to numerous factors beyond control. India's trade deficit is being financed largely by borrowing, both government and commercial, foreign institutional investors, foreign direct investment, NRI deposits and other inflows. All borrowing, both government and commercial, in the long run has to be paid back in foreign currency, which can be done only through the generation of additional export earnings. A good part of money flowing from abroad is volatile, and its flow slows down when economic conditions in the country are not favourable. During the past few years India's current account balance (CAB), which measures receipt and payment of commodity trade, as well as services, has been adverse, resulting in a steep fall in the value of the rupee in relation to the dollar.

Table 6.1 Export–import imbalance, IT exports and NRI remittance

Year	Export ($ billion)	Import ($ billion)	Trade deficit ($ billion)	Extent exports finance imports percentage	IT exports ($ billion)	NRI remittance ($ billion)
2007–8	166	258	–92	64	37	42
2008–9	189	309	–120	61	47	45
2009–10	182	300	–118	61	42	54
2010–11	256	383	–127	67	50	53
2011–12	310	500	–190	62	60	64
2012–13	307	502	–195	61	62	64
2013–14	319	466	–147	68	67	65
2014–15	317	461	–144	69	70	66

Source: Economic Outlook, Economic Advisory Council to PM, RBI Reports.

The current account balance (CAB/GDP) was around –1 per cent during 2005–6, ranged between –2.3 and –2.8 per cent during 2008–9 to 2010–11, jumped to –4.2 per cent in 2011–12 and was –4.8 per cent in 2012–13. (Mercifully it came down to –1.7 per cent in 2013–14 and –1.3 per cent in 2014–15). This resulted in the rupee tailspinning against the dollar from mid-2013 onwards, and its value falling to around Rs 60 to 65 to a dollar from around Rs 45 two years earlier, a fall of 25 per cent.

From the time we began economic planning in the 1950s, the 'India rupee' is a sorry story of a depreciating currency. In 1966, when Indira Gandhi had just taken over as prime minister, in an era of fixed exchange rate, India was forced to devalue its currency amidst intense international pressure, from the then prevailing rate of Rs 4 to a dollar to Rs 7.50. The 1970s marked the beginning of floating currency regime, and the rupee is continuously losing out on its value against hard currencies. In 1991–92, the value of a US dollar to a rupee was Rs 25; in 1992–97 its valued ranged between Rs 30 and 35, while between 1998 and 2012 its value hovered between Rs 43 and 47. There was sharp fall in value of the rupee towards June 2013, and it fell by more than 25 per cent to the range of Rs 60 to 65 and currently it is trading around Rs 66 to a dollar (April 2016). Steep depreciation of a currency can have a devastating impact on the economy and destroy the stability of society.

It is important to understand that the value at which a currency trades in the international market has nothing to do with its purchasing power. Any Indian who travels abroad knows that a cup of tea or coffee in the US costs $1 to $1.5 and in West Europe Euro 1, while in India in most roadside restaurants one can buy it for Rs 10 to 15, a fifth of the price abroad. In appreciation of the fact that the market-determined exchange rate does not reflect a currency's true worth, *The Economist* brings out The Big Mac Index based on prices of hamburgers sold in various countries by MacDonald's, the giant international fast-food chain. It is based on the theory of purchasing power parity (PPP). In the long range the exchange rates ought to adjust so that a basket of goods and services costs the same across countries. According to The Big Mac Index of January 2013, while one burger costs $4.37 in the US, it costs $1.67 in India.[2] Thus, the rupee was undervalued by 62 per cent. The Big Mac Index of January 2016 gives the price of a burger in the US to be $4.93, as against the price of $1.90 Maharaja Mac in India, thus undervaluing the rupee by 61 per cent.[3] The exercise of valuing currencies in terms of their purchasing power is not a fantasy. The United Nations Development Programme (UNDP) works out per capita income on the basis of PPP. India's per capita income based on PPP was $3,285 (Human Development Report [HDR] 2013), while as per World Bank data (2013), India's per capita income was $1,499. Thus, the rupee is undervalued by 55 per cent in relation to the dollar. According to UNDP (HDR 2015), India's per capita income was $5,497 for 2014, as against World Bank's per capita income of $1,582. Thus, the rupee is undervalued by a whopping 71 per cent if its purchasing power is used as criteria.

We need to understand that the value of a currency is determined by the iron law of supply and demand in the international market and not by its 'intrinsic value', that is its purchasing power of goods and services within a country. Therefore, in order to make a currency strong and stable, exports must balance imports, if not create a surplus. All dynamic economies, Japan, Germany and China, command huge trade surpluses, mainly on the strength of a strong manufacturing base.

Burgeoning imports

In India, no serious efforts have been made to cut down imports as the policymakers have become victims of a neoliberal economic philosophy, which advocates a free trade regime. Heavy imports on account of petroleum and gold were mainly responsible for worsening trade deficits. In 2011–12, 2012–13 and 2013–14 petroleum imports were of the order of $155 billion, $170 billion and $168 billion, respectively. Due to fortuitous circumstances, crude oil prices have fallen drastically in the past two years, from around $100 a barrel to $55 to $60, and touched an all-time low of $38 a barrel, proving a great boon to India in terms of saving of foreign exchange. India's crude import bill was $138 billion in 2014–15 and has dipped substantially to $83 billion in 2015–16. Due to the highly volatile nature of crude oil prices, India should have a long-term view and conserve on petroleum consumption, which requires complete reorientation of our energy policies. There is a need to go in for more indigenous production, use flexi-fuel such as ethanol and corn and rely on renewable energy sources such as wind, biomass and, more particularly, solar, which has a huge potential. Gold imports are another big drain on the economy and were an all-time high at $57 billion in 2011–12 and $54 billion in 2012–13, contributing to India's unsustainable current account deficit. Alarmed, the government took several policy measures to reduce import of gold, such as an increase in import duty and restriction of advances given by banks and non-banking financial company (NBFC). This resulted in substantial reduction of import bill to $28 billion in 2013–14, though it increased in 2014–15 to $35 billion – which shows that bold policy measures can help cut down wasteful imports.

India is a huge importer of vegetable/edible oil; almost 60 per cent of its annual demand of 21 million tonne (mt) is met through imports (palm oil accounting for 80 per cent, the remainder by soybean and sunflower oil). Imports bill was Rs 46,000 crore for 8.5 mt in 2011–12, Rs 56,500 crore for 10.1 mt in 2012–13, Rs 57,000 crore for 10.5 mt in 2013–14 and Rs 65,000 crore for 12.7 mt in 2014–15. There is a very low duty regime which gives a boost to imports and adversely impacts the economy of the entire domestic oil industry. (Duty on crude oil was nil and on refined oil was 7.5 per cent; it was raised to 2.5 per cent on crude and 10 per cent on refined oil in 2013. This was further raised to 12.5 per cent on crude and 20 per cent on refined oil in September 2015, against the background of a steep fall in international prices of palm and other edible oils.) In 1994–95

India was practically self-sufficient in edible oil production, importing only 3 per cent of consumption. The government can impose much higher duty permissible under the WTO (World Trade Organization)-bound rates rules and encourage domestic production. But its shortsighted policy has prevented national self-sufficiency, and the flood of imports has played havoc with the livelihoods of farmers who grow oilseeds.

India consumes huge amounts of fertilizers but is unable to meet its demand through domestic production and imports almost one-fourth of its requirement. Imports were of the order of Rs 53,000 crore during 2011–12, Rs 48,000 crore during 2012–13, Rs 38,000 crore during 2013–14 and Rs 45,000 crore during 2014–15. We have huge reserves of coal but are unable to produce enough quantity to meet the full demand, due to years of policy paralysis and corruption, in what is known as Coalgate, and forced to import huge quantities of costly coal. India has been importing almost 25 per cent of its coal consumption – its imports were a whopping Rs 99,000 crore in 2013–14 and Rs 109,000 crore in 2014–15. Domestic production of urea as well as thermal coal has shown marked improvement in FY 2015–16, which would inter alia curtail the burgeoning import bill.

India's self-goal

Our foreign trade policy is self-defeating, as it is unable to boost exports and protect both domestic industries and agricultural products from unfair foreign competition. A study by Sudip Chaudhuri[4] points out that India is facing de-industrialization as a result of economic liberalization. Drastic reduction of customs duty has led to heavy imports and virtually destroyed India's nascent capital goods industry. Duty on most industrial products is fixed very low at 10 per cent, and countervailing duty on a large number of imported goods does not fully neutralize domestic taxes, resulting in domestic manufacturers not able to compete with imported goods and equipment. On top of it there is zero duty on several products, such as electronics and semiconductors. India has voluntarily joined the international IT Agreement, which requires elimination of all duties on computers, semiconductors and telecom equipment, which has a devastating impact on electronic manufacturing. Two-thirds of the country's fast-growing consumer electronic and electronic hardware market ($90 billion in 2015) are met by imports. India has also entered several bilateral trade agreements, which require giving preferential market access to those countries. These include duty-free imports of power equipment and construction equipment for mega power projects and national highway development projects. In addition, China, which has become the world's industrial hub, is dumping its goods in the Indian market, by following unethical trade practices (see Chapter 5 for details).

The domestic power manufacturers, which include *navratna* PSU BHEL, are facing unfair competition from Chinese equipment manufacturers who are dumping their products.[5] A high-level committee headed by a member of the Planning Commission noted that the domestic power equipment producers suffered a price disadvantage and recommended levy of duty, to safeguard local producers, in the face of zero duty. This was rejected by the Ministry of Finance on the spurious ground that the cost of power-generating equipment on mega projects will increase. In the face of such unhelpful attitude of the government, how can the domestic power industry come up?

India is an efficient producer of steel, fourth largest in the world, and produced 86.5 mt (2014), after China, Japan and the US. It has, however, a liberal import regime and imported 5.5 mt steel in 2013–14, but imports jumped to 9.30 mt in 2014–15 and 11.70 mt in 2015–16, mainly from China, Korea and Japan. From 2014 onwards there was a slowdown of the global economy, particularly China's, which is dumping its surplus steel all over the world. China accounts for half of the world's steel production of 1,665 mt and exported 112 mt steel in 2015, more than the production of India or even Japan. This has resulted in global prices coming down by 50 per cent since 2012, prompting domestic players to sell at a discount, and they have not even been able to recover variable cost and are running at losses. To safeguard the domestic industry, the government has increased duty and has also set temporarily a floor price for imports of steel products (January 2016) to deter countries such as China from undercutting local mills. Due to China's cheap steel, the operations of British Steel, run by Tata, have become unviable, and it has decided to sell off the plant, which has created a political storm in Britain, with calls of governmental intervention to save the basic industry (April 2016). Prakash Kumar Singh,[6] chairman, SAIL, observes: 'Cheap imports from China are not only grave for domestic steel market, which employs around 20 lakh people, but poses a threat to entire global industry.' If India is to become an industrial nation, the government has to support this foundation industry through strong tariff and non-tariff measures.

There has been a huge surge in import of fruits and vegetables in the past few years. The import bill was Rs 4,000 crore in 2010–11 and Rs 5,100 crore in 2011–12; it went up to Rs 6,800 crore in 2012–13 and jumped to Rs 8,300 crore in 2013–14 and 10,200 crore in 2014–15, an increase of 2.5 times in five years. The government's policy to import fruits and vegetables, ostensibly to please urban consumers, is seriously flawed. Agriculture expert Devinder Sharma[7] faults the decision of August 2014 to import potato for the first time on the apprehension that there will be a shortfall in production. The government did not provide any relief to farmers in 2011 and 2012, when prices crashed due to bumper production, and they were forced to sell at throwaway prices and even dump them on road sides, incurring huge losses. In August–September 2014, India imported vast quantities of dry tomato, tomato ketchup, pulp and juice worth $376,000 from China, $94,000 from Nepal and $44,000 from the Netherlands. This was in the face of bumper production of tomato in the country, a few months back, with prices slumping and farmers doing distress sale, feeding cattle or just throwing it away. The import of pasta from Italy is growing every year at the rate of 40 per cent and jumped from Rs 340 crore in 2003–4 to Rs 1,720 crore in 2013–14.

Customs duty has been drastically reduced on pasta following free trade agreement with the European Union (EU). Pasta, a simple product made from wheat, which needs no technology, can be easily made in the country. The government has asked PEC, a state-owned company, to import 5 lakh tonne maize and reduced duty to zero from the prevailing rate of 50 per cent, acting under pressure from the poultry industry (January 2016).[8] Maize has been contracted at $193 per tonne, below the minimum support price of Rs 1,325 per quintal, without giving consideration to the fact that the shortfall in the country's maize production is due to severe drought conditions and such imports are detrimental to farmers' interest and will lead to price crash.

The fraud of international trade theory

The New Liberalized Economic Policy embraced by India in 1991, which basically means easing the flow of goods, services and capital, has been largely responsible for India's current economic woes. The doctrine of free trade is deeply embedded in economic theory. Adam Smith, considered the father of free trade doctrine (1776), expounded it when England was a staunch mercantilist country. Subsequently, David Ricardo built the theory of comparative advantage, as the foundation of free trade doctrine. Stated simply, it means that each country has an advantage in production of commodities, in which it has an abundant supply of factors of production that go in its making. Thus, a country with high proportion of labour should produce labour-intensive goods and those with abundance of capital should produce capital-intensive goods (manufactures), and thus, all countries trading with each other would gain, and overall income and welfare would be maximized. The theory based on the premise of free and open markets has no relation to the real-life situation. Distinguished Latin American economist Raúl Prebisch established the fallacy of theory of comparative advantage and its inapplicability to ground reality. Making an empirical study, he demonstrated that the long-term terms of trade of primary product – exported by developing countries – are continuously declining vis-à-vis industrial goods, and thus, the net effect of global trade is to siphon off income from developing countries to industrialized countries. Nobel Prize–winning economist Gunnar Myrdal observes that while international trade theory argues that it has an equalizing effect on factor prices, leading to equalization of income between countries, in practice international inequalities are growing and have become a pressing concern in international politics.

The economic history of developed countries demonstrates that by protective measures and state support they have built their industrial muscle. Britain was the most protective country during much of its economic rise during the 1720s–1850s. Britain adopted free trade only in the 1860s, when its industrial dominance was absolute, and by 1870, it accounted for 45 per cent of world trade in manufactured goods. Michael Barratt Brown[9] comments, 'Britain's industries were reared behind protective walls, nourished on imperial tributes and encouraged by the destruction of competition from the East. But once established they no more needed protection, plunder and protected markets.' Protection became a drag on development. 'Free trade was the instrument of Britain's industrial supremacy holding back development elsewhere.' However, two early industrial powers, Germany and the US, were not impressed by Britain's free trade doctrine. The young German industry developed its own lobby and had economist Friedrich List to espouse its cause and propagate 'infant industry' doctrine. The German industry thrived under protection and overtook Britain.

The US was the most protective country in the world during most of the phase of its industrial ascendency from the 1830s to the 1940s. This is what Ulysses Grant,[10] the president of the US, had to say in 1891:

> For centuries England had relied on protection, had carried it to extremes, and had obtained satisfactory results from it. After two centuries, England had found it convenient to adopt free-trade because it thinks that protection can no longer afford any thing. Very well, then, Gentleman my knowledge of my country tells, when America has gained all it can out of protection, it too would adopt free trade.

Distinguished scholar Noam Chomsky[11] observes: 'There is not a single case on record in history of any country that has developed successfully through the adherence to "free-market" principles: none. Certainly not the United States.' The Industrial Revolution took off in the US because of high protective tariff to keep British goods out. In the late 19th century when European countries were advocating laissez-faire, American tariffs were five to ten times as high as theirs – and that was the fastest economic growth in American history. In the 19th century, it was cotton textiles which had fuelled the Industrial Revolution. When Egypt, which had its own cotton resources, wanted to start the Industrial Revolution, Britain thwarted it by use of force. Chomsky has the following to say about India:

> India generally was a real competitor with England; as late as the 1820s, the British were learning advanced technique of steel – making there, India was building ships for British navy at the time of Napoleonic war (1803–15), they had a developed textile industry, they were producing more iron than whole of Europe combined – so the British just proceeded to de-industrialize the country by force and turned it into an impoverished rural society.[12]

Cambridge economist Ha-Joon Chang[13] explains how all of today's rich countries used protectionism, subsidies and other state-supported measures to promote industrialization. Japan, Finland and Korea severely restricted foreign investment, while France, Austria, Finland, Singapore and Taiwan used state-owned enterprises to promote key industries. Journalist-economist Jeff Madrick, speaking similar language, says, 'The economic development of today's rich world since 1800s was mostly accompanied by: high tariffs, government investment in industry, financial regulation, and fixed value of currency.'[14] He argues that ideas of mainstream economists such as elimination of tariff, minimization of government intervention, allowing value of currency to be determined by floating it and free play of market forces have damaged America.

Today the star performers among the developing countries such as South Korea, Taiwan, Singapore and China, which have become export powerhouses, have done so on the foundation of a strong manufacturing base. They did not open up their economies but followed sequenced industrial and trade strategies which helped industrial development and growth. While export expansion can help in expediting economic growth, the same cannot be said about import liberalization. There is no systematic relationship between a country's average level of tariff and non-tariff restrictions and its subsequent economic growth. The sub-Sahara African and Latin America countries that followed the orthodox reform agenda under the structural adjustment programme administered by the International Monetary Fund and World Bank, which led to indiscriminate trade liberalization, had to face the consequence of de-industrialization and marginalization of their economies in the international division of labour.

Agriculture

Agriculture in the developing countries is particularly vulnerable to competition from abroad. India was a huge importer of food grains during the 1950s and 1960s, and was going around the world with a begging bowl and facing humiliation. Cheap PL 480 food imports from the US in the 1950s and 1960s had a deleterious effect on India's wheat economy, which created price repression, and farmers lost interest in its production. During the Indo-Pak war of 1965, the US stopped food supply as a political offensive and forced the country to give attention to food grains production. The leadership provided by Prime Minister Lal Bahadur Shastri and Agriculture Minister C. Subramanian, coupled with the development of a high-yielding variety of wheat and price support for farm products, spurred agricultural production in the country and brought about national self-sufficiency. In my book *Foreign Money in India*,[15] I have demonstrated how import of cheap food grains ruined Indian farm economy, and only when bold reforms were taken was there spectacular growth of food production. Today India not only feeds its vast population but also exports high-quality rice and occasionally wheat.

Economist Utsa Patnaik[16] questions the very foundation of free trade doctrine as it is based on wrong premise and says that specialization and enforced trade can lead to two very adverse outcomes. The first outcome is the re-emergence of an inverse relationship between agricultural exports and domestic food availability in developing countries, and the second one is de-industrialization. Tropical and subtropical regions are biodiverse and produce a large range of food and diverse products, which Western countries, with their temperate climate, cannot produce to sustain their high standard of living. In a typical Western supermarket there are an average of 12,000 items of food alone, and 60 to 70 per cent of these items have wholly or substantially tropical or subtropical import content. 'If these were to disappear from the super market shelves the standard of life in Northern population will plunge to the near-medieval level.' She calls for third-world countries to fight back against attempted re-colonization and the discipline of economics in India to get rid of 'intellectual servility to the self-serving ideas generated in the mainstream of theorizing in the Northern universities'.

WTO and West's bullying

The WTO came into existence in January 1995, replacing General Agreement on Trade and Tariff, and included in its ambit agriculture, which was earlier excluded from multilateral trading system. Termed Agreement on Agriculture, it was hammered after years of protracted negotiations, in what is known as Uruguay Round. The agreement is heavily loaded in favour of rich countries, which give billions of dollars as subsidy to their farmers, but have no obligation to reduce it, as it is classified under 'income subsidy' which is considered non-trade distorting. On the other hand, countries like India, which give what is classified as 'producers' subsidy', are required to reduce or eliminate it, with a provision that for public stockholding for food security, subsidy up to 10 per cent of the value of a particular crop can be given. However, there is a catch. The reference price at which subsidy is to be calculated is the price in 1986–88. The government was procuring rice in 1986–88 at Rs 3.52 per kg, while in 2012 the minimum support price fixed was Rs 19.65 per kg. Thus, subsidy becomes Rs 16.13 per kg, and the whole operation of India's vast Public Distribution System becomes a violation of WTO norms and invites its sanction, if WTOs 'unfair' rules are to be followed. This was the issue at stake in Bali WTO talk in December 2013, when India quite justifiably refused to sign the trade facilitation agreement.[17] India was dubbed a 'spoiler' for its principled stand. Subsequently, in Nairobi meeting of WTO (December 2015), India managed to secure an affirmative decision on public stockholding for food security purposes and engage in further discussion to find a permanent solution to this issue.

The developed world's perfidy would be apparent when we examine the huge subsidy they give to their agricultural produce. In the US domestic support to agriculture was $74 billion in 2000, but jumped to $130 billion in 2010 and $140 billion by 2012 – most of it on account of domestic food aid.[18] But it has notified WTO that its farm spending on trade-distorting subsidies is within the limits of $19 billion and compliant with its regulations. According to OECD's *Agriculture Policy Monitoring and Evaluation Report*,[19] in OECD countries 18 to 19 per cent of gross farm receipts stem from public policies that support agriculture. The total support estimate (defined as monetary value of all gross transfers from taxpayers and consumers arising from policy measures that support agriculture) for 2015 was $355 billion for OECD countries, $88 billion for the US and Euro 93 billion for the EU (for 2013 it was $409 billion for OECD countries, $144 for the US and Euro 89 billion for the EU), while production support estimate (defined as monetary value of gross transfers from consumers and taxpayers to agricultural producers) for 2015 was $258 billion for OECD countries, $32 billion for the US and Euro 79 billion for the EU (for 2013 it was $257 billion for OECD countries, $32 billion for the US and Euro 76 billion for the EU). This shows that agriculture in rich countries club is highly subsidized and farm support measures are not coming down despite overseeing mechanism of WTO. Some of the highest providers of subsidy are rich countries such as Japan 56 per cent of gross farm receipts, Korea 54 per cent, Norway 63 per cent and Switzerland 57 per cent. Middle-income countries such as Russia, Brazil and China also give huge subsidy – China's subsidy is around 17 per cent of gross farm receipts.[20]

There is a huge surplus production of agriculture and dairy products in the US and EU. They dump it in the international market at low prices and cause havoc with the farm economy of developing countries. The US subsidies go to crops like corn, wheat, cotton and soybean, and EU subsidies go for milk, butter and sugar. Dumping cheap products in African and other developing countries' markets depresses prices, undermines the livelihoods of poor and small-scale farmers and destroys their economies.

US double standard

India produces 3,100 MW of electricity (March 2015) from solar power, which is a little more than 1 per cent of total power installed capacity. It has an ambitious programme of increasing production capacity to 100,000 MW by 2022, increased from the earlier target of 20,000 MW. In order to develop indigenous capacity, Jawaharlal Nehru National Solar Mission has made it a requirement that 50 per cent of the 750 MW power generated, in the first batch, be produced from solar cells and modules made domestically (in the second batch of 1,500 MW, domestic content requirement [DCR] has been reduced to 33 per cent; in third batch of 2,000 MW, it has been reduced to 10 per cent; and in fourth batch of 5,000 MW, there is no mention of DCR. Thus, effectively DCR is 11 per cent – 1,000 MW out of 9,250 MW). The US has raised a huge outcry against India's DCR, on the ground that it discriminates against US business and dragged India to WTO in 2013. WTO in September 2015 gave a ruling against India that DCR contravened 'international rules of import'. India appealed against the ruling, but WTO again ruled against India (February 2016). It may be worth noting that the US, China, Brazil, Germany and Denmark, which have achieved success in production of renewable energy, have been granting substantial subsidies to domestic producers of renewable energy.[21]

The US, and China mainly, but also Malaysia and Taiwan are dumping solar cells and modules in the Indian market. Following investigation, the Ministry of Commerce had recommended levying of anti-dumping duty in September 2015, but the government (Ministry of Finance), in its wisdom, did not approve it.[22] India has a fledgling solar industry. The country's manufacturing capacity for cells is about 1,400 MW and that of solar modules 2,800 MW, but only a fifth of the cell manufacturing capacity and half of module capacity is operational. In the face of such unfair trade practices, international blackmail and lack of governmental encouragement, how can domestic solar industry come up? Solar energy is clean, can be supplied off grid and can solve rural areas' pent-up demand. It needs a great vision to create a policy environment so that solar energy can be produced domestically and meet India's huge energy demand.

The US is upset with India's laws facilitating manufacture of generic drugs and India's efforts to promote access to cheap health care. The Indian Supreme Court has ruled that Glivec, a cancer drug made by Novartis, cannot be granted patent under the Indian Patent Act, as it is merely a derivative of the known substance for treating cancer that did not enhance the efficacy and safety of the original version. Big Pharma and the US government have been making repeated attempts to declare India as the worst IPR (intellectual property rights) offender, that is a Priority Foreign Country, which would allow the triggering of unilateral trade sanctions. After a long period of intense investigation, whether India would be downgraded to the Priority Foreign Country category, the US Trade Representative (USTR) decided (May 2014) to let India stay put in the Priority Watch List (India has consistently featured on this list since 1979).[23] Nevertheless, USTR decided that it will be conducting an Out of Cycle Review, which is described as a 'tool' to encourage progress on IPR issues of concern, but in reality, it is a part of a larger coercive measure entailing periodic reviews of the IP policy of a country and mount pressure on governments to make them compliant to the practices approved by the US. Special 301 is highly biased and meant for promotion of US industry interests. The 301 programme was initiated by the US in the 1980s, much before the WTO came into existence, but after WTO formation with its dispute settlement mechanism, it has no business to exist. The Special 301 law is used as a bullying tactic by the US government to pressurize India (and other countries) into becoming a better market for drugs, undermining indigenous efforts to increase access to affordable drugs.

While the US thwarts national self-reliance efforts of developing countries, on the pretext of trade distortion, it violates the principle of free trade with impunity by giving massive export subsidy to boost foreign sales of its products. Its 80-year-old Export–Import Bank provides loan, loan guarantees and credit insurance worth billions of dollars for every product, including jumbo jets made by Boeing. *The Economist* describes it as 'one of the most pervasive and enduring instrument of mercantilism in the world trading system'.[24]

Need for pragmatic policy

India should recognize the reality of the world's trading system and intelligently calibrate its policy to suit the nation's vital economic interests. Nobel Prize–winning economist Thomas C. Schelling had observed that 'trade is what most of international relations are about. For that reason trade policy is national security policy'.[25] While economists like to believe that trade policy is guided by rational calculus, wielders of power and policy know that it is an instrument of economic power. While India should pay lip service to the doctrine of free trade, in practice it should provide strong protection to its domestic industry and agriculture and vigorously promote exports, as is being done by Western countries and the emerging powerhouse, China. There is an old saying in Hindi, *hathi ke do dant, ak khane ke, aur ak dhekhne ke* (an elephant has two teeth one for show and another for eating). We should have a clear understanding that forces of globalization and free trading regime prevent building of an industrial base and a strong economy and are meant to hoodwink developing countries like India, who are late starters on the industrialization path.

A huge trade imbalance, as we are currently having, implies that we are exporting jobs abroad, unable to create a competitive economy and employment opportunities in the country. Therefore, serious national efforts are required to boost exports, reduce imports and generate trade surpluses, which will strengthen the rupee and make the economy strong and vibrant.

Notes

1 Ha-Joon Chang, *Things They Don't Tell You about Capitalism*, New York: Bloomsbury Press, 2010, p. 73.
2 'The Big Mac Index-Bunfight', *The Economist*, 2 February 2013, pp. 60–61.
3 Ibid., 9–16 January 2016, p. 60.
4 Sudip Chaudhuri, 'Import Liberalisation and Premature Deindustrialisation in India', *Economic and Political Weekly*, 24 October 2015, Vol. L, No. 43, pp. 60–69.
5 'Chinese imports: MOF sees no need for duty on power equipment', *The Indian Express*, 22 October 2010, p. 19.
6 'Steel companies unable to recover variable costs', *Times of India*, 22 February 2016, p. 19.
7 Devinder Sharma, 'Unjustified imports', *Dainik Jagran*, 25 October 2014, in Hindi.
8 Harish Damodaran, 'Is agriculture a business?', *The Indian Express*, 1 April 2016, p. 15.
9 Michael Barratt Brown, *After Imperialism*, London: Heinmann, 1963, p. 52.
10 Ulysses Grant, quoted by B. P. Mathur, *Foreign Money in India*, New Delhi: Macmillan, 1989, p. 266.
11 Noam Chomsky, *Understanding Power*, New Delhi: Penguin Books, 2003, pp. 251–258.
12 Ibid., p. 257.

13 Ha-Joon Chang, *Things They Don't Tell You about Capitalism*, New York: Bloomsbury Press, 2012, pp. 62–73.

14 Jeff Madrick, *Seven Bad Ideas: How Mainstream Economists Have Damaged America and the World*, New York: Alfred A. Knopf, 2014, pp. 164–188.

15 Mathur, *Foreign Money in India*.

16 Utsa Patnaik, 'The Cost of Free Trade', in *The Republic of Hunger*, Gurgaon: Three Essays Collective, 2007, pp. 17–50.

17 D. Ravikanth, 'WTO Upside Down: Trade Facilitation vs Agriculture', *Economic and Political Weekly*, 6 September 2014, Vol. XLIX, No. 36, pp. 21–25.

18 Data taken from Table 3, Biswajit Dhar and Roshan Kishore, 'Reality of US Farm Subsidies', *Economic and Political Weekly*, 13 February 2016, Vol. LI, No. 7, pp. 36–41.

19 OECD, *Agriculture Policy Monitoring and Evaluation 2015*, available at http://www.keepeek.com/Digital-Asset-Management/oecd/agriculture-and-food/agricultural-policy-monitoring-and-evaluation-2015_agr_pol-2015 (accessed 20 April 2016).

20 'Support to agriculture rising after hitting historic low, OECD says', available at http://www.oecd.org/newsroom/support-to-agriculture-rising-after-hitting-historic-lows-oecd-says.htm (accessed 14 November 2014); *OECD Agriculture Policy and Monitoring Evaluation 2013*; 'US violating norms but tries to reign in India', *Times of India*, 8 December 2013, p. 8.

21 'Crushing a Fledgling Industry', *Economic and Political Weekly*, 12 March 2016, Vol. LI, p. 7.

22 'Solar storm hits India – US relations', *The Hindu*, 12 February 2014, p. 10; 'US: Examining anti-dumping duty decision on solar panel', *The Indian Express*, 25 May 2014, p. 21; M. Ramesh, 'The solar war heats up', *The Hindu*, 11 February 2013, p. 15.

23 Anubha Sinha, *Special 301 Report: India Not Downgraded to Priority Foreign Country*, available at http://spicyip.com/2014/05/special-301-report-india-not-downgraded-to-priority-foreign-country-will-receive-ocr-though.html (accessed 14 November 2014); 'Bring the Special 301 Big Stick', *Economic and Political Weekly*, 8 March 2014, Vol. XLIX, No. 10, p. 7.

24 'Export agencies are an enduring instrument of mercantilism', *The Economist*, 5 July 2014, p. 63.

25 Thomas Schelling, quoted by Sanjay Baru, 'The real threat to WTO', *The Indian Express*, 31 July 2014.

7

INDIA'S PUBLIC FINANCE MISMANAGEMENT

Exploding debt and threat of bankruptcy

> All State activities depend first on the Treasury. Therefore the King shall devote his best attention to it.
>
> Kautilya: *The Arthashastra*[1]

> The dichotomy between ideals and reality, and even between enacted legislation and implementation, should be seen against the background that India, is a 'soft state'. There is an unwillingness among the rulers to impose obligation among the governed and a corresponding unwillingness on their part to obey rules laid down by democratic procedures.
>
> Gunnar Myrdal, Nobel Laureate, Economics[2]

Kautilya, the legendary statesman and philosopher of ancient India, had observed, 'A King with depleted Treasury eats into the very vitality of the citizens and the country.'[3] The UPA (United Progressive Alliance) government, in its ten-year rule, left an empty treasury due to its reckless financial policies. The NDA (National Democratic Alliance) government, which succeeded it in May 2014, is more or less following the same fiscal policies, as is evident from burgeoning public expenditure and soft taxation policy, resulting in heavy borrowing to meet the budgetary deficit.

In the wake of global economic meltdown of 2008, the US and West European countries incurred huge public expenditure, financed mainly by debt, but even today their economies have not been able to recover fully and continue to be afflicted with the problems of slow growth and unemployment. European countries have now learnt, to their dismay, that a policy of high public spending through budgetary deficit is counterproductive and will not help revive the economy. This has led to complete reversal of the earlier policy, and they have gone for severe austerity measures and cut public expenditure. Greece, Italy, Spain and Portugal reeling under the burden of heavy debt have slashed public expenditure, but their economies continue to stagnate with massive unemployment and loss of jobs, threatening their economic as well as political stability. A perceptive commentator observed (2011) in *Newsweek*,[4] 'Never outside periods of total war, has the debt of the world's most powerful states grown so immense. Never has it so heavily threatened their political systems and standards of living. Public debt cannot keep growing without unleashing terrible catastrophe.'

While India is facing a huge problem of debt explosion, threatening the stability of the economy, our policymakers refuse to recognize the gravity of the problem and remain in denial mood. If we do not recognize the problem, how are we going to find a solution?

Part I

The UPA government just before the election of May 2009 went on a spending spree, throwing fiscal rectitude to the wind. Up to 2007–8, the government was following prudent norms and borrowing constituted only 18 per cent of total expenditure, with over 90 per cent of it being spent on capital expenditure. However, keeping an eye on election of mid-2009, the UPA I government jacked up steeply the expenditure by over 20 per cent in revised estimates (RE) of 2008–9, all of which was met out of borrowing, which jumped two and a half times. Thus, 38 per cent of overall expenditure was financed by borrowing, of which only 27 per cent was spent on capital works. During the five-year tenure of the UPA government, the same trend continued, and on an average 35 per cent of public expenditure was met out of borrowed funds. Due to lack of fiscal rectitude, a huge debt repayment liability was created with serious adverse consequences for the economy.

Former finance minister P. Chidambaram admitted belatedly (March 2015) that the stimulus package given in 2008–9 was responsible for loss of election by his government.[5] Table 7.1 gives details from 2007–08 onwards.

From Table 7.1 it may be seen that out of every rupee the government spends, 30 to 35 per cent is financed by loan. Further, out of money borrowed, only 35 per cent was spent on capital expenditure. (In the past two years it was around 40 per cent. Capital expenditure figure given in the budget includes 'grants for creation of capital assets', which are not monitored, and it is generally believed that capital expenditure figures are overstated.) It is the first principle of public finance, that borrowed funds should be used for capital expenditure, so that income-generating assets are created which can stimulate the economy.

Interest payments consume more than one-third revenue earned by the government. This drastically limits the money available for meeting the current expenditure and forces the government to resort to more and more borrowing, landing itself in a perpetual cycle of debt and falling into a debt trap. Table 7.2 illustrates this.

The problem of budgetary deficit has been a cause of concern for more than two decades. In order to rein in deficit, a Fiscal Responsibility and Budget Management Act (FRBMA) was passed in 2003, effective from 2004. The act had mandated that revenue deficit may be eliminated and

Table 7.1 Expenditure and borrowing of government

Year	Total expenditure (Rs crore) 1	Borrowing (Rs crore) 2	Capital expenditure (Rs crore) 3	Borrowing percentage of expenditure 2 per cent 4	Capital expenditure percentage borrowing 3 per cent 5
2007–8 AE	712,671	126,671	118,238	18	93
2008–9 BE	750,884	133,287	92,765		
2008–9 RE	900,953	326,515	97,505	38	27
2008–9 AE	883,956	336,992	90,158		
2009–10 AE	1,024,487	418,482	112,678	40	27
2010–11 AE	1,197,328	373,591	156,605	31	42
2011–12 AE	1,304,365	515,990	158,580	40	31
2012–13 AE	1,410,367	490,597	166,858	35	32
2013–14 AE	1,559,447	502,858	187,675	32	37
2014–15 AE	1,663,673	510,725	196,681	31	38.5
2015–16 RE	1,785,391	535,090	237,718	30	44
2016–17 BE	1,978,060	533,904	247,023	27	46

Note: AE: actual expenditure; RE: revised expenditure; BE: budget estimates. Italics indicate the year from which there was a major jump in public debt.

Source: Government of India Budgets, various years.

Table 7.2 Debt servicing – interest payment as percentage of revenue

Year	Revenue receipts (Rs crore) 1	Interest payments (Rs crore) 2	Interest payments percentage, revenue receipts 2 per cent 1
2007–8	525,098	171,971	33
2008–9	540,259	192,204	36
2009–10	683,312	248,664	37
2010–11	783,312	240,757	31
2011–12	751,437	385,083	36
2012–13	877,613	428,387	35.5
2013–14	1,014,724	374,254	37
2014–15	1,101,473	402,444	36.5
2015–16 RE	1,206,084	442,620	37
2016–17 BE	1,377,002	492,670	36

Note: RE: revised expenditure, BE: budget estimates.

Source: Government of India Budget, various years.

fiscal deficit be no more than 3 per cent of gross domestic product (GDP) by March 2009. (Fiscal deficit is total expenditure less total revenue, other than borrowing, while revenue deficit is revenue expenditure less revenue receipts.) While for the first few years of FRBMA enactment the government managed its finances prudently, from 2008–09 fiscal caution has been thrown to the wind and huge deficits are being incurred. Fiscal deficit was hovering around 5 to 6 per cent of GDP between 2008–9 and 2012–13, and has come down to around 4 per cent currently (4.1 per cent in 2014–15 and 3.9 per cent in 2015–16), while revenue deficit was running between 3 and 5 per cent and has currently come down to 3 per cent of GDP (2.9 per cent in 2014–15 and 2.5 per cent in 2015–16). Besides the central government, states are running deficit budgets. The fiscal deficit of states to state GDP has been running between 2 and 2.5 per cent during the past several years. Thus, the combined fiscal deficit of centre and states had been around 8 per cent of GDP for the past several years, which has somewhat come down and is currently between 6.5 and 7 per cent. Such huge deficits are unsustainable.

Budget deficit and economists

Budget deficits get the support of economists following Keynesian prescription to deal with an economy facing recession. Later, economists of all hue used it as a tool for supporting large public spending, particularly in developing countries, who are perpetually short of resources. Economist Martin Feldstein[6] observes:

> It is unfortunate therefore that, starting with the 1940s, economists developed a series of different arguments that encouraged the political process to accept larger and larger peacetime deficits. These analyses started with simple Keynesian arguments and were followed by new theories of economic growth, theories of household saving behavior, and models of the global capital markets. The arguments were intellectually quite different from each other but they all lead to the same conclusion: that budget deficits in peacetime were not a problem for the economy.

Feldstein argues that there are severe adverse effects of budget deficits on capital accumulation, economic growth, future tax rates and inflation which may lead to financial crises.

I have worked in the finance division of several ministries of the Government of India, besides handling financial management of many large public sector undertaking (PSUs), and have been actively associated with the government's budgeting exercise – its preparation, approval, monitoring and implementation. A correlation between income and expenditure is key to sound budget making. In personal finance or corporate finance, you invariably correlate expenditure with income while doing budgeting. Why not apply the same principle to government budget? It is therefore surprising that in all discussions relating to deficit in government budget, it is linked to GDP and not capacity or effort to raise revenue to meet the expenditure. GDP is simply a broad estimate of value of a country's goods and services which have been monetized, and its numbers are vague and based on guestimates of a country's real income and wealth (particularly in India with weak and unreliable statistical data). Linking deficit with GDP camouflages the real issue.

Modern-day economists are prone to build theoretical models in laboratory conditions, which have no relation to reality. Thus, they play into the hands of 'smart politicians', who seize such 'intellectual support' to advance their political agenda, and go on merrily on an expenditure spree, without resorting to the unpopular route of raising resources through taxation. While the Keynesian model of deficit in government budget to stimulate the economy may be theoretically sound, a more rational course is to prescribe a limit related to government revenue, beyond which expenditure cannot be incurred – thus, say, in a particular year, expenditure cannot be more than 10 per cent of what is raised by way of revenue. Such an approach would keep a check on politicians who distribute freebies as political gimmickry without bothering its budgetary implications.

Many economists themselves are aware of the limitation of their profession to prescribe public policy. Paul Krugman,[7] an economics Nobel Prize winner, castigated the profession of economists for constructing mathematical models which have no relation to reality and their culpability in creating situations which resulted in the economic crisis of 2008. Ronald Coase,[8] another Nobel laureate in economics, faults economists for their theoretical approach of economization and for isolating themselves from the ordinary business of life.

Porous tax regime

It is through taxes, both direct and indirect, that public expenditure is financed. While expenditure is increasing every year, there has not been commensurate growth of tax revenue. Desperate for revenue, both the UPA and NDA have been selling shares of profitable PSUs, without any economic justification. These sales fetched Rs 18,253 crore in 2013–14, Rs 32,620 crore in 2014–15 and Rs 25,300 crore in 2015–16, and the sale is budgeted for Rs 56,500 crore for 2016–17. It is pointless to sell shares of profitable companies such as ONGC, NTPC, BHEL, SAIL, RINL and NALCO, which are national jewels. All these years PSUs were bringing substantial dividends to the government's coffer – Rs 25,921 crore in 2013–14, Rs 31,692 crore in 2014–15 and Rs 44,400 crore in 2015–16. Selling shares of profitable PSUs is tantamount to selling the family silver to pay for grocers' bill and killing the goose that lays the golden egg.

Tax revenue is financing only around 50 per cent of expenditure, as it has not kept pace with the burgeoning expenditure, as is evident from Table 7.3.

The main reason for lack of buoyancy in taxes is the government's lack of 'will' to raise taxes by taking hard and unpopular decisions. Tax revenue of the central government as a percentage of GDP is 10 to 11 per cent, while it is 6 to 7 per cent for states and 17 to 18 per cent of GDP for both central and state governments. In comparison tax-GDP ratio is 25 to 30 per cent in the US, Canada, Australia and Japan, around 35 per cent in the UK and Germany, 45 per cent in Belgium, Sweden and France and as high as 49 per cent in Denmark. Overall average of tax-GDP ratio in OECD (Organization for Economic Cooperation and Development) countries was

Table 7.3 Tax revenue as percentage of total expenditure

Year	2007–8	2008–9	2009–10	2010–11	2011–12	2012–13	2013–14	2014–15	2015–16 RE	2016–17 BE
Tax revenue (Rs crore)	439,547	444,339	456,536	563,685	629,765	742,115	815,854	903,615	947,508	1,054,101
Tax-revenue percentage, government expenditure	62	52	55	46	48	51	52	54	53	53

Note: For government expenditure, see Column 1, Table 7.1; RE: revised expenditure; BE: budget estimates.

Source: Government of India Budget, various years.

34 per cent (2012–14), with Denmark recording the highest tax-GDP ratio of 51 per cent in 2014.[9] In India with such low tax recovery, it is wishful thinking that it can provide food and employment security to its citizens.

India has a very soft tax regime for personal income tax. India has a large number of millionaires and billionaires earning crores annually. These super-rich are taxed at the same rate as an average citizen, as the highest tax rate is only 30 per cent (with 3 per cent educational surcharge). Even liberal economies of Europe and OECD known for low taxation structures have high tax rates for the rich. The highest marginal income-tax rate is 39 per cent in Norway, 45 per cent in Belgium and the UK, 47 per cent in Germany, 49 per cent in Australia and the Netherlands, 54 per cent in France, 55 per cent in Japan and Denmark and 57 per cent in Sweden (2015).[10] It may be worth noting that before the globalization era which began in the 1980s, the top marginal rates in OECD countries ranged between 60 and 80 per cent, with Sweden touching a peak rate of 87 per cent (1975).[11] In OECD countries, taxes on income (personal and corporate) are the main sources of public revenue and account for around 11 per cent of GDP.

Corporates in India are also taxed low. The tax rate on companies is 30 per cent and with surcharge it comes to around 33 per cent. However, due to various concessions, exemptions and so on, the effective rate came to 23.22 per cent in 2013–14 and 24.67 per cent in 2014–15 on those companies, which report profit (only about 55 per cent companies report profit). A large number of companies 'avoid tax' due to creative accounting practices. The owners and top management of these companies siphon off huge amounts of salary, allowances and bonus and use numerous other techniques, rather than ploughing back profits in the company for productive investment. One fails to see the logic of the finance minister in his budget speech of February 2015, proposing reduction of corporate tax to 25 per cent in the next four years.

There are several reasons for low tax collection. A large number of tax preferences have been given by way of special tax rates, exemptions, deductions, rebates, deferrals and credits, as a result of which huge revenue is foregone. Every year the revenue budget document gives information about revenue foregone. In 2011–12, Rs 533,500 crore (direct and indirect taxes) was foregone, which was around 60 per cent of estimated gross tax collection of Rs 889,000 crore, and in 2012–13, Rs 574,000 crore was estimated to have foregone, which is 55 per cent of gross collection of Rs 1,038,000 crore. During 2013–14, the revenue foregone was Rs 549,984 crore, which was 48 per cent of gross tax collection of Rs 1,138,734 crore, and in 2014–15, Rs 554,349 crore was foregone, which was 44.5 per cent of gross tax collection of Rs 1,244,884. For 2015–16, Rs 611,128 crore is estimated to have been forgone, constituting 42 per cent of a gross revenue of Rs 1,459,611 crore (for 2015–16 budget, the finance ministry is using the nomenclature 'Revenue Impact of Tax Incentive' to camouflage its soft tax policy). Table 7.4 gives the estimated tax revenue forgone, which ranged between 42 and 60 per cent

Table 7.4 Tax revenue foregone (Rs crore)

	2007-8	2008-9	2009-10	2010-11	2011-12	2012-13	2013-14	2014-15	2015-16
Personal income tax	38,057	37,570	45,142	36,826	39,375	45,464	35,254	53,525	59,928
Corporate tax	62,199	66,901	72,891	57,912	61,765	68,007	57,793	65,067	68,710
Excise tax	87,468	128,293	169,121	192,227	195,590	206,188	196,223	196,789	224,940
Customs duty	153,593	225,772	195,288	172,740	236,852	253,967	260,714	238,967	257,549

Source: Government of India Receipt Budget, various years.

of the gross tax collection of the central government during the past five years.

Due to the policy of liberalization, customs duty rates have been reduced on a large number of items, which not only reduces revenue collection but also has serious adverse effects on the economy, both in agriculture and in industrial sectors. For example, India is a very large importer of gold, edible oil and electronic equipment. The duty on gold and edible is very low, while on electronics it is nil. Customs duty needs to be properly calibrated to raise revenue, prevent foreign exchange outgo and encourage domestic production (see Chapters 5 and 6).

Black money is a huge problem in the country, estimated to be 50 per cent of the economy, which results in large tax leakage. Corruption is the most important reason for low tax collection in India. Raising revenue by better tax compliance, rationalizing the taxation structure and curbing the menace of black money are some of the important steps needed to generate more tax revenue. A major step in tax reform is passage of Goods and Service Tax bill in Parliament in August 2016, after years of parliamentary logjam. It needs a great deal of political will to bring fundamental reform in tax policy and administration and raise revenue to meet the country's burgeoning public expenditure.

Burgeoning public expenditure

The wage burden of public employees

The government's expenditure on salary and allowances of its employees has steeply increased due to the Sixth Pay Commission award (2008–9) and had been a contributory factor in unsustainable fiscal deficit. In 2007–8, the salary and pension bill of the employees (including defence forces) was a little over 16 per cent of the central government's revenue, but after the Pay Commission award it has jumped to more than 25 per cent of revenue. Table 7.5 illustrates this.

The Sixth Pay Commission has given a huge bounty to government servants. Besides, more than doubling the pay, it has indexed salary to inflation, and every six months, the employees get a pay rise based on the rise of the cost of living index. Today the dearness allowance of a government servant is 125 per cent of basic salary (April 2016). Huge benefits – such as enhanced house rent allowance, travel by air on Leave Travel Concession for employees above a certain pay band and eligibility of two years' leave with full pay for women employees to rear children, have been given. Similar bonanza has been given to pensioners – an employee on retirement can draw full pension after 20 years of service, instead of 33 years earlier; and get an escalation of 25 per cent of pension every five years on attaining the age of 80.

The figures of expenditure of civilian employees, given in the budget document, do not reflect the full extent of the government's wage bill, as it does not include the cost of employees of autonomous institutions

Table 7.5 Wages and pension of civil employees of central government and defence forces

	Pay and allowances, civilian employees (Rs crore) 1	Pay and allowances, defence (Rs crore) 2	Pension, civil + defence (Rs crore) 3	Wages and pension, civil + defence (Rs crore) 4	Wages + pension (Cl 4) percentage, government revenue (Column 1, Table 7.2) 5
2007–8	44,000	18,800	24,300	86,700	16.5
2008–9	71,700	29,400	32,900	134,000	24.8
2009–10	93,800	45,100	56,100	195,000	28.5
2010–11	89,750	44,000	53,240 (15,900 + 37,340) C + D	187,030	24
2011–12	95,980	49,540	55,500 (17,935 + 37,565) C + D	201,020	26.75
2012–13	107,900	56,890	62,920 (19,555 + 43,365) C + D	227,710	26
2013–14	117,914	62,503	68,284 (22,790 + 45,494) C + D	248,701	24.5
2014–15	133,984	70,758	85,708 (25,258 + 60,450) C + D	290,450	26
2015–16 RE	114,108	75,758	86,966 (26,728 + 60,238) C + D	276,832	23
2016–17 BE	179,531	86,568	113,351 (31,018 + 82,333) C + D	379,450	28

Notes: (1) Number of civilian employees was 33.06 lakh in March 2015 and 34.94 lakh in March 2016; (2) Defence includes army and auxiliary forces, navy and air force; (3) C is civilian pension and D is defence forces pension; RE: revised expenditure; BE: budget estimates.

Source: Extracted from budget documents, various years.

who are controlled/funded by the government and enjoy the same terms and conditions of service as central government employees and are fully or partially funded by the government. Teachers and staff working in colleges and universities have also been given salary increases, in line with central government employees, which has added a huge burden on the exchequer. In addition to salary and allowances, public servants enjoy perks such as free medical treatment under the Central Government Health Scheme (on nominal payment), subsidized housing, staff car, guest houses and free ration for defence personnel. (Salary bill does not include expenditure on official travel.) The wage bill and perks of not only government employees but also autonomous bodies and universities have to be ultimately picked up by the government. No computation regarding the full cost of the employees funded by the government is available – but as a guesstimate, it may run up to even 50 per cent of the revenue receipts of the government.

The position of states is more precarious. Due to competitive politics, most states have been adopting central pay scales, irrespective of the availability of resources. According to data available in the 13th Finance Commission report (2009–10), the percentage of expenditure on salary and pension of its employees to the state's own revenue (tax and non-tax) runs between 50 and 60 per cent in West Bengal, Uttar Pradesh and Punjab, 70 per cent in Orissa and 130 per cent in Assam and Bihar. The 14th Finance Commission (December 2014) has skirted this issue but notes in passing that in 2012–13, the share of expenditure on pay and allowances of employees as a proportion of revenue expenditure (net of interest payments and pension) among the states ranged from 29 to 79 per cent.

The 7th Pay Commission, which was appointed by UPA government, has in its report (applicable from January 2016) given another huge bonanza to government employees. An additional outlay of Rs 1,03,000 crore has been provided in the budget 2016–17. Government has accepted the recommendations of the Pay Commission (July 2016). This will result in jumping of expenditure on wages and pension of government employees from present 25 per cent of revenue receipts to over 30 per cent and will seriously stress government finances. It is therefore not surprising when people of the country say that the government exists for the benefit of the government servants alone.

MPLADS: There is a close nexus between bureaucracy and politicians, who both thrive at the cost of public exchequer. Our parliamentarians have given themselves not only liberal salaries, allowances and perks but also what is known as Member of Parliament Local Area Development Scheme (MPLADS). Each Member of Parliament has been allocated Rs 5 crore per year (increased from Rs 2 crore during 2012–13), and he or she can select works to be implemented in his or her constituency (in case of Rajya Sabha members, anywhere in the state). This imposes a burden of Rs 3,950 crore annually on the exchequer, and Rs 38,800 crore has been spent till March 2016 from December 1996, when it was introduced. The bulk of money spent under the scheme is not efficiently utilized, as the report of the Comptroller and Auditor General (CAG) and other expert bodies has shown. Experts say that the scheme is ultra vires of the constitution and a blot on democratic governance, as legislators assume the role of the executive and call for its abolition.

It is apparent that the government has no interest in economizing expenditure.

Part II

Poor outcome of public expenditure

From the time India started development planning, a huge sum of money is spent on five-year plans, but public funds are not optimally used and that is the main reason for dismal performance of the economy. During the 12th Five-Year Plan (2012–17), the central government is spending on an average Rs 470,000 crore annually as plan expenditure (which includes plan assistance to states). (The central plan expenditure was Rs 413,600 crore in 2012–13, Rs 453,000 crore in 2013–14, Rs 463,000 crore in 2014–15 and Rs 478,000 crore in 2015–16, and it is budgeted at Rs 550,000 for 2016–17 – altogether Rs 2,357,000 crore for the 12th Five-Year Plan period.) A large chunk of this money is spent on social sector programmes in the areas of poverty alleviation, rural development, health, primary education and so on and operated as centrally sponsored schemes (CSSs) such as Mahatma Gandhi National Rural Employment Guarantee Act (MGNREGA), Sarva Shiksha Abhiyan, Mid-Day Meal, National Health Mission, Pradhan Mantri Gram Sadak Yojana and Pradhan Mantri Awas Yojna. The practical working of CSSs is extremely complicated and creates difficulty in implementation. There are 66 CSSs (reduced technically from 137) with varying sizes, objectives and formulaes for expenditure sharing between the centre and states. Consequent on the 14th Finance Commission award, the states' share of taxes has gone up to 42 per cent from 32 per cent, and more resources are available to them with greater flexibility for its usage. This has necessitated changes and reduction in central assistance to state plans, which is now classified into three categories: schemes fully supported by the union government, schemes to be run with changing sharing pattern and schemes for which no assistance will be given.

The performance audit conducted by the CAG, the social audit conducted by non-governmental organizations and numerous studies by experts show that there is huge wastage and leakage of funds in the plan schemes. N. C. Saxena,[12] former civil servant and expert on rural development, points out that due to poor designing of MGNREGA, the states such as Bihar, Uttar Pradesh and Orissa, which have the largest number of poor people, are not benefitting and the bulk of funds have been cornered by better-off states such as Kerala and Tamil Nadu.

One of the reasons for poor implementation of plan schemes is the highly centralized system, under which all powers are concentrated in the erstwhile Planning Commission and the central government, with very little discretion to states. The NDA government has abolished the Planning Commission. This is a good step, in the sense that the Planning Commission had taken upon itself the responsibility to allocate funds for various development programmes and micro-managed them, which was unworkable. It should have limited its role to long-term strategic planning. The development schemes and projects would yield best results only when there is effective delegation to state governments, as well as decentralization within the central government to individual ministries, directorates and field outfits. The 14th Finance Commission has allocated more funds to states, keeping in view the principle of fiscal federalism. While this is a welcome step, states in turn should delegate more powers to Panchayati Raj Institutions and urban local bodies, as well as field outfits, and show greater fiscal responsibility. The productivity of the government departments is abysmally low. Public expenditure will secure best value for money only when both central and state governments improve their governance and financial administration.

Reforming budgetary systems

One of the main reasons for poor outcome of public expenditure is the outdated budgetary and financial management practices followed by the government. Several high-powered commissions and committees – such as the Second Administrative Reforms Commission (2008–9), Expenditure Reform Commission (2000–2001) and Fifth and Sixth Pay Commissions (1997 and 2008), have come out with laudable suggestions to reform the public administration systems, but they have remained unimplemented. The administrative ministries, departmental heads and field outfits face two major problems in efficient utilization of money:

1   The system of annual budgeting leading to lapse of money at the end of the fiscal year and rush of expenditure in the month of March.
2   The centralized control of the finance ministry and absence of delegation to administrative ministries and field outfits, responsible for the implementation of policies, and delivery of services.

Paradoxical though it may appear, while the government is perennially short of money for its various programmes and schemes, huge amounts of money allocated in the budget get surrendered every year as they cannot be utilized. The audit report of CAG on Union Government Accounts every year points out to large sums surrendered by various ministries every year. Thus, for example, as per CAG report for 2014–15 (No. 50 of 2015 on Union Government Accounts), there was a provision of Rs 94,300 crore as capital outlay for defence services, out of which Rs 12,500 crore (13 per cent) was surrendered. There is a huge requirement of funds for defence equipment, but due to slow decision making and bureaucratic rigmarole, funds lapse. (There is no overall savings at the end of the fiscal year, due to large supplementary grants taken every year.)

There are two reasons why ministries and departments are unable to use the allocated money: first, even when money is provided in the budget, there are numerous procedural formalities, such as clearance of schemes by the Standing Finance Committee/Expenditure Finance Committee/ Public Investment Board, sanction of posts and fulfilment of many procedural formalities, before money can be spent. These clearances do not come speedily and the money lapses; second, the tendering and contracting procedure for purchase of equipment, goods and services is long and tortuous, and it takes considerable time to complete the prescribed formalities of placing orders and taking delivery of supply and services.

Learning from best international practices

Most developed countries have resolved the problem of efficient utilization of budgetary allocation by modernizing expenditure management systems and shifted to the medium-term expenditure framework.[13] The UK, Australia, New Zealand and Scandinavian countries have moved to multi-year budget, with a proper linkage with annual budgets. End-year flexibility removes the perverse incentive for the departments to use up their provisions as the year end approaches without getting value for money. Departments have the flexibility, inside overall limits, to reprioritize expenditure to meet their objectives most efficiently. In order to realize value for money, we need to have a medium-term expenditure framework. Budgets should be approved for a three-year cycle with an annual review. All unspent money should be allowed to be carried forward to the next year within the three-year budgetary cycle, and the rule of lapse should be discarded. For capital projects, budgeting should be done for the full life cycle of the project, integrated in a three-year budgetary envelope, and funds saved at the end of the financial year should be allowed to be carried forward from year to year till completion of the project.

A major problem in expenditure optimization is lack of delegation to administrative ministries and departments. At present, the functioning of the finance ministry is highly centralized. It tightly controls spending of money through line-item budgeting, which implies that expenditure limits for every item are fixed, giving no flexibility to a particular department or field outfit to spend money as per its priority. Administrative ministries have very limited powers to reappropriate funds from one head to another. Both the Eswaran Committee of the Ministry of Finance (1996) and the Fifth Pay Commission (1997) had recommended that once the budgetary ceilings are determined, the administrative ministries and departmental heads should be given full control, authority and flexibility over the money allocated to them in respect of each scheme approved in the budget.

The UK, New Zealand, Australia and many other countries have developed a new philosophy of expenditure management, which shifts the existing practice of 'input orientation' when funds are sanctioned and correlates it to 'output' and 'results'. In a half-hearted approach, the

Ministry of Finance has prescribed presentation of Outcome Budgets and from the period 2007–8, every ministry is required to present an Outcome Budget to Parliament. However, due to poor designing and want of genuine commitment on the part of public servants to increase efficiency and productivity of public expenditure, the scheme has remained on paper only and is meeting the same fate as zero-based budgeting introduced with much fanfare in 1987–88.[14]

Performance-based organizations: During the past three decades, several developed countries, which have faced the problem of inept bureaucracies and fiscal profligacy, have met the challenge by taking some bold reform measures, in what has come to be known as the philosophy of New Public Management (NPM). The NPM emphasizes deregulating internal management of public bureaucracies and decentralizing and streamlining various management processes such as budgeting, personnel and procurement. As part of budgetary reform, the NPM envisages change in the existing budgetary practice of 'input' orientation, where funds are sanctioned without correlating it to the 'output', and shifts emphasis on what 'results' are delivered when funds are parcelled out.

As part of NPM, Britain, New Zealand, Australia and Canada have all revamped their bureaucratic systems and migrated to professional management of the bulk of government activity through creation of 'agency' or 'performance-based organization' and given them wide powers in personnel, operational and financial matters. In Britain, New Zealand and several other countries the Chief Executive of Agency and top functionaries are selected by the Public Service Commission, through competition open to both public- and private sector candidates and hired on the basis of a contract. They enjoy full freedom to manage operations within their framework document and annual agreements. Many scholars in India, including B. P. Mathur, have supported the introduction of NPM for India.[15] NPM promises to transform bureaucratic management into professional and performance-oriented management. There is need for embracing the philosophy of New Public Management and Agencification model for revamping governance in India as it brings efficiency in public administration and makes government servants accountable for delivering results (see Chapter 14).

Part III

Budgetary deficit and inflation

One of the biggest problems that an individual faces in the country is high inflation in the economy, which erodes his or her real income. Nobel Prize–winning economist Milton Friedman[16] had said, 'Inflation is always and everywhere a monetary phenomenon, in the sense that it cannot occur without a more rapid increase in the quantity of money than in output.' Are huge public spending and deficits in government budget responsible for high inflation in the Indian economy?

According to historic data of the consumer price index (CPI) brought out by the EU, India has one of the highest inflation rates in the world.[17] CPI is a measure of the average price which consumers spend on a market-based 'basket' of goods and services, measured as an average of monthly inflation rates of the particular year. The average inflation in India was 10.92 per cent in 2013 and 6.37 per cent in 2014 (a year's average inflation rate is average of monthly inflation rates in the calendar year). Compare this with the average inflation rate in 2013 of some leading economies: China, 2.57 per cent; Denmark, 0.78 per cent; France, 0.86 per cent; Germany, 1.51 per cent; Great Britain, 2.56 per cent; Japan, 0.36 per cent; Sweden, –0.04 per cent; and the US, 1.47 per cent. The average inflation rate in 2014 was as follows: China, 2.06 per cent; Denmark, 0.57 per cent; France, 0.51 per cent; Germany, 0.91 per cent; Great Britain, 1.46 per cent; Japan, 2.74 per cent; Sweden, –0.18 per cent; and the US, 1.62 per cent. In developed countries, the average annual inflation rate over a long period of time has remained within a range of 1 to 2 per cent. In Europe inflation averaged around 2 per cent in 20 years up to 2013. In 2015 the global economy slowed down, and inflation rates in developed countries such as France, Germany, Great Britain and the US, based on CPI, were below 1 per cent. In India CPI for 2015 was 5.88 per cent.

In India the average inflation based on CPI during the past 20 years was around 7 to 8 per cent annually. The average of CPI rates during the past five years was 8.25 per cent (2015 – 5.88 per cent, 2014 – 6.37, 2013 – 10.92, 2012 – 9.30, 2011 – 8.87). Thus, in five years' time the value of the rupee has come down to around 70 paisa. According to the formula adopted by the Income Tax Department for levy of Capital Gains tax, the cost index for 2014–15 is 1024, with 1981–82 as the base year, for which it is 100. Thus, in a 33-year period the real value of the rupee has come down to 10 paisa.

High inflation can cause havoc in an economy. Germany learnt a bitter lesson after the First World War, when currency notes were stuffed in a bag to buy a loaf of bread, and public anger against unfair peace treaty terms became a contributory factor in Hitler's rise to power, Germany's rearmament and triggering of the Second World War. Celebrated economist J. M. Keynes[18] in his book *Economic Consequences of Peace* quoted Lenin, who had observed,

> There is no subtler, no surer means of overturning the existing basis of society than to debauch the currency. The process engages all the hidden forces of economic law on the side of destruction, and does it in a manner which not one man in a million is able to diagnose.

Expressing his own serious misgivings about inflation, Keynes observed,

> By continuing the process of inflation, governments can confiscate, secretly and unobserved, an important part of the wealth of its citizens. By this method, they not only confiscate, but they

confiscate arbitrarily; and while the process impoverishes many, it actually enriches some.

High inflation that we are facing in India has a disastrous effect on the poor and fixed-income groups. While the real income of the poor keeps decreasing, the assets of the rich and powerful, who are holders of physical assets and major borrowers of money from banks, keep increasing, while the borrowing cost keeps decreasing. It needs to be seriously debated whether the government's huge spending through borrowed funds is a principal factor behind the country's high rate of inflation.

The way forward

In order to improve the finances of the country, we have to take bold action on both fiscal policy and its implementation. It is only through improved governance and curbing corruption that we can prevent large-scale evasion of tax and curb the generation of black economy. For reduction of large deficits in the budget and heavy public debt burden, the following measures are suggested:

1   A legislation should be passed by Parliament placing a ceiling on government borrowing. Article 292 of the Constitution has a provision to that effect.
2   The provision of FRBMA should be strictly enforced. There should be no revenue deficit, and fiscal deficit should be no more than 3 per cent of GDP. A still more effective course is to mandate that in a year, both the central and state governments should not incur expenditure above a certain percentage of revenue (e.g. 10 per cent) they collect. However, in emergency situations, such as drought, the government can have a deficit in revenue budget. A long-term objective should be a balanced budget with zero deficit.
3   There should be a law that the government should not borrow for current consumption, and all borrowings should be only for capital works and projects. As a general rule, the government should incur expenditure on any new schemes and activities above a certain level (e.g. Rs 1,000 crore) only when it shows how additional money will be raised to finance it through fresh taxation or other revenue-generating measures.
    New Zealand's FRMBA states, 'Once prudent level of total crown debt has been achieved, maintain these levels by ensuring that, on an average, over a reasonable period of time, the total operating expenses of the Crown do not exceed its total operating revenues' (prudent debt level is interpreted to mean net public debt in the region of 20 to 30 per cent of the GDP). Germany has passed a constitutional amendment called Schuldenbremse, or debt break, that outlaws deficit in national budget beginning 2016.

4   Additional resources should be raised by plugging the loopholes in taxation law and withdrawing unjustified exemptions and concessions. Income-tax rates should be hiked for the super-rich and those earning high incomes without 'sweat of their labour'. Customs and excise tariff should be rationalized to give incentive for domestic production and national self-sufficiency and prevent unnecessary imports.

   Tax policy should aim at a central government tax-revenue realization of 15 per cent of GDP, with the long-term objective of achieving a target of 20 per cent. The overall tax revenue of the government (centre and state) should target at 25 per cent of GDP, with a longer-term objective of 30 per cent.

5   Serious attempts should be made to curb the menace of black money, which is estimated to be 50 per cent of the economy and escapes tax payment.

6   There is a need to have medium-term expenditure framework. Budgets should be approved for a three-year cycle with an annual review. All unspent money should be allowed to be rolled over to the next year. For capital projects, funds should be provided for full life cycle of the project.

7   There should be budgeting for results – mission-driven budgets or Outcome Budgets. Budgets should become contract for performance. In exchange for agreed resources, ministries/departments should produce specified targets set for them. This is possible when the institutional framework of autonomous performance-based organization, with full operational autonomy, is created. This would simultaneously ensure accountability of public officials to deliver results.

Restoring fiscal balance

Large fiscal deficits have a variety of adverse consequences for the economy: they reduce economic growth, lower real incomes and increase the risk of financial and economic crisis. India should not lull itself into belief that as a sovereign state it can keep on accumulating excessive debt with impunity. In a globalized world, a state can lose the confidence of the market, which may result in a financial cut-off and derail the entire economy. Contemporary historian Niall Ferguson[19] argues that in the past civilizations have collapsed due to financial bankruptcy. He cites Spain in the 16th century, France in the 18th century – a major factor contributing to the French Revolution of 1789 – and disintegration of the Ottoman Empire in the 19th century. He elaborates that the declining influence of Britain after the Second World War and the US currently has been due to their unsustainable debt liability, particularly to foreign creditors.

It is important to remember that most cases of civilizational collapse are associated with fiscal crises as well as war. [They] were preceded by sharp imbalances between revenue and expenditures, as well as by difficulties with financing public debt.[20]

It is time the country wakes up to the reality of fiscal discipline. The government must take drastic action to cut wasteful expenditure, mercilessly prune schemes which have no utility and impose severe austerity measures on public services. Simultaneously, it should take tough and coercive action to impose and collect more taxes and generate revenue surplus. The government's foremost agenda should be freedom from crippling debt and restoring fiscal balance. That is the only way we can build a strong and robust economy and acquire a dignified place in the international economy.

Notes

Note: Most data has been taken from Government of India Budgets (various years), Economic Survey, RBI Handbook of Statistics on Indian Economy.

1 L. N. Rangarajan, *Kautilya, The Arthashastra*, New Delhi: The Penguin Books, 1992, p. 253.
2 Gunnar Myrdal, *Asian Drama*, Vol. I, Middlesex, UK: Penguin Books, 1968, p. 277.
3 Kautilya, *The Arthashastra*, p. 253.
4 Jacques Attali, 'The West and the tyranny of public debt', *Newsweek*, Special Edition 2011: The Key to Power, p. 56.
5 'PC blames Pranab's stimulus package for UPAs 2014 rout', *Times of India*, 8 March 2014, p. 10.
6 Martin Feldstein, *Budget Deficit and National Debt*, RBI: L. K. Jha Memorial Lecture, 13 January 2004, available at http://www.rbi.org.in/Scripts/PublicationsView.aspx?Id=5915 (accessed 25 June 2015).
7 Paul Krugman, 'How Economists Get It So Wrong', *The New York Times* Magazine, 2 September 2009, available at http://www.nytimes.com/2009/09/06/magazine/06Economic-t.html?pagewanted=all (accessed 25 June 2016).
8 Ronald Coase, 'Saving Economics from the Economists', *Harvard Business Review South Asia*, December 2012, p. 34.
9 OECD Revenue Statistics, available at http://www.oecd.org/ctp/tax-policy/revenue-statistics-ratio-change-latest-years.htm (accessed 23 April 2016); List of Countries by Tax Revenue as Percentage of GDP, available at http://en.wikipedia.org/wiki/List_of_countries_by_tax_revenue_as_percentage_of_GDP (accessed 20 March 2015).
10 OECD Statistics, available at https://stats.oecd.org/Index.aspx?DataSetCode=TABLE_I7 (accessed 22 April 2016).
11 Tax Policy Centre, Urban Institute & Brookings Institution, Available at http://www.taxpolicycenter.org/taxfacts/displayafact.cfm?Docid=105 (accessed 25 March 2015).
12 N. C. Saxena, 'Why are some programmes doing better than others: PMGSY vs MGNREGS', *The Indian Express*, 23 March 2016, p. 7.
13 For detailed discussion, see B. P. Mathur, 'Productivity of Public Expenditure', *Indian Journal of Public Administration*, July–September 2005, No. 3,

pp 448–464; B. P. Mathur, 'Streamlining Budgetary Systems', in *Governance Reform for Vision India*, Chapter 7, New Delhi: Macmillan, 2005; also see A. Premchand, *Control of Public Money*, New Delhi: Oxford University Press, 2005.

14 B. P. Mathur, 'Outcome Budget: An Exercise in Futility', in K. N. Kabra (ed.), *Alternative Economic Survey: Two Decades of Neo-Liberalism*, New Delhi: Daanish Books, 2012, pp. 451–463.

15 Pradip N. Khandwalla, *Transforming Government through New Public Management*, Ahmedabad: Management Association, 2010; S. K. Das, *Building a World-Class Civil Service*, New Delhi: Oxford University Press, 2010; B. P. Mathur, *Governance Reform for Vision India*, New Delhi: Macmillan, 2005; and *Ethics in Governance*, New Delhi: Routledge, 2014.

16 Milton Friedman quoted by Niall Ferguson, *The Ascent of Money*, London: Allen Lane, 2008, p. 100.

17 'EU world wide inflation data', available at http://www.inflation.eu/inflation-rates/cpi-inflation-2013.aspx and http://www.inflation.eu/inflation-rates/cpi-inflation-2014.aspx (accessed 28 March 2015) and http://www.inflation.eu/inflation-rates/cpi-inflation-2015.aspx (accessed 25 April 2016).

18 J. M. Keynes, *Economic Consequences of Peace*, London: Macmillan, 1920, extract available at https://en.wikipedia.org/wiki/The_Economic_Consequences_of_the_Peace (accessed on 27 May 2016).

19 Niall Ferguson, *Civilization: The West and the Rest*, London: Allen Lane, 2011, pp. 309–312.

20 Ibid, p. 309.

Part II

THE CURRENT ECONOMIC IDEOLOGY AND ITS PROBLEMS

8

FREE MARKET IDEOLOGY
AND ITS PERILS

We have for over a century been dragged by the prosperous West behind its chariot, choked by the dust, deafened
by the noise, humbled by our own helplessness, and overwhelmed by the speed. We agreed to acknowledge that this
chariot-drive was progress, and the progress was civilization. If we ever ventured to ask, 'progress towards what,
and progress for whom', it was considered to be peculiarly
and ridiculously oriental to entertain such ideas about the
absoluteness of progress. Of late a voice has come to us
to take count not only of the scientific perfection of the
chariot but the depth of the ditches lying on its path.
Rabindranath Tagore, *Civilization and Progress*[1]

Right now, one can only conclude that growth is the enemy of
environment. Economy and environment remain on collision.
James Speth, Environmentalist[2]

From the time of independence and more particularly post-1991 economic liberalization, India has been looking towards developed countries
as a model of economic development, largely due to the wealth they have
generated and lifted people out of poverty and basic deprivation. The
current ruling economic ideology in the West is known as free market
economy or capitalism. This ideology creates its own set of problems, as
we see in this chapter. We should not therefore blindly copy it and should
devise a model of development which suits our unique economic and
social conditions.

Modern capitalism

The principal characteristics of modern capitalism, as it has emerged
today, are materialistic values, consumer society and giant corporations and its huge production apparatus. Inherent in the dynamics of

capitalism are free markets and the powerful drive to earn profits, invest, innovate and grow the economy in an exponential manner. This ideology of capitalism and free markets reached its zenith in the US, the UK and other developed countries from the 1980s onwards, when Ronald Regan in the US and Margaret Thatcher in the UK came to head their respective governments. The philosophy derived its inspiration from the Chicago school, whose chief protagonist is Milton Friedman, and it is powerfully advocated by the World Bank, International Monetary Fund and World Trade Organization and what has come to be known as neoliberal model of economic development. The ideology gives great emphasis on deregulation, liberalization, privatization and globalization, with the state exercising minimal interference in economic activities.

The global economic meltdown of 2008 has exposed the hollowness of the philosophy of unfettered capitalism with its belief in free and unregulated markets. There has been a return to Keynesianism, with the state investing billions of dollars in the economy to stimulate demand. In the US, the General Motors and the housing finance giants Fannie Mae and Freddie Mac were practically nationalized to save them from collapse. The deregulation of the banking sector led to financial engineering, with big banks trading worthless securities, under all kinds of innovative products, making huge profits and their executives cornering astronomical salaries and bonuses, until the bubble burst, and banks such as Lehman Brothers collapsed. Nobel Prize–winning economist Paul Krugman[3] blamed the profession of economists for being blind to the possibility of catastrophic failures in a market economy and said that most macroeconomics of the past 30 years was 'spectacularly useless at best, and positively harmful at worst'.

David C. Korten,[4] a crusader against corporate power, says that free market gives the opportunity to unscrupulous corporates to commit fraud,

> The term free market is a code word for an unregulated market that allows rich to consume and monopolize resources for personal gain free from accountability for broader social and environmental consequences. A free market rewards financial rouges and speculators who profit from governmental, social and environmental subsidies, speculation, the abuse of monopoly power, and financial fraud, creating an open and often irresistible invitation to externalize costs and increase inequality.

While capitalism claims that it has faith in free markets, through globe-spanning mega-corporations,

> capitalism has distorted market theory beyond recognition to legitimize an ideology without logical or empirical foundation in the service of narrow class interest. Wearing the mantle of market, capitalism's agents vigorously advance public policies that create conditions diametrically opposed to those required by markets to function in a socially optimal way.

Despite pouring huge public money, the US and EU economies are not showing robust economic growth and are burdened with huge unemployment problems. Massive public expenditure financed by borrowing has landed these countries in a huge burden of debt. Lately there has been reversal of these policies, and fiscal discipline has become the new policy prescription. Several European countries have been forced to launch austerity programmes and cut public expenditure. This has further compounded the problem. Countries such as Greece, Italy, Spain and Portugal are confronted with a stagnant economy coupled with high unemployment, leading to social unrest.

Much of the problem of Western countries is with their fetish with economic growth. The obsession with economic growth is often termed 'the secular religion of the advancing industrial societies', and some macroeconomists declare it 'the summum bonum of their craft'. Leading environmentalist James Gustav Speth severely criticizes obsession with growth and says this is the main reason for environmental degradation.[5] Growth is built in the capitalist system of production as there is need to continuously make profit, which can come only through growth of the economy. The corporates and businesses have deep vested interest in the existing system of ever-rising production and consumption. 'Corporations are the principal actors on capitalism's stage. They are capitalism's most important institutions, perhaps the most important institutions of our time. If capitalism is the growth machine, corporations are doing the growing.'[6] In the US the largest Fortune 500 companies account for over half the gross domestic product. The corporate and business sectors wield great economic and political power and can influence government policies. As they are driven solely by profit motive, they do this by maximizing production and sale of goods and services irrespective of its environment and other costs. So long as production and sales are increasing, the GDP number would grow and keep the corporate and business sectors happy.

The problem with current economic model

The current economic model based on free market system, creates serious socio-economic problems. The most critical ones are as follows:

1 Ecological disaster
2 Inequality in society
3 Consumerist culture
4 Unemployment, particularly of educated youth

The looming ecological disaster

The vast expansion of human economic activity in the world, together with growth in population, is proving disastrous to environmental sustainability. The world population is increasing at an amazing pace despite reduction in fertility rates. Global population was 1 billion in 1800, increased to 3 billion in 1960, jumped to 6 billion at the beginning of this century in 2000 and touched 7 billion in 2012 – an increase of 1 billion in 12 years. On the other hand, production and consumption is increasing on a much faster rate than population growth. According to the data presented in a Club of Rome study *Limits to Growth*,[7] while the world population increased from 2.5 billion in 1950 to 6 billion in 2000, in this 50-year period, the increase in production activities has been phenomenal as the following indicates: registered vehicles from 70 to 723 million; oil consumption from 3,800 million barrels per year to 27,600 million barrels; electricity generation capacity from 154 million kilowatts to 3,240 million kilowatts; steel production from 185 million metric tonnes per year to 290 million metric tonnes; and aluminium production from 1.5 million metric tonnes per year to 23 million metric tonnes. In five decades from the mid-1950s to mid-2010s, while consumption rose sixfold, human numbers grew by a factor of 2.2 – thus consumption expenditure per person almost tripled. Another estimate of increase in human activity points out that from 1890 to 1990, while the world population increased four-fold, the world economy grew 14-fold, water use grew nine-fold and energy consumption grew 16-fold.[8]

Due to rising consumption, more fossil fuels, minerals and metals have been mined from earth, and more trees have to be cut down and more land has to be ploughed to grow food. As a result of huge human activity, half the world's tropical and temperate forests as well as wetlands have gone, and many species have disappeared from the earth. Human impact has led to depletion of the earth's stratospheric ozone layer and has pushed atmospheric carbon dioxide by more than a third and has started the dangerous process of warming the planet and disrupting climate. The current global industrial system is leading us to a situation where we are running out of resources that support life such as clean air and drinking water.

The world is confronted by several other ecological crises such as climate change; destruction of ocean fisheries and coral reefs; growing shortage of freshwater; depletion of top soil in prime agricultural areas; the cutting and burning of ancient forests including rain forests; introduction of toxicants into the biosphere; accumulation of toxic waste from chemical processing, mining and other industrial activities (see Chapter 9).

According to environmentalist James Speth, mindless pursuit of growth is responsible for ecological devastation. Questioning its very rationale, he observes:

> [We] live in a world where economic growth is generally seen as both beneficent and necessary – the more the better; where past growth has brought us to a perilous state environmentally; where we are poised for unprecedented increments in growth; where this growth is proceeding with wildly wrong market signals, including prices that do not incorporate environment costs or reflect the need of the future generations; where a failed politics has not meaningfully

corrected the market's obliviousness to environment needs; where economies are routinely employing technologies that was created in an environmentally unaware era; where there is no hidden hand or inherent mechanism adequate to correct the destructive tendencies. So, right now, one can only conclude that growth is the enemy of environment. Economy and environment remain on collision.[9]

Economic inequality

A free market economy creates vast disparity in income and wealth in society, as has been the experience of the US and other Western countries. The corporate owners and executives appropriate most of the profit to themselves, sharing very little with workers who are equal partners in wealth creation. In the US in the past three decades before the economic crisis, the workers' wages remained stagnant despite rising labour productivity. In the US, in 1980 the CEO of a typical major corporation received 42 times the compensation of an average factory worker; by the end of 2000 it was a whopping 475 times more.[10] Wall Street bankers appropriated for themselves a bonus of $20 billion in 2008, when the banks were being bailed out by state aid, which made President Obama to castigate them, soon after taking office. Even as banks have started making profit from late 2009, the bankers have again started making payment of huge bonuses to themselves. Unions were outraged at IBM boss being paid $21 million in 2009, when his firm laid off 10,000 American workers the previous year, due to recession.[11]

The top 1 per cent of the population in the US owns 40 per cent of the nation's financial wealth, the bottom 80 per cent owning just 9 per cent.[12] After the Second World War until 1980, the bottom 90 per cent Americans earned about 65 per cent of national income, and the top 10 per cent earned about 35 per cent, of which 10 per cent went to the top 1 per cent. From 1981 to 2010, the numbers changed, as the bottom 90 per cent share fell to 52 per cent, and the top 10 per cent rose to 48 per cent, with almost all those gains going to the top 1 per cent whose income share increased to 21 per cent.[13]

An article in *Yes Magazine*[14] cites Pulitzer Prize–winning author Hedrick Smith, who demonstrates how labour is losing out in the current capitalist system. Between 1945 and 1973, US workers' productivity grew by 96 per cent, and they were rewarded with a 94 per cent increase in their wages. However, between 1973 and 2011, years that parallel a collapse of the middle class, US workers' productivity grew by 80 per cent, yet employees saw only a 10 per cent increase in their wages. Millions who created that wealth were thus pushed into poverty or to its precipice, while billions in profits were transferred to the upper rich class.

Nobel Prize–winning economist Joseph Stiglitz notes that in America, while the top 1 per cent was doing fantastically, most Americans were growing worse off. 'The simple story of America is this the rich are getting richer, the richest of the rich are getting still richer, the poor becoming poorer and more numerous, and the middle class is being hallowed out.'[15] The growing inequality is destroying the social fabric.

The Credit Suisse 'Global Wealth Report'[16] estimates that overall in the world there were 24.2 millionaires (one whose net assets exceed $1 million) in mid-2010, about 0.5 per cent of the world's adult population. They control $69.2 trillion in assets, more than a third of world total. Some 41 per cent of them live in the US, 10 per cent in Japan and 3 per cent in China. The richest 1 per cent of adults control 43 per cent of the world's assets; the wealthiest 10 per cent have 83 per cent. The bottom 50 per cent have only 2 per cent. Credit Suisse reckons that there are about 1,000 dollar billionaires in the world. A study by *Oxfam* (January 2014) finds that almost half of the world's wealth is now owned by just 1 per cent of the population, and the bottom half of the world's population owns the same as the richest 85 people in the world. Further, the richest 1 per cent increased their share of income in 24 out of 26 countries, for which data is available between 1980 and 2012. This massive concentration of economic resources in the hands of fewer people presents a significant threat to inclusive political and economic systems.[17] The growing income disparity is a worldwide phenomenon. A survey by *The Economist*[18] on inequality notes that not only in America but in many countries such as Britain, Canada, China and India, the share of national income taken by the top 1 per cent has risen.

Oxford economist Anthony B. Atkinson, a leading authority on inequality, has presented a comprehensive set of policies that could bring a genuine shift in distribution of income. He has worked out the Gini coefficient (which measures inequality) for 'equalized disposable household income' for countries across the world in terms of their income per head.[19] Nordic countries such as Sweden, Norway and Denmark have the lowest inequality, with Gini coefficient less than 25, followed by continental European countries such as the Netherlands, Germany and France, where Gini coefficient is between 25 and 30 per cent. The Anglo-Saxon countries such as UK and the US have a much higher inequality, with the Gini coefficient around 35 per cent. India's Gini coefficient is around 49 per cent, China's is 51 per cent and South Africa's is the highest at 59 per cent, showing that they are very unequal societies.

Income inequality has serious economic and social consequences. It slows growth, causes financial crises and results in social unrest.

Rising inequality in India

One of the disquieting aspects about the economic growth in our country is that it is following the same pattern as in the US and other Western countries, creating vast social problems. This is due to the fact that there is a huge income disparity in investment between urban and rural areas, which favours the better-off educated urban population, as noted by the National Commission for the Enterprises in the Unorganised Sector. The commission noted that 83.6 crore Indians are poor and vulnerable living on less than Rs 20 per day. The chairman of the commission Arjun Sengupta pointed out that the whole thrust of the economy caters to middle and higher income group, whose number works out to about 225 million.[20] Studies by Asian Development Bank (ADB) shows that during the past two decades, income inequalities have vastly increased in our country.

In India the benefit of economic growth is getting unevenly distributed. According to Forbes, India had as many as 54 dollar billionaires, with combined net worth of 100 richest Indians equal to $276 billion, around one-fourth of the country's GDP (2009).[21] Another study called Hurun Report released in 2014 estimated that India has 109 billionaires and their total wealth is $422 billion, 22 per cent of India's GDP.[22] A Rich List by Raymedia (2015), which combines Indians, non-resident Indians and persons of Indian origin, found that there are 145 individual, families or partnership with minimum net worth of $1 billion.[23] Their aggregate net worth is estimated at $440 billion, which is equal to 23 per cent of India's GDP. In 2011–12, more than 100 CEOs took home an annual compensation package of more than a million dollars (Rs 45 crore). Promoter executive Naveen Jindal pocketed over Rs 73 crore, and professional executive Y. C. Deveshwar around Rs 10 crore as annual salary.[24] According to a survey by Ramstand[25] (2012), a global recruitment firm, the average annual salary of an Indian CEO below the age of 50 was Rs 7.9 crore and was higher than that taken by his or her American and European counterparts. Another report notes that Infosys CEO Vishal Sikka will be the highest-paid professional CEO of an Indian company, drawing Rs 30 crore as annual package.[26]

Thomas Piketty's new insight into inequality

Thomas Piketty,[27] a young French economist, has assembled massive amounts of data, spanning more than two centuries, relating to income distribution in developed countries. He concludes that wealth–income ratio and the associated inequality was high in industrially advanced countries until about the First World War, then declined and stabilized in the period 1910–70, and has been rising since then in terms of inequality of both income and wealth. This is due to the fact that the rate of return on capital significantly exceeds the growth rate of the economy. Piketty estimates over a long period of time the rate of return on capital is around 4 to 5 per cent per year, against 1 to 2 per cent growth rate of the economy. However, in the inter-war years and the period up to 1970, there was a substantial reduction in inequality due to higher growth rate of economy (the global economy grew at 3.5 to 4 per cent in the second half of the 20th century). In most European countries such as France, Germany, Britain and Italy, the richest 10 per cent own 60 per cent wealth, while the bottom 50 per cent own just 5 per cent (2010). In France, the richest 10 per cent command 62 per cent of national wealth and the poorest 50 per cent only 4 per cent, while in the US, the top decile own 72 per cent wealth and the bottom half just 2 per cent (2010–11).[28]

Piketty examines the functional distribution of income, and the share which goes to labour and capital, and finds that owners of wealth get a larger share than those who earn by dint of their labour. Thus, owners of capital become rentier and dominate those who own only their labour. One can find Marxist overtones in Piketty's analysis. As inherited wealth grows faster than output and income, it leads to concentration of wealth in the hands of few and is totally incompatible with meritocratic values and principle of social justice in a democratic society.

> The consequences of long term distribution of wealth is potentially terrifying especially when one adds that the return on capital varies directly with the size of initial stake and the divergence of wealth distribution is occurring on a global scale.[29]

In order to create a social state, Piketty suggests a progressive annual tax on wealth and a global tax on capital. Piketty's final conclusion is that a market economy based on private property contains powerful forces which threaten democratic societies and the value of social justice on which they are found. His findings have drawn worldwide attention and shaken the foundation of Western economic thought for whom free market is idée fixe of the economic system.

The consumerist society

A consumer society is one in which consumerism and materialism are central aspects of dominant culture, where goods and services are acquired not only to satisfy common needs but also to secure identity and meaning.

> Consumerism is a pillar of modern capitalism. It involves a powerful, socially sanctioned commitment to ever increasing purchase of goods and services on the market. Consumerism in this sense is paired with materialism, an approach to life and social well-being that elevates the material conditions of life over spiritual and social dimension.[30]

It was spending binge on consumer goods and houses, fuelled by credits and mortgages by recklessly indulgent banks, that was responsible for the global financial meltdown in 2008. According to economist Raghuram Rajan,[31] the root cause of the global economic recession of 2008 was growing income inequality in the US, as policymakers made indiscriminate advance of credit to the deprived sections of the population to keep them happy, which eventually boomeranged. Americans have been saving only 2 to 3 per cent of their income; the household debt was as high as 100 per cent of GDP in 2007. The British amassed even a larger debt; by 2008 the household debt was 183 per cent of annual disposable income, the highest level in any major economy. Indians traditionally have a habit of saving, about 30 to 35 per cent of GDP, so is China which saves 38 per cent of

GDP. But the culture of Western-style consumer credit is spreading rapidly across India and China, as also to other emerging markets. The middle class in these countries is picking up credit cards, auto loans and home mortgages lured by easy availability of credit by banks. Studies show that the habits of spending, saving and debt have little to do with national traits; profligacy breeds through easy access to credit. The growing credit booms in these countries pose a great risk to financial stability, if not supported by rising individual income and an ever-expanding economy.

In India, the disparity in wealth, with a large part of it being cornered by a privileged section of society, is leading to conspicuous consumption. Acquisition of palatial houses and luxury cars, the culture of five-star hotels and holidays abroad and ostentatious display in marriages and other social functions are all symbols of fast-spreading consumerist culture. Top cricketers command crores of rupees as fees, thanks to the advertisement industry which lures them to advertise products of dubious value, promoting consumerism and youngsters wanting to emulate them to make fast bucks, without realizing that only 11 can make it to the national team.

There is no doubt virtue in consumer movement all over the world, as it has empowered households to secure better value for money for the things they buy. No one will prefer shoddy, outdated goods and disdainful and inefficient services, which characterized those provided by monopolistic suppliers, in either the public or private sector. The liberalization of the Indian economy in 1991 has allowed consumers a whole range of choices from fuel-efficient cars to latest-technology television, refrigerators and cellphones. Competition and choice over goods and services help people to lead a comfortable life, especially in developing countries like India, where they were deprived of these basics of life earlier. However, consumerism is a two-edged sword. A society faces social instability when consumerism becomes a status symbol. In a consumer culture, material values overtake life values, such as love, sharing and community spirit. The cost of consumerism includes stressful inducement to consume more even if the quality of life declines. Unless there is a balance between material values and life values, consumerism can threaten the social fabric of society.

Unemployment

One of the most serious problems facing the world today is unemployment, particularly the poor quality of job for a large number of people. According to the International Labour Organization's *World Employment and Social Outlook 2016*,[32] global unemployment rate in 2015 was 5.8 per cent, with 197.1 million persons unemployed, an increase of 1 million over the previous year. Due to slowing down of the global economy, the unemployment is expected to rise by 2.3 million in 2016 and an additional 1.1 million in 2017. Vulnerable employment with hardly any social security accounts for 46 per cent of employment, affecting roughly 1.5 billion people globally. Decent work is at the heart of sustainable development and elimination of poverty. The bulk of the world's unemployed live in developing counties, and structural unemployment and underemployment is a fact of life for the labour force there. In India, for example, 90 per cent of the workforce is employed in informal/unorganized sectors of the economy, with no stability of job and social security (see Chapter 4).

In developed countries, following adoption of welfare state post-1950s, full employment has become the main plank of economic and social policies. High unemployment, with which EU and US economies are currently afflicted, has become a very serious national issue, with voters throwing out governments which have not been able to make a dent on the problem. Following the economic crisis of 2008, European Union countries (28) are facing serious unemployment problem. In 2013 there were 26.4 million persons unemployed, with an unemployment rate of 10.9 per cent. Since then there has been a marginal decline in the number of unemployed, estimated at 21.6 million at the beginning of 2016, with an unemployment rate of 10.4 per cent.[33] (An unemployed person is one between the ages of 15 and 74 years who has actively sought work, and unemployment rate is the people unemployed as a percentage of labour force.) Countries which suffer very high unemployment rates are Greece – 24 per cent, Spain – 20 per cent, Portugal and Italy – 12 per cent and France – 10 per cent (January 2016). An alarming aspect is youth unemployment (between the ages 15 and 25), which ranged between 22 and 24 per cent in 2013 and 2014 in EU-28. During these two years, youth unemployment ranged between 52 and 58 per cent in Greece, 53 and 55 per cent in Spain, 43 and 49 per cent in Italy, 35 and 38 per cent in Portugal and 24 and 25 per cent in France. In the US the unemployment rate was 7 per cent at the end of 2013, much lower than EU average. However, in the US, the employment rate among population aged 16–64 years dropped 5 percentage points from 72 per cent in 2007 to 67 per cent in 2010 and has remained close to that level. One-third of this decline is due to joblessness and the remaining two-thirds due to people dropping out of the labour market because of various reasons such as discouraged job seekers and women taking up unpaid work. Lately, there has been an improvement in the US employment situation, and the unemployment rate came down to 6.3 per cent in 2014 and 5.3 per cent in 2015.

Two factors have contributed to this mass unemployment: long-term slowdown in the West and population explosion in developing countries such as India and Egypt. Growing unemployment is largely due to structural problems in the global economy. Big firms and multinational corporations that account for a substantial portion of global production and trade have profit as their sole motive and, due to competitive pressure, constantly cut costs, upgrade technology and shed labour. The digital revolution has completely disrupted the global job market. The prosperity unleashed by the digital revolution has gone overwhelmingly in favour of the owners of capital and high-skilled workers. Over the past three decades, labour's share of output has shrunk globally from 64 to 59 per cent. A study by academics at Oxford University suggests that

47 per cent of today's jobs in developed countries could be automated in the next two decades, further disrupting the job market.[34] Between 1991 and 2012, the average annual increase in real wages was 1.5 per cent in Britain, 1 per cent in America, 0.6 per cent in Germany and practically no increase in Japan and Italy. Real pay for most workers remained flat or even fell, whereas for highest earners, it soared. *The Economist*[35] observes that new technology is empowering talented individuals as never before, but at the same time it is creating a large pool of unemployed labour. The effect of technological revolution is changing the tried methods of economic development, and poor countries can no longer count on a growing industrial sector to absorb unskilled labour from rural areas. High unemployment in developed countries has now become structural, and unless there is a fundamental rethink about the current model of development, it is difficult to foresee how the problem can be resolved.

Markets and commodification of life

Most of the problems rich countries are facing are due to the fact that market-oriented thinking has entered every aspect of life, and they have slid into hyper-commercialism, untethered by ethical, religious or philosophical constraints. Today markets are used to allocate health, education, public safety, national security, criminal justice, environmental protection, procreation and many other social goods, which were unheard of earlier. Michael J. Sandel,[36] a distinguished Harvard scholar, in his perceptive study observes that today everything is for sale in the US. By paying money you can get a prison upgrade in California and a surrogate mother to carry pregnancy, cellphone number of your doctor for same-day appointment by paying yearly fees, admission for your child in a prestigious university and the right to immigrate to the US by investing certain amount of money. By paying money you can get a licence to emit carbon in the atmosphere – European Union runs a carbon emissions market where companies can buy and sell the right to pollute atmosphere. The value of a product is judged by its ability to be bought and sold in the market.

Sandel argues that when market reasoning is applied to sex, procreation, education, health, criminal punishment and environment protection, it raises serious moral issues. Financial incentives corrupt attitudes and norms and threaten the existence of a good society. When markets reach the sphere of life where they do not belong, it raises two fundamental issues. The first one is *inequality* – life becomes harder for people with modest means.

> If only advantage of affluence were the ability to buy yachts, sports cars, and fancy vacations, inequalities of income and wealth would not matter very much. But as money comes to buy more and more – political influence, good medical care, a home in a safe neighborhood rather than crime ridden one, access to elite schools rather than failing ones – the distribution of income

and wealth looms larger and larger. Where all the good things of life are bought and sold, having money makes all the difference in the world.[37]

The second problem with market triumphalism is that it *corrupts good things of life*. Paying children to read makes it a chore and destroys the joy of reading and learning. Top universities admit students on the basis of talent and promise, not those who offer the most money in a freshman class. Hospital emergency rooms treat patients according to the urgency of their condition, not according to the order of their arrival or their willingness to pay extra to be examined first. Kidneys are not allowed to be sold, as they prey on the poor, whose choice to sell their kidney may not be truly voluntary. If allowed, it would promote a degrading view of human lives, as a collection of spare parts. Hiring foreign mercenaries to fight wars destroys the meaning of good citizenship and nationalistic pride.

Trading in life and death: Sandel points out how life and death itself has become a subject of commerce in the US and cites numerous cases in support of his contention.[38] In the US it is legal for companies to buy insurance for their employees in what is known as 'janitors insurance'. Big companies invest millions of dollars in corporate-owned life insurance (COLI) policies, which has become a multi-million dollar industry. Corporates are lured to this, as yearly premium and death benefits are tax free. COLI policies cover the lives of millions of workers and account for a substantial portion of all life insurance sales. Such policies give perverse incentives to corporates to skimp on health and safety measures of workers. The spread of janitors insurance throughout corporate America has morphed from a safety net for the bereaved family into a strategy of corporate finance. In the US, you can bet on your life, by selling your life insurance policy to a third person who would take responsibility for premium payment, known as viaticals. If a person has terminal illness and the doctor tells that he or she has a year to live, that person can sell his or her policy of $100,000, say, for $50,000, and if the person dies as per the doctor's forecast, the buyer of the policy would make a cool profit of $50,000. Such policies are based on the investor's hope, that the person whose life insurance he or she buys dies sooner than later. There have been many lawsuits where investors lost out due to the person living long. Such policies are morally reprehensible as they are wagers of death, giving investors an interest in prompt passing away of the people whose policies they have bought. 'The lines separating insurance, investment and gambling have all vanished. Today, the markets in life and death have outrun the social purposes and moral norms that once constrained them.'[39]

Market triumphalism and commercialization change the character of goods they touch and change the conception of good life that society has traditionally valued. We need to create a good society where markets do not honour and money cannot buy moral and civic goods which the society values.

Summing up

The present problems of world economy are largely due to the manner in which production and distribution is organized in capitalist free market economies, with profit as the sole motivating factor of economic activity and a push to boost growth exponentially. This results in environmental degradation, accentuation of income disparity and widespread unemployment, causing great dissatisfaction and suffering to people at the lower end of the economic bracket. It is time we devise a more human-centric model of development.

Notes

1 Rabindranath Tagore, 'Civilization and Progress'. Lecture delivered in China, 1924, available at http://www.swaraj.org/tagorecivilization.htm (accessed 2 March 2015).

2 James Gustave Speth, *The Bridge at the Edge of the World: Capitalism, the Environment, and Crossing from Crisis to Sustainability*, New Haven, CT: Yale University Press, 2008, p. 57.

3 'The state of economics', *The Economist*, 24–29 July 2009, pp. 58–60; Paul Krugman, 'How did the economist get it so wrong', *New York Times*, 2 September 2009.

4 David C. Korten, *Agenda for a New Economy: From Phanthom Wealth to Real Wealth*, San Francisco, CA: Berrett-Koehler Publishers, 2009, pp. 30–32.

5 Speth, *The Bridge at the Edge of the World*.

6 Ibid., p. 165.

7 Donella Meadows, Jorgen Randers and Dennis Meadows, *Limits to Growth: The 30 Year Update*, London: Earthscan, 2005, p. 8.

8 Speth, *The Bridge at the Edge of the World*, p. 50.

9 Ibid., p. 57.

10 Ira Katznelson, Mark Kesselman, Alan Draper and Thomson Wadsworth, *The Politics of Power*, Belmont, CA: Thomson Higher Education, 2006.

11 'Executive pay in America', *The Economist*, London, 13–19 March 2010, pp. 68–69.

12 For a detailed discussion on inequality, see 'Special report on Global Elite' and 'Unbottled Gini', *The Economist*, 22–28 January 2011, pp. 1–20 and pp. 79–80.

13 Data from Bill Clinton, *Back to Work*, London: Hutchinson, 2011, pp. 85–86.

14 'Poverty Is Not Inevitable, Dean Paton', *Yes Magazine*, August 2014, quoting Hedrick Smith, available at http://www.yesmagazine.org/issues/the-end-of-poverty/why-poverty-is-not-inevitable (accessed 2 March 2015).

15 Joseph E. Stiglitz, *The Price of Inequality*, London: Allen Lane, pp. 2, 7.

16 *The Economist*, 22–28 January 2011.

17 'Working for the few', *Oxfam*, 20 January 2014, available at http://www.oxfam.org/sites/www.oxfam.org/files/file_attachments/bp-working-for-few-political-capture-economic-inequality-200114-summ-en_1.pdf (accessed 2 March 2015).

18 *Oxfam*, 'Special report, World economy: For richer, for poorer', *The Economist*, 13-19 October 2012.

19 Anthony B. Atkinson, *Inequality: What Can Be Done?* Cambridge, MA: Harvard University Press, 2015, pp. 21–23.
20 National Commission for Enterprises in Unorganised Sector, *The Challenge of Unemployment in India – An Informal Economy Perspective, Volume I*, April 2009, http://dcmsme.gov.in/The_Challenge_of_Employment_in_India.pdf (assessed 8 November 2013).
21 *Forbes*, available at http://www.ibnlive.com/news/business/forbes-list-2-328953.html (accessed 2 March 2015).
22 'Adani breaks into top 10 rich club as wealth jumps 152%', *Times of India*, 17 September 2014, p. 21.
23 'To be in a rich man's world', *Hindustan Times*, Lucknow, 16 March 2015, p. 7.
24 'More professionals in million $ pay club', *Times of India*, 26 October 2012.
25 'Younger CEOs paid more in India than US', *Times of India*, 19 September 2012.
26 'Sikka top-paid professional CEO in India with Rs 30 cr pay', *Times of India*, 3 July 2014, p. 22.
27 Thomas Piketty, *Capital in the Twenty-First Century*, Cambridge: The Belknap Press of Harvard University Press, 2014.
28 Ibid., Table 7.3, pp. 249, 257.
29 Ibid., p. 571.
30 Speth, *The Bridge at the Edge of the World*, p. 147.
31 Raghuram G. Rajan, *Faultlines*, Noida: Harper Collins Publishers, 2010.
32 ILO, *World Economic and Social Outlook Trends 2016*, available at http://www.ilo.org/wcmsp5/groups/public/---dgreports/---dcomm/---publ/documents/publication/wcms_443480.pdf (accessed 29 April 2016).
33 Eurostat Unemployment Statistics, available at http://ec.europa.eu/eurostat/statisticsexplained/index.php/Unemployment_statistics (accessed 29 April 2016).
34 'Coming to an office near you' and 'The future of jobs: The onrushing wave', *The Economist*, 18–24 January 2014, pp. 9–10, pp. 23–26.
35 'Wealth without workers, workers without wealth', and 'Special report, The World Economy: The third great wave', *The Economist*, 4–10 October 2014, p. 14, pp. 1–26.
36 Michael J. Sandel, *What Money Can't Buy: The Moral Limits of Markets*, London: Penguin Books, 2013. This section is based on Sandel's book.
37 Ibid., p. 8.
38 Ibid., pp. 130–141.
39 Ibid., p. 149.

9

ENVIRONMENTAL UNSUSTAINABILITY OF INDIA'S ECONOMIC GROWTH

> Earth provides enough to satisfy every man's needs, but not every man's greed.
>
> Mahatma Gandhi[1]

> The only meaningful and effective solution to climate crisis involves massive changes in human behavior and thinking.
>
> Al Gore[2]

Human civilization and the earth's ecological system are on a collision course. Al Gore, environment crusader and former US vice-president, observes: 'The violent impact human civilization has on earth's eco-system add up to a worldwide ecological crisis that threatens the habitability of the world', and if it is not quickly addressed, 'it has the potential to end human civilization as we know it'.[3] Astrophysicist Martin Rees[4] warns of more dire consequences of new science and 21st-century technology, which is advancing at an exhilarating rate; it has a dark side and has the potential to destroy our species. Environmental changes induced by human activities may be graver than age-old hazards from earthquakes, eruptions and asteroid impacts.

The most serious and destructive threat is climate crisis. Climate is not just weather. Climate is the fundamental support system that determines whether we can live on this planet. It is generated by the *atmosphere* – the air we breathe; *hydrosphere* – planets water; *cryosphere* – ice sheets and glaciers; and *biosphere* – planets, plants and animals. The Intergovernmental Panel on Climate Change has noted that increase in air and ocean temperatures leads to widespread melting of snow and ice and rise of average sea level. The availability of freshwater will shift; some areas will get much water, while others will become dryer. Rising sea level will increase coastal erosion, flooding and wetland loss. Human health will suffer in various ways, particularly those with low adaptive capacity.

All around the earth human activity is the cause of extraordinary amounts of air pollution – greenhouse gases (GHG) that trap heat and raise the temperature of the air, oceans and the surface of the earth. There are several pollutants, but the biggest global warming is caused by carbon dioxide. It is produced primarily from burning coal for heat and electricity, from burning oil-based products (gasoline, diesel and jet fuel) in transportation and from burning coal, oil and natural gas in industrial activities. For this reason, most discussions on how to solve the climate crisis tend to focus on producing energy in ways that do not produce dangerous emissions of carbon dioxide. The next major pollutant is methane, which comes from fossil fuel, cattle raising, rice growing and landfill emissions. Another pollutant causing global warming is black carbon, which is produced by burning forests and grassland, cooking fires and other artificial sources. Industrial agriculture is the largest source of nitrous oxide and carbon monoxide. A number of specialty chemicals in the halocarbon family, which include chlorofluorocarbons that deplete the ozone, are also potent GHGs. The solution to global warming is that emissions of air pollutants – carbon dioxide, methane, black carbon, halocarbons, nitrous oxide and carbon monoxide – must all be reduced dramatically.

The most important solution to climate crisis requires the accelerated development and deployment of low carbon dioxide substitute for producing energy, as the single largest source of man-made global warming pollution is the production of energy from fossil fuels – coal, gas and natural gas. The global effort to tackle climate change is being made under the auspices of the United Nations. To date industrial nations have contributed far more to the build-up of GHGs than developing countries. The developed countries with 20 per cent of the world's population have contributed more than 75 per cent of the cumulative carbon dioxide emissions and are responsible for today's 60 per cent emissions. Today, the main polluters are China which accounts for 28 per cent and the US which accounts for 16 per cent of the annual GHG emissions. India stands third, though its contribution is only 6 per cent. Per capita India's contribution in GHGs is very low. The Kyoto Protocol of 1997 had envisaged imposing legally binding caps on GHG emissions, but no progress could be made, as developed countries were not willing to accept the historical liability for carbon emissions made by them. Under the Paris Convention of December 2015, held under the United Nations Framework Convention for Climate Change, an agreement has been reached by accepting a voluntary and more inclusive approach. A total of 188 countries have submitted their 'intended nationally determined contribution', showing what they are prepared to do and build climate resilience. The national climate plans will be reviewed every five years beginning 2018. The Paris Agreement has emphatically stated that the increase in global temperature has to remain well below 2°C and the world will pursue efforts to limit such increase to 1.5°C. Experts doubt that the target of 1.5°C could be achieved; nevertheless, it marks a major advance. The secretary general of the United Nations Ban Ki-moon has hailed it as a health insurance policy for the planet as 'every country of the world has pledged to curb their emissions, strengthen resilience and act internationally and domestically to address climate change'.[5]

Besides climate, the world is facing several other environmental challenges.[6] *Losing the forests*: about half of the world's tropical and temperate forests are already lost, mostly to clear land for agriculture. Deforestation leads to species loss, climate change, loss of economic value, landslides, flooding and soil depletion. *Losing the land*: desertification involves more than spreading deserts. It includes degradation of productive land, turning it into wasteland due to soil erosion, salinization, and de-vegetation. The process is most prevalent in arid and semi-arid land, which accounts for 40 per cent of the planet's land surface. *Losing freshwater*: natural water courses and the vibrant life associated with them have been extensively affected by dams, dykes, diversions and canal diversion. There is a serious problem of freshwater supply to meet the drinking demand as well as the need for agriculture, which has increased severalfold. The most serious problem relates to pollution as all kinds of pollutants are discharged into the world's waters, which reduces the capacities of water bodies to support life in the water. Contamination denies a large portion of the world's population access to clean water supply. *Loss of marine fisheries and loss of biodiversity*: overfishing driven by the powerful fishing industry is a serious problem. Many species of birds and animals are threatened with extinction. Almost 95 per cent of the weather-backed turtles have disappeared in the world, and the tiger population is on the verge of extinction. *Toxic pollutants*: numerous organic pollutants and pesticides are serious threats to human health. They can cause cancer and birth defects and can interfere with hormonal and immune systems' functioning. These global-scale environmental problems do not exist in isolation; they constantly interact with each other, worsening the situation.

India's environment challenge

The problem of environment protection in India has a much wider dimension, as compared to the West, where it initially stemmed from protection of endangered natural species and natural habitat. In India it is directly linked with the livelihood and survival of a large section of the population. Majority of India's population is self-employed – farmers, fishermen, craftsmen, pastoral and nomadic occupation, and they are going through severe crisis due to ecosystem disruption. They have seen their lands, forests and grazing fields being diverted for commercial exploitation by mega hydroelectric projects, mining and fishing of costal sea belt by large commercial trawlers. This has resulted in conflicts over natural resources' rights – conflicts over forests, fish and pastures; conflicts over people losing their land due to large dams; and conflicts over social and environmental impact of unregulated mining. These conflicts have given birth to an environmental movement in India.

Unfettered development has damaged the ecology, making life difficult for people. Post-economic liberalization, the policies of the government have been leading to deprivation of land and natural wealth of people, who are solely dependent on land and forests for their livelihood. In many parts of India, land is being forcibly acquired, rivers are being privatized, forests are being sold to private companies and tribal people are being displaced from their traditional habitat, with the result that weaker and vulnerable sections of the population are being deprived of their only means of livelihood and survival. Distinguished social scientist and environmentalist Ramchandra Guha says,

> India today is an environment basket-case, marked by polluted skies, dead rivers, falling water tables, ever increasing amounts of untreated wastes, disappearing forests. Meanwhile, tribal and peasants communities continue to be pushed off their lands through destructive and carelessly conceived projects.[7]

During the 1970s and 1980s there was a big resistance to destruction of forests in Uttarakhand, Himalayas, and a movement known as *chipko* was launched, under the leadership of veteran Gandhians, Sundarlal Bahuguna and Chandi Prasad Bhatt. Forests play a critical role not only in providing food, fuel and fodder but also in stabilizing soil and water resources. The movement embraced hundreds of decentralized and locally autonomous initiatives. The impact of the movement led to banning of felling of trees and later passing of forest protection act. Another major environment protection movement was against construction of large dams, such as Narmada Valley Project, Tehri Dam and Silent Valley Project. The movement against Narmada Valley Project was led by veteran social activists Medha Patkar and Baba Amte, who highlighted that large numbers of poor and underprivileged communities, mostly tribals and dalits, are being dispossessed of their livelihood and even their ways of living, while the claimed benefits of the project in terms of additional production of electricity and water are based on dubious facts. The matter finally reached the Supreme Court, which, after several stoppages of the project, allowed its completion with a proviso that a monitoring mechanism for resettlement of tribals and other oustees be put in place and the concern raised about raising the dam and submerging vast tracts of land under water be addressed. The *Narmada Bachao Andolan* (movement to save Narmada) helped in creating a high level of awareness about the environmental, rehabilitation and relief aspects of not only Sardar Sarovar but also other big dams. Prof. G. D. Agarwal, former professor of engineering at IIT, Kanpur, who is now known as Swami Gyan Swaroop, launched a crusade to stop the construction of hydroelectric projects on Ganga in Uttarakhand region, so that the river flow is not diverted through a series of tunnels and reservoirs, resulting in destruction of the ecology of the river and its self-purifying properties. The movement led to stoppage of projects on Bhagirathi River and constitution of Ganga River

Basin Authority for comprehensive management of Ganga River Basin. Another protest movement which drew countrywide attention was the Kudankulam atomic power project in Tamil Nadu, as the fishermen and villagers in nearby areas feared that the plant has the potential of nuclear disaster. The plant has been commissioned, as the government claims that its safety aspects have been taken care. Environmentalists, however, question its justification and say that when the world is moving towards sustainable and renewable energy sources which have become increasingly more efficient and viable, there is little logic in going for nuclear power.

Deprivation of land and natural wealth

Today one of the most serious hardships people are facing in the country is over land and natural rights, resulting in conflicts and unrest. Nothing exemplifies it better than the story of special economic zone (SEZ). Till the end of 2013 land was being acquired using an anachronistic piece of legislation from colonial times (Land Acquisition Act of 1894) in the name of 'public purpose', invoking the power of 'eminent domain', and given to influential lobby of real estate developers, industrialists, businessmen and politicians. In the name of industrialization, SEZs have been created for construction of commercial complexes, residential areas, hotels, shopping malls and entertainment centres. SEZs are responsible for displacement of people and loss of livelihood, threaten food security due to diversion of fertile agriculture land and are responsible for loss of revenue due to tax concessions. People affected by SEZs have launched agitations all over the country. The Nandigram agitation in West Bengal (2007) turned violent and many people were killed. People have expressed huge dissent and agitated against aggressive mining and industrialization policy of the Orissa government, wherein land and water sources of farmers and forest dwellers have been given to powerful corporates for setting up steel and aluminium plants.

The government very often acts in an illegal and arbitrary manner, favouring builders and land mafia lobby. This is evident from the judgement of the Allahabad High Court, which cancelled the land acquisition made by Noida and Greater Noida Authority, on petition by the aggrieved farmers. Farmers in Gopalganj village in Khandwa district in Madhya Pradesh launched *jal-satyagraha* (non-violent peaceful agitation relating to water) by standing in waist deep water for 17 days to protest against displacement and submerging of their land by the Omkareshwar hydroelectric project (September 2012). This forced the state government to respond and offer a suitable rehabilitation and resettlement package. The *Economic and Political Weekly*[8] called it another story of displacement and pauperization of people and an illustration of 'destructive development'. A countrywide land reform movement was launched by 'Ekta Parishad' headed by P. V. Rajgopal.[9] Its main demand is protection of land rights of dalits, adivasis and the weaker and marginalized sections and provision of agricultural land and homestead rights to the landless poor. It threatened to organize *jal satyagraha* in which thousands of landless people from all over the country would assemble at Gwalior and march on foot to Delhi to press their demand (October 2012). The government diffused the situation by signing an agreement with them for bringing in comprehensive land reforms package.

After the countrywide uproar, finally a Right to Fair Compensation and Transparency in Land Acquisition, Rehabitation and Resettlement Act was passed by Parliament in September 2013, effective from 1 January 2014. However, the new NDA government felt that provision of the act makes it very difficult to acquire land for 'development' purposes and amended it through the issue of an ordinance. This has caused a fresh round of protests all over the country. Fearing its political impact, the government has allowed the ordinance to lapse. Nevertheless, it has created an impression that those in power are pro-big business and unsympathetic to farmers and small land-holders.

Environment laws and apathy towards enforcement

The environmental movement has led to enactment of several legislations to safeguard ecology: the Wildlife (Protection) Act of 1972, the Water Act of 1974, the Air Act of 1981, the Environment (Protection) Act of 1986, the Forests Right Act of 2006 and the National Greens Tribunal Act of 2010. However, the question is whether these laws are going to be enforced or whether they are just to adorn the statue book. *The State of India's Environment 2015* report observes: 'The regulatory framework in India is effectively geared towards giving clearances and consents. But the assessment and monitoring of environment, social and health conditions that go with these approvals are usually missing.'[10] Jairam Ramesh, former minister for environment in UPA II government, known for his sensitiveness to environment issues, candidly admits that laws have not been observed. In his book *Green Signals*, he states, 'Industry has assumed that somehow these laws can be "managed" and government too have not insisted that the laws be implemented both in letter and spirit.'[11] Ramesh observes that the industry due to its vested interest has hijacked the debate by making it an 'industry versus development' issue, rather than one of whether law is to be followed. Ramesh explains,

> The 'growth first at all costs and environment later' approach is clearly unacceptable. India needs to press into its development all that modern science and technology has to offer. At the same time, the notion that we can impose technological fixes without caring for their larger ecological consequences and without addressing larger social concerns is clearly untenable, but more so in an open argumentative society like ours.[12]

The environment has today become a major public health issue. The levels of air pollution in Indian cities are shockingly high. The huge industrial and vehicular pollution and dumping of chemicals and sewage waste in rivers and water bodies are creating a public health catastrophe. Environmental deterioration has emerged as a major cause of illness. The NCR (National Capital Region) of Delhi is a classic example of pollution and unsustainable growth of a fast-expanding metropolis. Delhi is bursting at the seams with a population of about 15 million due to unchecked migration, with a vast majority of people living in pathetic conditions in slums with no basic amenities. The huge growth of vehicular traffic is polluting the atmosphere, causing lung diseases to school children, and the heavy traffic on roads is resulting in unbearable snarls, taking hours to commute a short distance. The most visible symbol is the pollution of River Yamuna, an integral part of India's cultural history, which has been reduced to a *nalla* (narrow drain) and its water unfit for human consumption, due to thousands of gallons of toxic industrial effluent discharged in it every day. I have myself experienced fast deterioration in the quality of life in Delhi, during the past three decades, which is a nightmare to go on the streets, with traffic jams, garbage piled all over, stinking drains, slums all over and air unfit to breathe. The position is no better in other big cities.

India is currently on an unsustainable path of development. Assem Shrivastava[13] and Ashish Kothari in their perceptive study *Churning the Earth* vividly explain how globalization and market-oriented policies are damaging the ecology and observe that in the name of development 'the state has sponsored or backed the appropriation of fields, pastures, forests, wetlands, groundwater and other natural resources by the corporate sector or other elites'.[14]

Ramchandra Guha observes that economic development in India during the past 60 years has destroyed nature while failing to remove poverty. The process of development has been characterized by basic asymmetry between omnivores and ecosystem people. This is largely due to 'channelizing of an ever increasing volume of natural resources, via the state apparatus and at the cost of the exchequer, to serve the interests of rural and urban omnivores'.[15] Guha says that the central feature of the development process is the concentration of political power/decision making in the hands of omnivores and use of state machinery to divert natural resources to islands of omnivore prosperity, especially through use of subsidies and indifference of omnivores to the environmental degradation caused by them. The displacement of millions of people from their homes has resulted in widespread protests all over the country. The ecological refugees have been forced to live in slums in cities in subhuman conditions.

Environment protection – ethics and culture

The Western development model that India has embraced, and called 'modernization', is creating a huge dichotomy in the lifestyles of a large section of the urban population. This has helped create a class of super-rich who lead a lavish lifestyle, indulge in unabashed consumerism and are totally indifferent to the environment. We need to abandon this model and adopt a model of sustainable development. Development Alternatives,[16] an NGO headed by Ashok Khosla, which works at grass-roots level, has successfully experimented with environment-friendly technologies at the village and small community levels. It emphasizes that sustainable development is one in which environment, social equity and empowerment are goals of equal importance. Shrivastava and Kothari observe that many struggles of socio-economic and ecological justice and thousands of real-life experiments in sustainable living give us hope.

> The way of economic future for the vast majority of people is ecological, is rooted in the local and the regional and is built in the past. It depends critically on the best traditions of Indian cultures, even while rejecting the worst, and combining these with the best of modernity.[17]

Ethics, human rights and equity are at the very centre of environmental issues. According to Prof. M. V. Nadkarni,

> An ethically insensitive people are not likely to be unduly concerned to tackle issues confronting humanity – poverty, hunger, illiteracy, environmental degradation. The basic reason for our failure on these fronts is not lack of economic resources, but simply our lack of ethical concern and seriousness. . . . It shows an irrational lack of concern for our own future. We prefer to drift in current tendency, unable to think of our future, our children's future, and do not show enough evidence of having any urge or energy to face our responsibilities.[18]

There are two ways to tackle environmental crisis. One is to improve technological efficiency so that less pollution is produced while generating energy and undertaking other productive activities. The second is to reduce our wants and modify our lifestyle as preached by most religions of the world. The main strategy adopted by the advanced countries is to improve technological efficiency, and they have achieved a greater degree of success by controlling to some extent emission of carbon dioxide and other GHGs. However, improving technological efficiency as the main or only strategy is not going to solve the problem, unless we change our consumerist, energy-intensive lifestyles.

The basic philosophy of the West is to master and control nature. On the other hand, the Indian culture pleads for living not only in harmony with nature but also with reverence towards nature and respect for all life forms, including animals and plants. Restraint on wants and self-control is a highly regarded value in all Eastern religions. Gautama Buddha advocated a middle path, between the two extremes of self-indulgence and total abstinence. Bhagawad Gita's main message is to exercise control over wants and desires, so that they do not turn into greed, and maintain balance in all activities. Mahatma Gandhi's philosophy was a product of Indian ethos. He advocated labour-intensive production rather than energy-intensive production and emphasized on a decentralized village economy and living in harmony with the natural habitat. He had observed, 'Nature produces enough for our wants from day today; and if only everybody took enough for himself and nothing more, there would be no pauperism in this world, there would be no dying of starvation.'[19]

India's ancient scripture, Vedas, has considered earth as living mother – *bhoomata*. Many of its verses glorify Mother Earth on which we are born, and one of the hymn passionately ends with the lines, 'O Earth, my mother, set me thou happily in a place secure. Of one accord with heaven, O sage set me in glory and in wealth.'[20] Another verse of Atharvaveda offers the following prayer, 'O Mother Earth, let Thy bosom be free, from sickness and decay; May we through long life, be active and vigilant, and serve Thee with devotion.'[21] In India reverence for nature did not remain only at the level of preaching in scriptures but had percolated down to people. In villages and traditional communities, people lead a simple life in tune with their natural surroundings.

There is an imperative need for India to move towards a sustainable development model which should be environment friendly and rooted in the principles of ethics and social justice. It should embrace our ancient cultural values of 'simple living and high thinking' and respect not only human beings but all life forms, as well as nature.

Notes

1 M. K. Gandhi's quotes, available at http://www.wisdomquotes.com/quote/mohandas-k-gandhi-54.html (accessed 25 March 2016).
2 Al Gore, *Our Choice: A Plan to Solve Climate Crisis*, London: Bloomsbury, 2009, p. 315.
3 Ibid., p. 32.
4 Martin Rees, *Our Final Century*, London: Arrow Books, 2004.
5 Ban Ki-moon, 'A new era of opportunity', *The Times of India*, 19 December 2015, p. 26.
6 James Gustav Speth, *The Bridge at the Edge of the World: Capitalism, the Environment, and Crossing from Crisis to Sustainability*, New Haven, CT: Yale University Press, 2008, for a detailed discussion, see pages 17–45.
7 Ramchandra Guha, *Environmentalism: A Global History*, Gurgaon: Allen Lane, 2014, p. xix. Also see Ramchandra Guha, 'The past and present of Indian environmentalism', *The Hindu*, 27 March 2013.
8 'Damned by the Damn', *Economic and Political Weekly*, 22 September 2012, Vol. XLVII, No. 38, pp. 7–8.
9 Bharat Dogra, *Land Reforms and the Significance of Jan Satyagraha*; P. V. Rajgopal, 'Proposal from Bottom to Address Land-related Problems', *Mainstream*, 22 September 2012, Vol. L, No. 40, pp. 7–9; and 'Document: Agreement between the Ministry of Rural Development (GOI) and Jan Satyagraha', *Mainstream*, 27 October 2012, Vol. L, No. 45, pp. 3–4.
10 Centre for Science and Environment, *A Down to Earth Annual: State of India's Environment 2015*, New Delhi, 2015, p. 177.

11 Jairam Ramesh, *Green Signals: Ecology, Growth and Democracy in India*, New Delhi: Oxford, 2015, p. 97.
12 Ibid., pp. 98–99.
13 Assem Shrivastava and Ashish Kothari, *Churning the Earth: The Making of Global India*, New Delhi: Penguin and Viking, 2012, pp. 121–165.
14 Ibid., p. 146.
15 Ramchandra Guha, *How Much Should a Person Consume?* Gurgaon: Hachette India, 2006, pp. 302–303.
16 Development Alternatives, *To Choose Our Future*, New Delhi: Development Alternative Group and Academic Foundation, 2015.
17 Shrivastava and Kothari, *Churning the Earth*, p. 330.
18 M. V. Nadkarni, *Ethics for Our Times: Essays in Gandhian Perspective*, New Delhi: Oxford, 2011, p. 101.
19 M. K. Gandhi, *India of My Dreams*, compiled by R. K. Prabhu, Ahmedabad: Navjivan Publishing House, 2011, p. 69.
20 Pandit Satyakam Vidyalankar, *The Holy Vedas*, Delhi: Clarion Books, 1998, p. 18.
21 Ibid., p. 319.

10

A NEW DEVELOPMENT
SCENARIO

Human development is the expansion of people's freedom to live long, healthy and creative lives; to advance other goals they have reason to value; and to engage actively in shaping development equitably and sustainably on a shared planet. People are both the beneficiaries as well as drivers of development, as individuals and in groups.

UNDP, Human Development Report[1]

Most environmental deterioration is a result of systems failure of the capitalism that we have today and long term solutions must seek transformative change in the key features of this contemporary capitalism.

James Gustave Speth, Environmentalist[2]

Intellectuals, public-spirited persons and think tanks all over the world are seriously concerned with the existing model of economic development and have come out with alternatives to create a sustainable and egalitarian society, based on respect for nature, universal human rights and economic and social justice. In this chapter we discuss the views of some of the leading think tanks.

Limits to growth – the Club of Rome

Since 1972, the Club of Rome has been in the forefront of the movement which has been pointing out that there are ecological constraints in the existing development pattern, and the planet's physical limit in the form of depletable natural resources and its finite capacity to absorb, exploitation done to meet the ever-increasing need of agriculture and industry. In further studies over the next three decades, the analysts at the Club of Rome[3] emphasized that *the world is in an overshoot phase*. This is measured in terms of *ecological footprint* of humanity and compared with the 'carrying capacity' of the planet. The ecological footprint can be defined as the land area that would be required to provide resources such as grain, feed, wood, fish and urban land and absorb the emissions (carbon dioxide) of the global society. Unfortunately, today, even when humanity is already in unsustainable territory, the ecological footprint is still increasing. Ecological footprint could be reduced by altering consumption norms, implementing resource-efficient technologies and stabilizing population.

The Club of Rome study points out that the exponential growth of population and industrial production is built into the self-generating structure of the global economy. It swings in developed parts of the world towards slow population growth accompanied by fast industrial growth, and in the developing world towards slow industrial growth and fast population growth. But in both cases, population and physical capital keep growing. The growth in population and capital increases the ecological footprint of the economy. Once the footprint has reached beyond the sustainable level, as it already has, it must eventually come down – it must come down through a managed process or through the work of nature. *The Club of Rome pleads for a managed process to limit growth* and projects different scenarios through computer modelling to drive home its point.

What we need to do is to move towards a sustainable society. According to World Commission on Environment and Development, 'A sustainable society is one that meets the needs of the present without compromising the ability of future generations to meet their own needs.'[4] In a sustainable society there are informational, social and institutional mechanisms to keep in check exponential population and capital growth. To be sustainable, the economy's throughputs would have to meet three conditions:

1 Their rates of use of renewable resources do not exceed their rates of regeneration.
2 Their rates of use of non-renewable resources do not exceed the rate at which sustainable new substitutes are developed.
3 Their rates of pollution emission do not exceed the assimilation capacity of the environment.

Sustainability does not mean 'zero growth'.

> A sustainable society would be interested in qualitative development not physical expansion. It would use material growth as a considered tool, not a perpetual mandate. Neither for nor against growth, it would begin to discriminate among kind of growth and purposes of growth. It would even entertain rationally the idea of purposeful negative growth, to undo excess. To get below limits, to cease doing things that, in full accounting of natural and social costs actually cost more than they are worth.[5]

The Club of Rome suggests several steps to move in the direction of sustainability: (1) extend the planning horizon; (2) improve the signals that monitor the real welfare of the human population and the real impact on the world ecosystem; (3) speed up response time – look actively for signals that indicate when the environment or society is stressed; (4) minimize the use of non-renewable resources such as fossil fuels and minerals; (5) prevent the erosion of non-renewable resources; the productivity of soils, surface waters, rechargeable groundwaters and all living things including forests, fish and game should be protected, restored and enhanced; (6) use all resources with maximum efficiency; and (7) slow and eventually stop exponential growth of population and physical capital.[6]

The Club of Rome underlines the fact that to attain sustainability the most important step is to secure cultural commitment to remove poverty and unemployment and to meet non-material needs such as community, identity, self-esteem, love and joy. Showing optimism, the report says that after first the two revolutions of agriculture and industry, the next global revolution will be sustainability. Its tools will be visioning, networking, truth telling, learning and loving.

UNDP – human development in all dimensions

UNDP's Human Development Report, since its first publication in 1990, has been emphasizing that development is primarily and fundamentally about people. Celebrating 20 years of its publication, UNDP's Human Development Report 2010[7] observes that at the core of human development are sustainability, equity and empowerment. Future generations must be treated justly; therefore, development must be sustainable. Human development is also about addressing structural disparities and should be equitable. People should also be able to exercise individual choice and should be able to shape and benefit at the household, community and national levels and need to be empowered. Human development has three components: *well-being*: expanding people's real freedom so that people can flourish; *empowerment and agency*: enabling people and groups to act – to drive valuable outcomes; and *justice*: expanding equity, sustaining outcomes over time and respecting human rights and other goals of society.

UNDP has been articulating the idea that GDP growth is meaningless if it does not improve quality of people's lives. It laid down the criteria of 'good' economic growth – that promotes human development in all its dimension. Human Development Report 1996[8] observes that growth is good when it generates full employment and security of livelihoods, fosters people's freedom and empowerment, distributes benefits equitably, promotes social cohesion and cooperation and safeguards future human development. UNDP faulted the current obsession with GDP growth, which is leading to the following:

- *Jobless growth* – where the overall economy grows but does not expand opportunities for employment
- *Ruthless growth* – where the fruits of economic growth mostly benefit the rich

- *Voiceless growth* – where growth in the economy has not been accompanied by an extension of democracy or empowerment
- *Rootless growth* – where growth causes people's cultural identity to wither
- *Futureless growth* – where the present generation squanders resources needed for future generations

UNDP has constructed a Human Development Index (HDI), which compares country achievements across the most basic dimension of human development and takes into account literacy level, longevity and GDP adjusted to purchasing power parity. UNDP has been publishing the HDI index every year since 1990. India's position was 134 out of 182 countries in 2009, 136 out of 186 countries in HDI 2013 and 130 out of 188 countries in HDR 2015. Since 2010 UNDP has introduced three new measures, capturing multidimensional inequality, gender disparities and extreme deprivation. India continues to be at the lower end of the international league of what constitutes a 'good economic well-being'.

Genuine Progress Indicator

Social scientists all over the world are realizing that we need to measure progress by improvement in well-being rather than expansion in market-based economic activity. Economic progress needs to be measured by how little we can consume and achieve a high quality of life. We need to measure progress by how quickly we can build a renewable energy platform, meet basic human needs, discourage wasteful consumption and invest rather than deplete natural and cultural capital.

The World Watch Institute under the stewardship of John Talbert[9] has developed a set of indicators balanced across economic, environmental and social domains to measure sustainable development for the 21st century. The index is called Genuine Progress Indicator (GPI). GPI adjusts a nation's personal expenditure upward to account for the benefits of non-market activities such as volunteering and parenting and downward to account for costs associated with income inequality, environmental degradation and international debt. GPI has the following five macroeconomic objectives:

1 Promoting genuine progress based on multiple dimensions of human well-being. This includes aggregate index of life well-being based on life satisfaction, life expectancy, health, education, income, knowledge and community support.
2 Fostering a rapid transition to a renewable energy platform. This includes carbon footprints, which provide for spatial and intensity measures of life cycle carbon emissions and energy intensity, that is energy used per unit of output.

3   Equitable distribution of both resources and opportunities. Gini coefficient measures the extent to which income distribution deviates from an equitable distribution norm.
4   Protecting and restoring natural capital. If civilization is to survive, it must live on interest, not on the capital of nature. Nature's interest is the flow of goods and services received from stocks of natural capital. Ecological footprint, which compares the surface area of the earth needed to sustain current consumption patterns and absorb waste, is the best measure of natural capital depletion. When the footprint exceeds biological capacity, the world is engaged in unsustainable ecological overshoot and depletion of natural capital.
5   Economic localization. This is the process by which a region, country or city frees itself from overdependence on the global economy and invests in its own resources to produce a significant portion of the goods, services, food and energy it consumes from its local endowment of financial, natural and human capital. The present global distribution system is based almost exclusively on cheap fossil fuel, with huge hidden cost.

A breakdown of GPI contributions and deductions for the US for 2004 shows that a GDP of $10.8 trillion gets reduced to a GPI of $4.4 trillion, implying that well over half the economic activity in the US was unsustainable and did not contribute to genuine progress. It is apparent that after a particular threshold, environment and social costs of economic growth are more than offset by rising environment and social costs.

Erik Assadourian[10] of the World Watch Institute says that to understand real progress, we should construct GPI. As indicated earlier, GPI measures consumer purchases, government spending and business investments, but it subtracts out some bad forms of economic activity, such as pollution and resource degradation, costs of accidents and expenditures on fighting crime, and adds in some good ones such as the estimated dollar value of hours spent volunteering or parenting. A group of economists have constructed the global GPI for the 17 countries which make up 53 per cent of the world's population and 59 per cent of global GDP. The analysis shows that while GDP has nearly doubled since 1970, GPI has stayed essentially flat, suggesting little progress has been made in the past four decades.

World Watch Institute emphasizes that the planet's ecological limits make limitless growth and consumption a mathematical impossibility. Degrowth and the responsible stewardship of resources go hand in hand with a new definition of true progress. Today we are living on one planet and yet we use the resources of 1.5 planet earths, according to the ecological footprint. This indicator measures the amount of land area used around the world to produce humanity's food, materials and infrastructure and to absorb our carbon emissions, and compares this total land needed to the land available. If we are really going to live within earth's limits, we have to drastically reduce our consumption. There is need for major contraction in human consumption, in human energy use, in material goods produced and even in human numbers. The question is only whether that contraction comes proactively, through economic degrowth, or reactively, through an economic contraction brought on by climate change, the collapse of ocean systems, the mass die-off of pollinators or the breakdown of some other essential ecosystem services.

Developing a new matrix of development

Stiglitz Commission[11] has emphasized that our obsession with GDP growth should end and we should be more focused on economic well-being. Quality of life depends on the objective conditions and opportunities available to people. How societies are organized makes a difference to people's lives, as can be seen in measures of people's health and education, their daily work and leisure activities, citizens' political participation and responsiveness of institutions, people's social connections and their environmental conditions and physical and economic insecurity that shapes their lives.

We need to realize that an economic model based on relentless consumerism is fundamentally flawed and is responsible for current global economic crisis, as well as the ecological and social problems. We should work towards a model of development focused on reducing consumption and ostentatious living and maintain ecological sustainability. The present economic model of the West, which India is blindly following, is increasingly irrelevant and out of touch with great humanitarian and environmental costs at which development takes place and masks inequities in the distribution of income and fails to register declines in well-being that stem from loss of community, culture and environment. We need to develop a new matrix of economic development, in which progress is measured in terms of development of human capability, dignified employment for everyone, equitable distribution of income and wealth and ecological sustainability and social well-being of the community.

Notes

1 UNDP, *Human Development Report 2010: The Real Wealth of Nations*, New York: 2010, p. 22.
2 James Gustave Speth, *The Bridge at the Edge of the World: Capitalism, the Environment, and Crossing from Crisis to Sustainability*, New Haven, CT: Yale University Press, 2008, p. 9.
3 Donella Meadows, Jorgen Randers and Dennis Meadows, *Limits to Growth: The 30 Year Update*, London: Earthscan, 2005.
4 Ibid., p. 254.
5 Ibid., p. 255.
6 Ibid., pp. 235–263.
7 UNDP, *Human Development Report 2010*, pp. 1–9.

8 UNDP, *Human Development Report 1996*, pp. 43–65.
9 John Talbert, 'A New Bottom Line of Progress', in *World Watch Institute: State of the World 2008: Innovations for a Sustainable Society*, London: Earthscan, 2008, pp. 18–31.
10 Erik Assadourian, 'Degrowing Our Way to Progress', *World Watch Institute*, available at http://archleague.org/2013/10/degrowing-our-way-to-genuine-progress/ (accessed 1 December 2014).
11 Joseph Stiglitz, Chairman, 'Commission on the Measurement of Economic and Social Progress', November 2009, available at http://www.stiglitz-sen-fitoussi.fr/documents/rapport_anglais.pdf (accessed 6 April 2016).

11

SAVING THE ECONOMY FROM THE ECONOMISTS

Pothi parh parh jag muha, pandit bhya na koi,
Aek achar prem ka, parhe so pandit hoi.

People world over read voluminous books, but no one attains wisdom.
It is only by imbibing love (for humanity), one acquires wisdom.

Sant Kabir[1]

A mind all logic is like a knife all blade. It makes the hand bleed that uses it.

Rabindranath Tagore[2]

A large part of economic woes that we face today is the result of policy prescription given by an influential section of economists, who have dominated policy space, in management of global economy as well as national economies, more particularly in India, during the past three decades.

Adam Smith,[3] the father of economics, famously said in *Wealth of Nations* (1776) that it is self-interest that guides human behaviour and holds the society together. 'It is not from the benevolence of the butcher, the brewer, or the baker that we expect our dinner but from their regard to their own interest.' According to this philosophy, the market beautifully harnesses the energy of selfish individuals thinking only of themselves and their families to produce social harmony. Self-interest promotes competition, competition promotes markets and markets promote provisioning of goods and services and creation of wealth. This theory, which holds sway to this day, believes in an 'invisible hand', which provides automatic corrective to excesses and inefficiency of the markets. Many of society's ills that we face today are because of this ideology. An ideology which glorifies self-interest and Mammon worship is fundamentally flawed as it is contrary to basic human nature and human behaviour. Human beings

142

are guided by many noble motives such as honesty, love, sense of duty, faith and loyalty, and this has helped life become meaningful and is holding the society together since time immemorial.

In the ancient Vedic philosophy, the universe exists on the principle of *ritam* (the word 'right' is derived from it), which implies that the right moral order is built into it. From this follow certain virtues: honesty, rectitude, charity, non-violence, modesty and purity of heart. On the other hand, we have to condemn selfishness, falsehood, egoism, cruelty, adultery, theft and injury to living beings. Because the eternal moral law is part of the universe, doing what is praiseworthy is to act in harmony with the universe. All the great religions of the world emphasize the need to curb baser human traits and develop nobler values such as truth, love, non-violence and service to society. The Enlightenment movement in Europe was based on human values of equality, freedom, liberty and fraternity among human beings.

If we proceed on the premise that everyone is advancing his or her self-interest, the world would come to a grinding halt as there would be cheating all around – in trading and in business – and people will avoid doing honest work and productive activities. An economic system designed on this assumption would result in lower efficiency, and a huge amount of resources would be needed in monitoring, judging and punishing people. Modern management theory completely belies self-interest as the main motive force of economists. All the successful companies run on trust and loyalty of their workers rather than suspicion and self-seeking. The Japanese production system, which revolutionized lean and efficient production, is based on goodwill and creativity of workers by giving them responsibilities and trusting them as moral agents. Corporate managers believe in human motivation and devise ways to bring the best out of workers and seek their goodwill and cooperation in advancing corporate and social objectives.

Fallacy of free markets and global economic crisis of 2008

Free market economists argue that individuals are rational beings, they know best what is to be done and should be left alone and government should not interfere with the markets. The financial crisis of 2008 showed that the working of the financial system was so complex that top bankers, high-flying fund managers and celebrated academicians did not understand what is going on. Robert Merton and Myron Scholes, who won Nobel Prize in economics (1997) for the asset-pricing model, were clueless of what was happening in the financial markets when the hedge and other funds they were associated with went bust. As we all know, the world is full of uncertainty, and therefore, 'rational behaviour', the foundation of modern economics, is impossible under this kind of uncertainty.

Herbert Simon, who won Nobel Prize in 1978 and whose ideas have changed the way we view a modern 'firm', has propounded a theory of 'bounded rationality'. Contrary to the tenets of classical economics,

Simon maintained that individuals do not seek to maximize their benefit from a particular course of action (since they cannot assimilate and digest all the information that would be needed to do such a thing). Not only can they not get access to all the information required, but even if they could, their minds would be unable to process it properly. The human mind necessarily restricts itself due to its 'cognitive limits'. The complexity of the world and uncertainty make rational behaviour – the foundation of modern economics – so difficult to practice. This makes out a case for regulation of free markets, which limits the complexity of the activities and enables the regulated to take better decisions.[4]

The financial crisis which griped the US and Western Europe in 2007–8 dealt a devastating blow to the entire discipline of economics as a guide to running an economy. Hitherto the ruling economic ideology was efficient-markets hypothesis – its essence is that the price of a financial asset reflects all available information that is relevant to its value. A blind adherence to this theory led to the emergence of the biggest financial bubble in history. The US had to pour billions of dollars of public money in the economy, in failing banks and in financial institutions and companies like General Motors to prevent them from collapse. Castigating economists, Nobel Prize–winning economist Paul Krugman observed in *The New York Times* that the profession was blind to the possibility of market failures: 'During the golden years, financial economists came to believe that markets were inherently stable – indeed, that stocks and other assets were always priced just right.' He elaborates, 'The economics profession went astray because economists, as a group, mistook beauty, clad in impressive-looking mathematics, for truth.'

> They (economists) turned a blind eye to the limitations of human rationality that often lead to bubbles and busts; to the problems of institutions that run amok; to the imperfections of markets – especially financial markets – that can cause the economy's operating system to undergo sudden, unpredictable crashes; and to the dangers created when regulators don't believe in regulation. . . . They will have to acknowledge the importance of irrational and often unpredictable behavior, face up to the often idiosyncratic imperfections of markets and accept that an elegant economic 'theory of everything' is a long way off.[5]

Analysing the cause of recession, Jeffrey Sachs, another distinguished economist and social crusader, observes that it is because of the narrow vision of economists that they could not foresee the problem, 'Economic issues can rarely be understood in isolation. An effective macroeconomist must look at the big canvas, in which culture, domestic politics, geopolitics, public opinion, and environmental and natural resource constraints all play important role in economic life.'[6]

The fraud of international trade theory

One of the biggest bogey of modern economics is the doctrine of free trade, which when applied by developing countries as a practical policy prescription causes a devastating impact on the economy. Distinguished academic Noam Chomsky asserts that there is not a single case on record in history of any country that has developed successfully through the adherence to 'free market' principles. The Industrial Revolution took off in the US because of high protective tariff to keep British goods out. Cambridge economist Ha-Joon Chang argues that free trade and free market policies do not work, and most of today's rich countries followed highly protectionist policies when they were industrializing. Free trade policies have slowed down growth and increased income inequalities in developing countries (see Chapter 6 for details).

As America is now having serious economic problems, many academics are pointing out that the mainstream theory of free trade is responsible for its economic woes. Jeff Madrick[7] of Century Foundation says that free trade creates winners and losers – and American workers have been among the losers. Free trade has been a major factor behind the erosion in wages and job security among American workers. It has created tremendous prosperity, but mostly for those at the top. Madrick says,

> The irony is that during the Industrial Revolution, today's rich countries – Britain, France and the United States – pursued the very opposite policies: high tariffs, government investment in industry, financial regulations and fixed values for currencies. Trade expanded, and capital flowed anyway.

Over the past few decades, powerful international institutions such as the World Bank and International Monetary Fund (IMF) are actively supporting free market and free trade policies, in return for financial help. They have received strong intellectual support of mainstream economists, though in practical operation they are positively harmful for developing countries. Brandt Commission[8] (1980), more than three decades ago, had emphasized on the failure of the world economic system to provide social and economic equality for humanity, and argued for reduction of growing economic disparity between the rich North and the developing South. It had noted that economic activity in industrialized countries has been sustained by a major recycling of financial surpluses in developing countries, which has helped to prevent unemployment, underutilization of capacity and inflation, without commensurate gain to developing countries. IMF's structural adjustment programme to developing countries facing foreign exchange crisis requires opening up the economy for imports, reducing social spending, cutting subsidies and dismantling the public sector, which have played havoc with some of the countries. The commission observed that IMF 'has tended to impose unnecessary and unacceptable political burdens on the poorest, on occasion leading to IMF riots and even the downfall of government'. Things have not changed in recent years. Cambridge economist Ha-Joon Chang has the following to say:

> Over the last three decades, economists played an important role in creating the conditions for 2008 crisis (and dozens of smaller financial crisis that came before it since the early 1980s, such as the 1982 Third World Debt crisis, the 1985 Mexican peso crisis, the 1997 Asian crisis and the 1998 Russian crisis) by providing theoretical justifications for financial deregulation and unrestrained pursuit of short-term profits. More broadly, they advanced theories that justified the policies that have led to slower growth, higher inequality, heightened job insecurity and more frequent financial crisis that have dogged the world for last three decades. . . . [t]hey supplied arguments that insist that all those economic outcomes that many people find objectionable in this world – such as rising inequality, sky-high executive salaries or extreme poverty in poor countries – are really inevitable, given human nature and the need to reward people according to their productive contribution. . . . Economics as it has been practiced in the last three decades has been positively harmful for most people.[9]

Economists culpability

Roland Coase,[10] a Nobel laureate in economics, observes that economics has isolated itself from the ordinary business of life. It has identified itself as a theoretical approach of economization, giving up the real-world economy as its subject matter, and now economists write exclusively for one another. The separation of economics from the working economy has severely damaged both the business community and the academic discipline. Economics offers little in the way of practical insight to managers and entrepreneurs. Economics has become a convenient instrument the state uses to manage the economy, but as it is no longer firmly grounded in systematic empirical investigation of the working of the economy, it is hardly up to the task. Coase says,

> It is suicidal for the field to slide into a hard science of choice, ignoring the influences of society, history, culture and politics on the working of the economy. It is time to re-engage the severally impoverished field of economics with the economy. . . . But knowledge will come only if economics can be reoriented to the study of man as he is and economic system as it actually exists.

Thomas Piketty, a young French economist, who has shaken the mainstream economic establishment, by his empirical study, which concludes that free market economy with private property as its foundation is

146

largely responsible for growing inequality in the world, castigates the discipline of economics for its theoretical approach, divorced from the real world. 'The discipline of economics has to get over its childish passion for mathematics and for purely theoretical and often highly ideological speculation, at the expense of historical research and collaboration with other sciences.'[11] The economists' so-called scientific methods and mathematical models are 'no more than an excuse for occupying the terrain and masking the vacuity of content'.[12] He pleads for economics to be studied alongside other social sciences such as history, sociology, anthropology and political science, more as a 'political economy', to be able to understand and provide solutions to the real-world problems.

Manufacturing 'consent'

While it is understandable that Western economists are great protagonists of free market and free trade doctrine, as it helps those countries in monopoly hold of global trade and finance, why majority of Indian economists 'parrot' the same theory when the practical application of the policy is proving so disastrous for our economic interests? The only explanation I can find is that the group of economists in India trained in the US/UK and other European universities have become 'intellectual slaves' of the West. Our economics teachers teach this biased economic theory to students in colleges and universities. Economics as a subject is highly sought at graduate and postgraduate levels, which some of our brightest students join. This is mainly due to attractive job opportunities in the World Bank, UN and other international organizations, besides multinational corporations (which worship unbridled freedom of market). Once these youngsters join these organizations, they are 'brainwashed' in the ideology of the organization they work and in due course become their most ardent champions. The global academic economics community dominated by the West is able to 'manufacture consent' to their ideas and ideology.

A prominent group of academic economists have backed student protests in Britain, against neoclassical economics teaching, to reform courses that are dominated by free market theories that ignore the impact of financial crises.[13] The academics from some of the UK's most prestigious institutions, including Cambridge and Leeds universities, protested in a letter to *The Guardian* that the way the neoclassical economics that is being taught, the students were short-changed, as it is based on dubious hypothesis of rational consumers and workers with unlimited wants and contrasts sharply with the openness of teaching in other social sciences. They pointed out the absurdity that students can complete a degree in economics without having been exposed to the theories of Keynes, Marx or Minsky, and without having learned about the Great Depression. Many economists, including the 2013 Nobel Prize winner Robert Shiller, have argued that mainstream economics is highly biased, teaching theories based on maintaining openly competitive markets, and that well-informed buyers and sellers eliminate the risk of asset prices rising beyond a sustainable level for a prolonged period. The academics observed that shortcomings in the way economics is taught are directly related to an intellectual monoculture and favour orthodoxy, instead of intellectual diversity.

Failure of Indian planning

Nobel laureate Gunnar Myrdal, who wrote the highly acclaimed *Asian Drama* (1970) analysing the socio-economic problems of developing countries, and was very sympathetic to India, said four decades ago (1973) that Indian planning has not been so successful as planners did not follow the fundamental teachings of Mahatma Gandhi:

> The main responsibility for this failure (planning) should be laid on my own profession, the economists, and in this respect there is no difference between the Western economists, the Asian economists and, indeed, also the economists from the Communist countries. All were too narrow minded in their approach, too 'materialistic' in a sense . . . t[he] approach to economic planning for development in underdeveloped countries was for a long time, and partly today, dominated by the concept of capital-output ratio. It implied always the narrow attention in economic planning merely to physical investment and to the financial and fiscal appropriations. It thus meant a non-consideration on a large scale of the 'human dimension of economic growth'.[14]

From the time planning has been initiated in our country, more particularly post-economic liberalization, the economists sitting in the Planning Commission and similar other policymaking bodies have come to acquire a dominant say in policymaking. Their policy prescription has caused great damage to the values we cherish in this country. Take, for example, education and health, the two most crucial sectors for national development. Economists classify higher education as 'non-merit good' and have encouraged propagation of ideas that has starved universities and other higher academic institutions of public funding and encouraged private institutions of dubious values to flourish. The standards of most private educational institutions are abysmally low; they charge heavy capitation fees and are virtual teaching shops for minting money. The entire higher education sector has been ruined, with long-term adverse consequences for the country. In the medical and health sectors, under the influence of free market ideology, the government has abandoned its responsibility of providing affordable medical care to citizens. Government hospitals and medical colleges are denied funding and are in a pathetic state of neglect. Instead, reliance is placed on private hospitals which are frightfully expensive, which only the rich can afford or those whose bills are picked by employers. The indiscriminate opening up of the economy and privatization and disinvestment of public enterprises, which we are following today, is a direct result of policy prescription of free market economists, with the result that a spectre of de-industrialization is confronting the country. These problems arise when economists meddle into policies of education, health or industrial production, which should be best left to specialists and professionals in their respective domains.

Professional economists did not have much say in policymaking in miracle economies of East and South Asia, which achieved spectacular economic growth in the second half of the 20th century. Economic policies in Japan and South Korea were run by lawyers and in China and Taiwan by engineers and scientists. In pre–Second World War Soviet Union, it was technocrats who had the dominant say in planning, which helped transform a backward peasant economy into a modern industrialized nation.

Commenting on the discipline of economics, Arun Maira,[15] a former member of the Planning Commission, who had a ringside view of economic policymaking, observes that 'mainstream economics has become like an ostrich with its head in the sand, unwilling to see what is around it'. Economists are caught in the trap of measurement, and time has come to reconstruct it as 'too much reality was being left out of economic models for them to explain the world'. The reconstruction of economics will require the inclusion of many disciplines of social and ecological sciences.

Economists' default – narrow vision

Sociologist Des Gaper[16] observes that mainstream economics views humans from a very narrow perspective and on the assumption that wants are unlimited, and people are self-interested, rational and best judge of their own well-being. Consumer sovereignty, a pet theme of economists, takes a nihilist approach to ethics as even wants such as gambling, smoking and prostitution are considered value-neutral. Due to such an approach, a perspective of economism has emerged, which can be explained in the following terms:

- The economy is a separate sphere, interrelated with the rest of the society only peripherally, and can be adequately analysed and planned irrespective of social, cultural and psychological factors.
- Society is primarily an economy; a system for the provision of saleable goods and countries is referred to as 'economies' as part of a larger 'world economy'.
- People are primarily 'economic men' driven by wants for material goods, and concerns for rights, justice, equity and so on are not important.
- Most of life should be understood, valued and measured in terms of economic calculation.
- Societal development can be measured by GDP/GNP and development means this economistic interpretation.
- Economy should be managed by its own technical interpretation, and there should be no political interference.

Most scholars of social science feel that economy is too important to be left to conventional economists, and part of mainstream economics requires considerable reconstruction. Harvard scholar Michael Sandel[17] questions the fundamental postulate on which the free market economics rests, as it does not make a distinction between material goods and civic goods. Free market economists love monetary incentives. They believe that all the problems of the world can be solved if a free hand is given to design a proper incentive system. Today markets are increasingly invading our life. Market reasoning is applied to sex, procreation, child rearing, education, health, criminal punishment, immigration policy and environmental protection. When market reasoning travels beyond the domain of material goods, it has to necessarily deal with issues of morality, an issue that economists duck. If commercialization is allowed to invade social and civic goods indiscriminately, it will lead to corruption of good things of life and will destroy the values on which a good society rests.

Commenting on the causes of downslide of the US economy from 2008, distinguished economist Jeffrey Sachs observed that 'at the root of America's crisis lies a moral crisis: the decline of civic virtue among America's political and economic elite'.[18]

Economics – ignoring ethical and human dimension

Most of the ills of modern economic development are the direct and indirect results of the narrow and non-ethical character of economic science. Mahatma Gandhi had emphasized that economics cannot be divorced from ethics. He was highly critical of the kind of economic development which was taking place in the world. It was propelled by continuous and insatiable hunger for wealth and greedy pursuit of worldly pleasure. Being a study of mankind, economics and its laws must find harmony with the laws of human behaviour. Albert Einstein had cautioned,

> Science cannot create ends and, even less, instill them in human beings; science, at most, can supply the means by which to attain certain ends. . . . For these reasons, we should be on our guard not to overestimate science and scientific methods when it is a question of human problems; and we should not assume that experts are the only ones who have a right to express themselves on questions affecting the organization of society.[19]

We should not place too much trust on economists, who construct theories and economic models which have no relation to real-life situations but in their practical application cause a great deal of suffering and damage to human beings. Human personality is not limited to physical and biological aspects, but has the psycho-spiritual dimension, and therefore, only a humane and ethical approach can help solve huge socio-economic problems that we face in the country today.

Notes

1 Ramkishore Sharma (ed.), *Kabir Granthawali (Kabir's Poetry Collection)*, Allahabad: Lokbharti Prakashan, 2010, p. 214, in Hindi.

2 Quoted by Udit Narayan Singh, 'Tagore in 21st Century', *India Perspective, Ministry of External Affairs, Rabindranath Tagore*, Vol. 24, No. 2, 2010, pp. 2–3.

3 For a detailed discussion of Adam Smith's self-interest theory, see Ha-Joon Chang, 'Assume the Worst about People and You Get the Worst', in *Things They Don't Tell You about Capitalism*, New York: Bloomsbury Press, 2010, Chapter 5, pp. 41–50; and M. V. Nadkarni, 'Ethics in Development', *Ethics for Our Times*, New Delhi: Oxford University Press, 2011, Chapter 3, pp. 77–99.

4 For a detailed discussion, see Ha Joon-Chang, 'We Are Not Smart Enough to Leave Things to the Market', in *Things They Don't Tell You about Capitalism*, New York: Bloomsbury Press, 2010, Chapter 16, pp. 168–177.

5 Paul Krugman, 'How did economists get it so wrong?', *New York Times*, 2 September 2009, available at http://www.nytimes.com/2009/09/06/magazine/06Economic-t.html?pagewanted=all&_r=0 (accessed 3 July 2014).

6 Jeffrey Sachs, *The Price of Civilization*, London: The Bodley Head, 2011, pp. 6–7.

7 Jeff Madrick, *Seven Bad Ideas: How Mainstream Economists Have Damaged America and the World*, New York: Alfred A. Knoff, 2014; and Jeff Madrick, 'Our misplaced faith in free trade', *New York Times*, Sunday Review, 3 October 2014, available at http://www.nytimes.com/2014/10/04/opinion/sunday/our-misplaced-faith-in-free (accessed 24 January 2015).

8 Brandt Commission Report, *North South: A Programme for Survival*, London: Pan Books, 1980, pp. 216, 238.

9 Ha Joon-Chang, *Things They Don't Tell You about Capitalism*, New York: Bloomsbury Press, 2010, pp. 247–248.

10 Ronald Coase, 'Saving Economics from the Economists', *Harvard Business Review South Asia*, December 2012, p. 34, available at http://hbr.org/2012/12/saving-economics-from-the-economists (accessed 3 July 2014).

11 Thomas Piketty, *Capital in the Twenty-First Century*, Cambridge: Harvard University Press, 2014, p. 32.

12 Ibid., pp. 573–575.

13 'Academics back students in protests against economics teaching', *The Guardian*, Monday, 18 November 2013, available at http://theeconomicrealms.blogspot.in/2013/11/academics-back-students-in-protests.htm (accessed 3 July 2014).

14 Gunnar Myrdal, 'Challenge of Stagnation in Developing Countries', in J. S. Mathur (ed.), *Gandhi in the Mirror of Foreign Scholars*, New Delhi: Gyan Publishing House, 2006, p. 59.

15 Arun Maira, *Redesigning the Aeroplane While Flying: Reforming Institutions*, New Delhi: Rainlight and Rupa, 2014, pp. 82–89.

16 Des Gaper, *The Ethics of Development*, New Delhi: Vistaar Publications, 2007, pp. 78–81.

17 Michael J. Sandel, *What Money Can't Buy*, London: Penguin, 2012, pp. 84–91.

18 Sachs, *The Price of Civilization*, p. 1.

19 Albert Einstein, 'Why Socialism', *Monthly Review*, May 1949, available at http://monthlyreview.org/2009/05/01/why-socialism (accessed 24 January 2015).

Part III

RETHINKING DEVELOPMENT

12

THE GANDHIAN ALTERNATIVE TO ECONOMIC DEVELOPMENT

India's destiny lies not along the bloody way of the West, of which she shows signs of tiredness, but along the bloodless way of peace that comes from a simple and godly life. India is in danger of losing her soul. She cannot lose it and live. She must not, therefore, lazily and helplessly say, 'I cannot escape the onrush from the West'. She must be strong enough to resist it for its own sake and that of the world.

Mahatma Gandhi[1]

Mahatma Gandhi's philosophy of truth, non-violence and *satyagraha* helped India to be liberated from British rule and is considered a perennial philosophy to fight injustice, oppression and suppression of human rights. Martin Luther King Jr effectively used non-violence as a weapon to secure rights and justice for the blacks in America. While Gandhi's philosophy has wide acceptance to deal with political and social issues, it did not have many followers in the area of economics and he was aware of it – 'Pandit Nehru wants industrialisation because he thinks that, if it is socialised, it would be free from the evils of capitalism. My own view is that evils are inherent in industrialism, and no amount of socialisation can eradicate it.'[2] Gandhi was not impressed by the two prevailing dominant systems of the management of the economy – the capitalist free market economy and the state–bureaucratic socialism of the communist countries.

Post-independence, India did not follow Gandhi's economic philosophy and adopted a mixed economy model, with the state commanding the heights of economy. As we know, this did not help in solving our gigantic problems of poverty and backwardness. Post-liberalization in 1991, we have adopted a free market economy model, but genuine progress and development has been eluding us. Today, the global economy, with free market as its mantra, is in a state of severe crisis. The political leadership, thinkers and intellectuals are all searching for the 'right model' of economic development, but it is nowhere in sight. Does Gandhian economics provide answer to some of the problems afflicting the world economy? Mainstream economists consider Gandhian ideas as utopian. This chapter questions this conventional wisdom and demonstrates that Gandhian philosophy, if properly understood, can provide valuable guidance in finding out solutions to our economic problems.

Gandhi's world view

Mahatma Gandhi had challenged the foundation of modern Western civilization and called it satanic. He was highly critical of technological and the materialistic aspect of Western civilization, rooted as it is in self-indulgence, multiplicity of wants, exploitation, enslavement of the individual, coupled with a mad race for capturing markets and conquering lands for raw materials. Gandhi's main mission was to secure India's freedom from foreign rule, and he was analysing the reason why Britain and other European industrial powers had enslaved India and vast tracts of Asia and Africa. It may be remembered that following British conquest, Indian (Hindu) culture and civilization was under severe attack, from the British rulers, and efforts were made to show it as 'inferior' and Indians 'unfit to rule themselves'. This was challenged by patriotic Indians, and there was an Indian renaissance based on India's cultural and spiritual heritage. Raja Rammohan Roy, Swami Dayanand Saraswati, Swami Vivekananda, Lokmanya Tilak, Sri Aurbindo Ghosh and many other savants pointed out the strength of India's ancient culture and civilization, which had stood the test of time. Mahatma Gandhi carried forward this legacy in his own inimitable manner.

Gandhi advocated total philosophy of life, of which politics, society and economics were all an integral part. His philosophy had deep religious underpinnings based on truth, *ahimsa* and service to society. He derived inspiration from ancient Indian philosophy espoused in the Ramayana, the Upanishads and the Bhagavad Gita, expounded the highest ethical standards and felt that religion and morality cannot be delinked from politics and economics. For Gandhi, 'civilization is that mode of conduct which points out to man the path of duty. Performance of duty and observance of morality are convertible terms. To observe morality is to attain mastery over our mind and our passions'.[3] He felt Indian civilization as superior to Western, 'The tendency of Indian civilization is to elevate the moral being, that of Western civilization is to propagate immorality' and wanted to preserve it at all cost.

While Gandhi was deeply influenced by Tolstoy, Ruskin and Thoreau, as well Christ's teachings, his core ideas were deeply embedded in India's religion and philosophy. His ideal of a society was *Ramrajya*. *Ramrajya* meant the Kingdom of God on earth, which ensures equal rights alike of the prince and pauper and sovereignty of people based on moral right.[4]

Philosophical foundation of Gandhian economics

Gandhi's view on economy emerged from his overall philosophy of life. He did not draw any distinction between economics and ethics. According to Gandhi,

> Economics that hurt the moral well-being of an individual or a nation are immoral and, therefore sinful. . . . That economics is untrue which ignores or disregards moral values.[5]

Gandhi's economic ideas flow from the Vedantic ideal of *aparigraha* – non-possession – renunciation of ownership. He derived his inspiration from *Ishopanishad*, which exhorts *Tena tyaktena bhunjeetha, Ma gridha kasyaswiddhanam* (enjoy wealth, but not covet it and not cling to possessions).[6] An individual should abstain from acquisitiveness. Civilization should not be equated with the multiplication of wants and accumulation of material goods to satisfy our increasing wants.

Gandhi's views are in total contrast to modern economic theory, which is based on wants and not on needs. Unlimited wants are the source of rat race that debases human beings by keeping them subject to their animal spirit. Want-oriented economies create a psychology of scarcity and poverty, as all wants can never be satisfied.

J. K. Mehta and the theory of wantlessness

Prof. J. K. Mehta,[7] a highly respected philosopher-economist of Allahabad University, has propounded a theory of wantlessness, which echoes Gandhi's views. We satisfy wants to get rid of pain and to derive pleasure. But this is not a permanent solution, as wants have a tendency to recur. It is to maintain mental equilibrium for which man satisfies wants, but all wants can never be satisfied.

> The prime mover of economic system today is the wanting self. The self exists and the self prospers. With each selfish act of want-satisfaction the self gathers strength. The process of condensation makes a speedy headway as the ego flattens, feeding itself on pampered wants.[8]

To permanently get rid of pain of want, we must sublimate wants, and we must conquer and not pamper them. Mehta argues that *karmayog* is the method of attaining wantlessness for an average man. 'Were all of us to follow the path of *karmayog* life would be simplified, though not altered materially in form and progress as we understand.'[9] He criticizes the narrow vision of economists,

> The science of economics sets for itself the goal of removal of all wants. It is not realized, however, that the way we proceed

to reach goal is self-defeating. For one thing, we secure merely fleeting pleasures of life; for another we create an atmosphere in which wants keep on multiplying. . . . The madding crowd's ignoble strife for pleasure continues and science is developed to explain human behavior that is directed to that end.[10]

The policy implications for the discipline of economics, whose main focus is on removal of wants, can be disastrous, 'Where the desire to satisfy wants is encouraged and efforts to raise the standard of people eulogized, man is robbed of mental peace and nations of peaceful existence.'[11] Suggesting a corrective to this distorted view Mehta says,

Economic theory was developed to explain human behaviour on the fundamental postulate that the man wants to satisfy his wants with least expenditure of the resources at his command. And that meant that it was assumed that in satisfying one want care must be taken that the fewest possible other wants were created. . . . The wider discipline of economics looks at human behavior in the light of complete mastery over wants.[12]

True economics should pull down barriers between economics and religion. The pampering of wants is not the final desideratum. For Prof. Mehta, true discipline of economics is 'the science of human activities considered as an endeavor to reach the state of wantlessness'.[13]

Gandhian economics

The fundamental postulate of Gandhi's economic philosophy is individual dignity and the welfare of the poorest of the poor. He felt that a man earns his dignity by working and earning his bread and livelihood. Work is a medium of self-sustenance and self-expression. Gandhi was echoing Bhagawad Gita's famous message: *karmavey adikarste, ma phaleshu kadachan* (your duty is to work only and not to the results thereof). Work is a duty cast on man. *For Gandhi, an ideal social and economic order should ensure this right to work for everyone.* Therefore, the economic system should be organized to provide employment for everyone:

According to me the economic constitution of India, and for that matter of the world, should be such that no one under it should suffer from want of food and clothing. In other words everybody should be able to get sufficient work to enable him to make two ends meet. And this ideal can be universally realised only if the means of production of the elementary necessities of life remain in control of the masses.[14]

Gandhi was against mass production and industrialization, which destroyed local industries, impoverished villages and reduced man to a cog in the machine – 'What I object is the craze for machinery, not machinery as such. Men go on saving labour till thousands are without work and thrown on the open streets to die of starvation.'[15] Gandhi did not oppose all machinery; he praised the invention of the Singer sewing machine, which saved the drudgery of housewives. His opposition to machines was particularly in the context of India, owing to the huge population and unemployment: 'Mechanization is good when the hands are too few for the work intended to be accomplished. It is an evil when there are more hands than required for work as in case of India.'[16] He was against India copying the West and its urban-centric civilization and pleaded for *gram-swarajya* (village self-reliance):

> I have believed and repeated times without number that India is to be found not in its cities but in its 7,00,000 villages. But we town-dwellers have believed that India is to be found in its town and the villages were created to minister our needs. The cities with their insolent tort are a constant menace to the life and liberty of the villages.[17]

Gandhi believed in a village *swaraj* (self-reliance) that was 'independent of its neighbours for its vital needs, and yet inter-dependent for many others in which dependence is a necessity'.[18] For Gandhi, village should be self-contained,

> If village perishes India will perish too. . . . We have to concentrate on the village being self-contained, manufacturing mainly for use . . . there would be no objection to villagers using even modern machines and tools . . . only they should not be used as a means of exploitation of others.[19]

Gandhi's idea of *gram-swarajya* was part of his gospel of *swadeshi*, which he described as 'that spirit in us which restricts us to the use of our immediate surroundings to the exclusion of more remote'.[20]

Although it is almost seven decades since we attained independence, the condition of our villages continues to be pathetic. Veteran Gandhian Ela Bhatt,[21] writing in January 2015, says that our potters, carpenters, weavers, dyers, embroiders and artisans of handicrafts, who work with their hands and carry generations of old knowledge, are living on the margins of society and can no longer live by their trade. 'The urban industrialized world is wreaking havoc on our rural economy'. Bhatt pleads for understanding the true spirit of khadi (hand-woven cloth), which means dignity of manual labour, self-sufficiency, employment, sustainability and local control.

Trusteeship

Gandhi criticized the capitalist system because it was based on ownership of the means of production and property. He argued that unlimited wants, greed and fear arise from capitalist property relations and advanced a theory of trusteeship, as an organizational structure under which production could be organized, instead of large industrial houses, where economic power was concentrated in the hands of few and was inherently exploitive. Socialist thinkers have for a long time been arguing that private property is at the root of exploitative process of production and distribution and called for its abolition. Proudhon termed 'property' as 'theft', and Karl Marx called for a revolt of the property-less proletariat, capture of state power by the working class, to be followed by classless society. Gandhi declared himself a socialist and repudiated the concept of private ownership of property. But he was opposed to the use of violence or hatred to bring social change. He wanted to do it by moral force and persuasion. The objective is to create a non-violent and non-exploitive property relationship. He equated private property in excess of basic needs of human existence with exploitation and, as private property was not a natural right but man-made privilege, it could be modified and altered by social action. Gandhi simultaneously proclaimed his profound belief in the rightness of economic equality. He did not visualize a world where there would be no property, but he would restrict the right of private property to what was necessary to yield an honourable livelihood, while for the excess he prescribed the principle of trusteeship. He asked those who owned money to behave like trustees holding their riches on behalf of the poor.

Gandhi promoted a six-point programme containing his ideas about trusteeship on the basis of a draft prepared by distinguished economist Prof. M. L. Dantwala.[22] Its salient features are:

1   Trusteeship provides a means of transforming the present capitalist order of society into an egalitarian one.
2   It does not recognize any right of private ownership of property, except in as much as it may be permitted by society for its own welfare.
3   It does not exclude legislative ownership and use of wealth.
4   Under state-regulated trusteeship, an individual will not be free to hold or use his or her wealth for selfish satisfaction or in disregard of the interest of the society.
5   Just as it is proposed to fix decent minimum wage, even so a limit should be fixed for the maximum income that could be allowed to any person in society.
6   The character of production will be determined by social necessity and not by personal whim or greed.

Elaborating on the concept of trusteeship, economist V. K. R. V. Rao says that it basically means

acceptance of the principle of private ownership of property, the limit imposed upon its use for sustaining minimum living standards, the major constraints it imposes by prohibiting its use merely for selfish satisfaction or in disregard of the social interest and the inclusion of legislative regulation for determining its ownership and use in the desired direction for non-exploitive purposes.[23]

According to Gandhian economist J.D. Sethi, 'Philosophically trusteeship is an economic conscience by which an individual when engaged in economic activity takes into account not only his own interests but also the interest of others.'[24] Four underlying ethico-economic principles of trusteeship are (1) non-possession, (2) non-exploitation, (3) bread labour and (4) equality of rewards. Thus, trusteeship is a theory of need-based production, equitable distribution and social justice.

Intermediate technology

E. F. Schumacher, author of *Small Is Beautiful*, draws inspiration from the Gandhian ideology of 'resisting the temptation of letting our luxuries become needs' and 'recognition of existence of the soul apart from the body'.[25] He argues that man's current pursuit of profit and progress, which promotes giant organizations and increased specialisation, has resulted in gross economic inefficiency, environmental pollution and inhuman working conditions. He proposes a system of *intermediate technology*, based on smaller working units, communal ownership and regional workplaces utilizing local labour and resources:

> The technology of mass production is inherently violent, ecologically damaging, self-defeating in terms of non-renewable resources and stultifying for the human person. The technology of production by the masses, making use of the best modern knowledge and experience, is conducive to decentralisation, compatible with the laws of ecology, gentle in its use of scarce resources, and designed to serve the human person instead of making him servant of machines.[26]

Intermediate technology is a technology with a human face, which is viable and integrates the human being with his or her skilful hands and creative brains, into a productive process.

From the point of modern economic theory, 'labour' or 'worker' is an item of cost to be reduced to the minimum and have output without employees. This approach is demeaning as work provides individual growth and fulfilment according to Buddhist as well as Vedanta (Gita) philosophy. However, there is a need to make a distinction between mechanization that enhances an individual's skill and power and one that that turns the work of an individual to a mechanical slave, leaving him or her to serve the machine:

> To organise work in such a manner that it becomes meaningless, boring, stultifying, or nerve racking for the worker would be little short

of criminal; it would indicate a greater concern with goods than with people, an evil lack of compassion and a soul-destroying degree of attachment to the most primitive side of this worldly existence.[27]

An economics which considers goods more important than people and consumption more important than creative activity is a surrender to the forces of evil. Schumacher faults the current philosophy of materialism under which the development of production and acquisition of wealth have become the highest goal of modern world, to which all other goals should be subordinated.

> It is of little use trying to suppress terrorism if the production of deadly devices continues to be a legitimate employment of man's creative powers. Nor can the fight against pollution be successful if the pattern of production and consumption continue to be of a scale, a complexity, and a degree of violence which, as is becoming more and more apparent, do not fit into the laws of universe, to which man is as much subject as the rest of creation.[28]

Schumacher calls for guiding our actions according to time-tested, four cardinal virtues of Christianity – prudence, justice, goodness and beauty – if the civilization is to survive.

Building social business

Nobel Prize winner Muhammad Yunus has pioneered micro-credit in Bangladesh, the innovative banking programme that provides poor people (mostly women) with small loans which they use to launch business and lift their families out of poverty. He has advanced the concept of social business to deal with the problems of capitalism. The existing economic theory portrays human beings in business as one-dimensional whose sole mission is maximization of profit. In reality, human beings are multidimensional; their happiness comes from many sources, including selfless service to fellow human beings. This spirit of human beings, combined with powerful technology available today, offers huge opportunity to do social business. Social business has seven principles:[29]

1　The business objective is to overcome poverty or similar problems relating to education and health, among others, and not to maximize profit.
2　The company will attain financial and economic sustainability.
3　Investors will get back only their investment amount. No dividend is given beyond the original investment.
4　When the investment is paid back, profit stays with the company for expansion and improvement.
5　The company will be environmentally conscious.

6   The workforce gets market wages with better-than-standard working conditions.
7   Work is done with joy.

The concept of social business has been successfully experimented in Bangladesh in diverse areas such as provision of mobile phone companies in rural areas, solar homes, affordable health care and modernization of handloom industry. Yunus, in partnership with some of the world's large business houses such as Danone, has been producing affordable nutritious yogurt for malnourished children. According to Yunus, if social business is developed and integrated into the main stream of economic theory, it can solve many of the world's problems of poverty, hunger and ill health and can address the problems which profit-making businesses create.

Internet as a tool

Political activist Sudheendra Kulkarni has developed a thesis that the Internet fulfils the expectations of a machine that Gandhi had been visualizing and fulfils the role of *charkha* (spinning and weaving wheel) espoused by him.[30] Gandhi was wedded to scientific spirit, contrary to the general perception about him. While the spinning wheel was at the centre of his economic and social campaign, he was not dogmatic about it and had contemplated a better substitute in changed socio-economic situations. Today, the spirit of *charkha* and *khadi* is fulfilled by digital technologies anchored in the Internet. Kulkarni pleads for people to become Internet *Satyagrahi*, as it is a latter-day avatar of the spinning wheel and, through service-oriented actions, creates a more humane and just society. The Internet is being used actively in public spheres, creating content to improve quality of education in schools and colleges, promoting best practices in environment protection and heritage conservation, educating people in disease control and healthy living and fighting the battle against corruption and abuse of human rights.

Sustainable development

Today the world is facing huge environment challenges, the most serious of which is climate change. Tremendous growth in human activities has increased the presence of greenhouse gases, more particularly carbon dioxide, which heats the atmosphere and threatens the existence of not only human life but also animal and plant life in our planet. The Club of Rome, a leading think tank, has been pointing out for the past 40 years that there are ecological constraints in the existing development pattern, due to ever-increasing need of agriculture and industry, and the planet's physical limit in the form of depletable natural resources. Former US vice-president Al Gore has produced a movie *An Inconvenient Truth*, which draws attention to dangers society faces from climate change. Its message is to change our lifestyle and reduce consumption, particularly fossil fuels, the main polluter of the atmosphere. Recognizing the gravity of the problem, the United Nations has set up a Framework Convention on Climate Change, and an agreement has been reached by member countries to voluntarily cut carbon emission (see Chapter 9).

Mahatma Gandhi argued for village-centric, decentralized development. He was against mindless industrialization and urbanization, which are today the main causes of pollution and environmental degradation. He believed in simple living and controlling one's desires and wants. 'Our civilization, our culture, our Swaraj depend not upon multiplying our wants – self-indulgence, but upon restricting our wants – self-denial.'[31] Economist A. K. Dasgupta points out that such limitation of wants was not intended as glorification of austerity but rather as an exercise in the optimization of individual welfare.

> In taking up such a position Gandhi anticipated a basic theme of recent literature against economic growth. Indeed he was one of the first writers to argue explicitly and in a systematic way that non economic aspect of welfare are important and that a single minded pursuit of the maximum satisfaction of material wants might not lead to best possible worlds.[32]

It is well recognized that if people in poor countries start enjoying the same material living standard as that of the US and Western Europe, it will exhaust all the natural resources of the world and the earth will soon become barren, unfit for human habitation. Gandhi anticipated this, when he said, 'God forbid that India should ever take to industrialization after the manner in the West. If the entire nation of 300 million took to similar economic exploitation, it would strip the world bare like locusts.'[33] Looking at today's global problem of environment sustainability, one has to admit how modern Gandhi's views were and how much ahead of time his thinking was. He can be described as an environmentalist par excellence.

The relevance of Gandhian ideology today

The Gandhian ideology, whose main focus is on welfare and dignity of individual, provides us a broad framework into the new philosophy of economic development that we need today. We first summarize the Gandhian economic principles:

1   The economic system should be so organized that every individual has an opportunity of getting a gainful employment, so that he or she can buy his or her own bread and essential means of living. Gandhi did not believe in the poor living on the charity or mercy of others and wanted eradication of poverty which is possible only when everyone has a fulfilling job.

2 Gandhi was opposed to mindless industrialization as it displaces labour and causes unemployment and is the main reason for rural poverty.

3 He supported rural-centric development, with agriculture and small-scale industries getting pride of place, as this was the only way the unemployment problem could be resolved in a labour-abundant country like India.

4 Gandhi was totally opposed to the current craze for economic globalization, as it displaces local labour and is contrary to the philosophy of helping one's neighbour first.

5 Gandhi believed in a decentralized development model as it helps benefits of development reach everyone and promotes equality and social harmony.

6 Gandhi was opposed to conspicuous consumption and luxurious living. He wanted people to have minimum needs and lead a simple life.

7 While Gandhi was not opposed to private ownership of large industries and business, he advocated social control of business so that profit generated is equitably distributed and prevents concentration of wealth in the hands of few people, which leads to exploitation.

We should not therefore look towards Gandhian economics as a rigid framework and view Gandhi opposing all 'machines and industrialization'. Prof. M. V. Nadkarni explains,

> He only wanted industrialisation in particular, and economic development, in general, to have a human face, without reducing humans to robots or depriving them of their livelihood and employment or making them some filthy rich and some abjectly poor.[34]

Gandhi was deeply aware of the social dimension of technology. Nadkarni says,

> This awareness led him to develop an ethics of technology, technological advance and industrialization. He wanted all these to be constantly subjected to ethical evaluation, monitoring and correction. . . . The criterion was whether technology and industrialization, combined with necessary social or State action, improved human welfare of all.

Gandhi's idea of trusteeship should not be viewed as impractical or utopian, wherein rich businessmen will voluntarily surrender their wealth and work towards social good. Gandhi had his own vision of socialism and did not believe in violent methods of controlling means of production advocated by Marxists and believed in change of heart of man for doing good to others. Gandhi was pragmatic and expressed views in the context of India's poverty, which he attributed largely due to British rule and its driving force, the industrialization and capitalist mode of production.

Schumacher has shown how use of simple and intermediate technology can help micro- and small-scale industries, as a rewarding and profitable occupation, in which millions of people can find employment. Muhammad Yunus with his social business model has demonstrated how successful businesses can be run without profit as motive and can lift people out of poverty. Internet and digital technology hold great promise of individual empowerment and decentralized development. Gandhian economic model offers solution to environment sustainability, one of the most pressing problems facing the global community.

The way forward

Policymakers all over the world are groping in the dark, trying to find the best economic model to build a stable and sustainable economy. It needs to be remembered that both capitalist and socialist paths of economic development have failed. Socialism, in its practical operation, implies control over means of production and distribution by the state, though the philosophy of socialism, when originally postulated, had its roots in the doctrine of equality and liberalism. The economists for a long time suffered from the illusion that state acts as a platonic guardian of the people. They forgot that it is the politician and the bureaucrat who control the machinery of the state and their main aim is to exercise power and authority with scant regard for people's welfare. Due to its inherent contradiction, the socialist model practised by the Soviet Union and its satellite Eastern European countries collapsed in the late 1980s and early 1990s.

Capitalism, with its philosophy of free and unregulated markets, leads to concentration of wealth in the hands of a few, causing widespread social disparity. It also encourages individual greed and avarice. For the past three decades, the US and other Western countries have been unabashedly pursuing the neoliberal economic model with liberalization, globalization and free play of market forces as their mantra. Its main objective is economic growth, without any thought given to its cost. This model based on relentless consumerism is fundamentally flawed and is responsible for current global economic crisis, mass unemployment and environmental degradation. It is time we abandon a model whose foundations rest on materialism, consumption and greed.

What we need today is to devise a new model of economic development based on Gandhian ideology, whose foundation rests on ethics and welfare of every individual in society. This, in practice, would mean that public policy's first and foremost priority should be dignified employment for everyone. This is possible only when massive support is given to agriculture and it is made a remunerative occupation, on par with the industry and service sectors. In addition, state policy should support in a big way thousands of micro- and small-scale industries through investment in research and development and upgradation of the capability of people in terms of education, knowledge and skill, with provision of credit and allied facilities. To create an egalitarian society, the 'Big Business' should be strictly regulated and converted into 'Social Business', so that they plough their profits back into the business for socially productive activities and are not allowed to extract huge surpluses by way of salary, dividend, bonus and other means, except what they need for a reasonable standard of living. Mahatma Gandhi's philosophy, applied in its true spirit, offers solution to most of the social and economic problems India is currently facing.

Notes

1 Quoted in R. K. Prabhu (compiler), *Mohan-Mala: A Gandhian Rosary*, Ahmedabad: Navajivan Publishing House, 2000 reprint, p. 95; *Young India*, 7 October 1926.

2 U. S. Mohan Rao, *The Message of Mahatma Gandhi*, New Delhi: Publications Division, Government of India, 1994 (1968), p. 54; *Harijan*, 19 September 1940.

3 Mahatma Gandhi, *Hind Swaraj*, New Delhi: Rajpal, 2010, pp. 49–52. The book was originally written in Gujrati in 1908, when Gandhiji was in South Africa. It was translated by him in English in 1909.

4 R. K. Prabhu and U. R. Rao, *The Mind of Mahatma Gandhi*, Ahmedabad: Navajivan Publishing House, 2010 reprint (1967), p. 326.

5 Mohan Rao, *The Message of Mahatma Gandhi*, p. 263; *Young India*, 13 October 1921, and *Young India*, 26 October 1924.

6 For a detailed discussion, see Ravindra Varma, 'Gandhi's Theory of Trusteeship', in J. D. Sethi (ed.), *Trusteeship: The Gandhian Alternative*, New Delhi: Gandhi Peace Foundation, 1986, pp. 45–75.

7 For a detailed discussion, see J. K. Mehta, *Rhyme, Rhythm, and Truth in Economics*, London: Asia Publishing House, Chapter 1, pp. 27–35; and J. K. Mehta, *Studies in Advance Economic Theory*, Delhi: Premier Publishing Co., 1950, Chapters I and II, pp. 1–22.

8 Mehta, *Rhyme, Rhythm, and Truth in Economics*, pp. 31–32.

9 Ibid., p. 32.

10 Ibid., p. 33.

11 Ibid., p. 35.

12 Ibid., p. 34.

13 Mehta, *Studies in Advance Economic Theory*, p. 22.

14 Prabhu and Rao, *The Mind of Mahatma Gandhi*, p. 264; *Young India*, 15 November 1928.

15 Ibid., p. 235; *Young India*, 13 November 1924.

16 Ibid., p. 236; *Harijan*, 16 November 1934.

17 Mohan Rao, *The Message of Mahatma Gandhi*, p. 73; *Young India*, 6 April 1921 and 2 April 1925.

18 Mohan Rao, *The Message of Mahatma Gandhi*, p. 78; *Harijan*, 26 July 1942.

19 M. K. Gandhi, *India of My Dreams*, Ahmedabad: Navjivan Publishing House, 2011 reprint (1947), p. 104; *Harijan*, 29 August 1936.

20 Gandhi, *India of My Dreams*, p. 120.

21 Ela R. Bhatt, 'The spirit of khadi', *The Indian Express*, 3 February 2015.

22 M. L. Dantwala, 'Trusteeship: Its Value Implications', in J. D. Sethi (ed.), *Trusteeship: The Gandhian Alternative*, New Delhi: Gandhi Peace Foundation, 1986, pp. 40–44.

23 V. K. R. V. Rao, 'Trusteeship as Gandhian Instrument for Socialist Change', in J. D. Sethi (ed.), *Trusteeship: The Gandhian Alternative*, New Delhi: Gandhi Peace Foundation, 1986, pp. 27–28.

24 J. D. Sethi, *Trusteeship: The Gandhian Alternative*, New Delhi: Gandhi Peace Foundation, 1986, pp. 76–94.

25 E. F. Schumacher, *Small Is Beautiful: A Study of Economics as If People Mattered*, London: Vintage and Random House, 1993.

26 Ibid., p. 121.

27 Ibid., pp. 39–40.

28 Ibid., pp. 249–250.

29 Muhammad Yunus, *Building Social Business: The New Kind of Capitalism That Serves Humanity's Most Pressing Needs*, New York: Public Affairs, 2010, p. 2; also see Muhammad Yunus, *Creating a World without Poverty: Social Business and the Future of Capitalism*, New York: Public Affairs, 2007.

30 Sudheendra Kulkarni, *Music of the Spinning Wheel*, New Delhi: Amaryallis, 2012.

31 Prabhu and Rao, *The Mind of Mahatma Gandhi*, p. 188; *Young India*, 23 February 1921.

32 Ajit K. Dasgupta, *Gandhi's Economic Thought*, London: Routledge, 1996, p. 18.

33 Prabhu and Rao, *The Mind of Mahatma Gandhi*, p. 242; *Young India*, 20 December 1928.

34 M. V. Nadkarni, *Ethics for Our Times*, New Delhi: Oxford University Press, 2011, p. 47.

13

REVISITING SOCIALISM
Solution to our socio-economic problems

> Socialism is a beautiful word and in so far I am aware in socialism all members of the society are equal – none low, none high. . . . Socialism was not born with the discovery of the misuse of capital by capitalists . . . socialism, even communism, is explicit in the first verse of *Ishopanishad*.
>
> Mahatma Gandhi[1]

> Poverty is not due to a weakness of individual character but is a problem of social structure and economic mismanagement.
>
> Beatrice Webb[2]

Gandhian philosophy, as well as all the great religions of the world, has deep socialistic underpinnings. They have been deeply concerned with problems of poverty, economic inequality and social injustice, although they never attempted to draw a blueprint of changing the existing economic and social order, and have been appealing to the moral conscience of human beings to create a good society.

'Socialism', as understood in the modern sense, is an 18th- and 19th-century European construct, when political philosophers such as Robert Owen, Proudhon, Saint Simon and Karl Marx noted the evils of industrialization and propounded theories for creation of a more just and equitable social order. However, socialism acquired a 'dubious overtone', as it came to be practised in the Soviet Union, under Stalin and his successors, and became a model for many countries after the Second World War in East Europe, China and elsewhere. It symbolized a system where the state controlled not only the means of production and distribution but every aspect of citizens' lives, suppressing individual liberty and freedom.

Post–Second World War, the leading economies of Europe, such as Britain and France, embraced the basic tenets of socialism, moved towards reduction of economic inequality and provided social security to their citizen. However, due to exigencies of cold war between the two post–Second World War superpowers, the US and its allies branded 'socialism', as practised by the USSR and its satellites, purely in terms of an economic system and claimed that their system of economic management which was described as 'free market economy' or 'capitalism' is superior. This was clearly wrong and misuse of socialist terminology and meant to obfuscate the issue. Philosopher Ludwig Wittgenstein has warned us how language can mislead and trap our thoughts. We should understand that 'socialism' is not limited to the manner in which economy is managed; its fundamentals are rooted in human values, which mankind has been cherishing from time immemorial.

What is socialism?

The most fundamental characteristic of socialism is the creation of an egalitarian society. A basic tenet of socialism is reduction of current inequality of income, wealth and power in society. Socialists maintain that under capitalism, vast privileges and opportunities derive from hereditary ownership of capital and wealth. A second feature of socialism is a belief in constructing an alternating egalitarian system based on the values of solidarity and cooperation. The third characteristic of socialism is a belief in human beings and their ability to cooperate with each other to create a good society. They have rejected views that stress individual self-interest and competition as the sole motivating factors of human behaviour.[3]

Karl Marx who had the most profound influence in the socialist movement believed in economic determinism and gave an economic interpretation to movement of society. He changed the concept of property, which had the effect of drawing a line between the classes that owned the means of production and the proletariat. If the exploitation of an individual by another individual is to be abolished, the means of production should be owned not by individuals but by the community. When Lenin seized power in the Soviet Union in 1917, as a faithful follower of Marx, he abolished private property in one stroke, and all the means of production and distribution were taken over by the state. The *Encyclopaedia Britannica* defines socialism as a 'social and economic doctrine that calls for public rather than private ownership or control of property and natural resources'.[4] This, of course, was a very limited view of socialism. Over 60 years of centralized planning showed that it failed to deliver the promised manna. In the late 1980s, economic disaster struck the Soviet Union and its Eastern former satellites, and their economies collapsed. The then Soviet president Mikhail Gorbochev gave a call for perestroika (restructuring) and glasnost (openness). Born of a commitment to remedy the economic and moral defects of capitalism, Soviet socialism far surpassed capitalism in both economic malfunction and moral cruelty.

Democratic socialism

India was never enamoured of socialism of the type practised by the Soviet Union. At the height of Soviet power, India's leading socialist thinker Jayaprakash Narayan expressed his disenchantment (1951) in no unmistakable terms.

> Communism has presented mankind with a kind of civilization, based on amoral ethics – a civilization in which every aspect of individual and social life is controlled by an irreplaceable ruling clique. The society has its own political and economic structure and its own theoretical rationalization, which is often far removed from reality as the north from the south pole.[5]

He made a distinction between totalitarian communism and democratic socialism, and condemned the former and lauded the latter. 'The central problem of socialism is to re-organise the economic and political life of society as to abolish exploitation, inequality and injustice on one hand, and preserve on the other, individual freedom and efficiency.'

Social democracy is a political ideology that has as its goal the establishment of democratic socialism through reformist and gradualist methods.[6] It is a policy regime involving a universal welfare state and collective bargaining schemes within the framework of a capitalist economy. Social democrats have advocated for a peaceful and evolutionary transition of the economy to socialism through progressive social reform of capitalism. Social democracy asserts that the only acceptable constitutional form of government is a representative democracy under the rule of law. It promotes extending democratic decision making beyond political democracy to include economic democracy to guarantee employees and other economic stakeholders sufficient rights of co-determination. It supports a mixed economy that opposes the excesses of capitalism such as inequality, poverty and oppression of various groups, while rejecting both a totally free market and a fully planned economy. Common social democratic policies include advocacy of universal social rights to attain universally accessible public services such as education, health care and workers' compensation, and other services, including child care and care for the elderly.

The Fabians and socialism in Britain

Karl Marx had little following in Britain. There was a strong socialist movement in Britain in the late 19th and early 20th centuries led by a small idealist group known as the Fabian Society. The Fabians rejected the Marxian doctrine. They concluded that a democratic state which was prepared to embark upon social reform, a working class well organized and politically informed and a nation with growing self-consciousness cannot be treated from the standpoint of revolution and class struggle. They believed in social transformation on the principle of 'inevitability of gradualism'. There were several schools of thought regarding common ownership of the means of production. One was the notion of workers' control, which found expression in guild socialism. The guilds were self-regulating autonomous bodies of producers and merchants. Another idea was consumer cooperatives. A third and more dominant idea was that centralized planning and control was necessary to avoid wasteful duplication of resources and to ensure adequate level of investment. One of the most powerful thinkers of the Fabian Society Sidney Webb believed that socialism essentially involved a powerful state machine, and it was his influence that helped shape the movement towards the state owning the major industries as the main method of socialist advance.

The Labour Party came to power in 1945 on the basis of the manifesto which called for ownership of key industries, and the then prime minister Clement Attlee's government carried out the main nationalization programme. The Labour government is also credited with creating a welfare state. It tackled five major problems afflicting the society: want, disease, squalor, ignorance and idleness. The aim was to end poverty and provide sickness and unemployment benefit, retirement pension and widow and maternity benefit. The reform also included provision of compulsory education up to the secondary level and tackling the housing problem. A national health service was created and the National Insurance Act was enacted. Britain became truly a socialist state to look after everyone from the 'cradle to the grave'. These reforms were based on Beveridge Report published in December 1942. Its bold social principles were universal coverage, full employment, family allowances, benefits in return for contributions, a national health service and the right to citizen welfare with the intention to win the peace and remake British society following the ravages of war. It was the intellectual influence of Fabian socialists which helped create the welfare state. Its most powerful voice was Beatrice Webb, who had a vision of creating a good society, free from poverty. In her 1909 Minority Report to the Royal Commission on Poor Law, she observed, 'Poverty is not due to a weakness of individual character but is a problem of social structure and economic mismanagement.'[7]

Over the years Great Britain and other developed countries, as also developing countries like India, faced a new set of problems with nationalized/sate-owned industries. Insulated from competition with powerful trade unions calling the shots, many of them became inefficient with management bureaucratized and a drag on the economy. When Margaret Thatcher became prime minster in the 1980s, she launched a large-scale drive of privatization and withdrawing of the state from economic activities, under the free market ideology, a doctrine she shared with US president Roland Regan. Privatization of state-owned enterprises was part of the neoliberal model of economic development. In two decades of practice of free market ideology, the world has moved full circle. The US and Western European countries faced the worst economic crisis, since the Great Depression of the 1930s, and were forced to turn Keynesian, with the state taking an active role in management of the economy.

Socialism and the state

Socialists, contrary to popular belief, were not committed to the glorification of the state or to the extension of its powers. The links of socialism are with liberalism and with anarchism, with emphasis on individual free-dom and opposition to the extended state. For instance, Guild Socialists and Syndicalists rejected the state. They believed that the state is an instru-ment of oppression. The revolution that has to be brought about is to be a double revolution – a revolution against the capitalists, the economic exploiters, and a revolution against the bureaucrats and the politicians, the exploiters of political life. Clarifying the socialists' attitude towards the state, Nobel Prize–winning economist Arthur Lewis observes:

> Socialism and nationalization of property are now commonly identified, but this is as great an error as the identification of socialism and the extended State. Socialism is not, in the first instance, about property any more than it is about the State. Socialism is about equality. A passion for equality is one thing that links all socialists; on all others they are divided. Because they are concerned about equality socialists have to be concerned with property, since the present system of property is the most important cause of inequality. But subject to over-riding claims of equality, socialism is not committed to any one way of dealing with property, and property can be handled in many ways that are not inconsistent with socialism.[8]

In Britain after coming to power in 1945, the Labour government nationalized all the key industries. This was largely due to the intellectual influence of Sidney Webb, an influential member of the Fabian Society, who was 'a worshiper of state'. When India began its planning in the 1950s, it was greatly influenced by the British model, and all major and heavy industries which were set up were in the public sector. But as noted earlier, the identification of socialism, with the state running the major industries, is an error. It is the doctrine of economic equality and social justice which is the core of socialist philosophy.

Keynesian and the state

Today most of the successful countries of the West have incorporated the values of socialism in their economic system. This has been largely due to the influence of Keynesian economics which made out a convincing case for government's direct intervention in the economy and manage demand. In Europe, the Keynesian economics, put into practice in post-war years up to the early 1970s, helped in the prolonged period of eco-nomic growth, leading to higher level of standard of living and a greater portion of national income devoted to welfare expenditure. Margaret Thatcher, when she became prime minster (1979), felt that the socialist policies of the Labour government were largely responsible for the slug-gish growth of the British economy and launched a massive drive of pri-vatization and reducing the size of the welfare state. Nevertheless, it was not possible to shrink the state beyond a point – as welfarism has become a universally accepted creed. In Britain public expenditure, which was 43 per cent of the GDP in 1980, came down to 40 per cent by 1990 as a result of ruthless cutting, but again jumped to 50 per cent in 2010 – largely due to massive public spending to fight the recession *and has only marginally come down thereafter*. Keynesian economics has dramatically transformed the nature of 'capitalist – free market' economies of the West. The US was able to fight the Great Depression of the 1930s under President Roosevelt's New Deal programme, which helped revive the economy and create jobs. This strategy was again put into practice in 2008 and 2009 to fight the meltdown afflicting the Western economies.

Today, we can say that most of the advanced countries of the West, with the possible exception of the US (where President Obama has made a bold attempt to introduce a state-supported medical welfare system), have become socialist democracies and incorporated their values in their political and economic systems.

Nordic countries and social democracy

The Nordic social democracy refers to the economic and social models of Denmark, Finland, Norway and Sweden, which involves a combination of a free market economy and a welfare state. Nordic countries are at the top of everything from economic competitiveness to social health to happiness. They have avoided both Southern Europe's economic downturn and America's extreme inequality. The Nordic model is distinguished from other types of welfare states by its emphasis on maximizing labour force participation and promoting gender equality, egalitarian and extensive benefit levels and a large magnitude of income redistribution. Some of the key characteristics of this model are an elaborate social safety net in addition to public services such as free education and universal health care and public pension plans and high percentage of workers belonging to labour unions.

The Nordic countries have a collective population of 26 million. They have a very high level of public spending to meet the welfare needs. Government expenditure as a percentage of GDP is 57 per cent in Denmark and Finland, 52 per cent in Sweden and 43 per cent in Norway (2014). High public spending is sustained by high tax collection. Tax burden as a percentage of GDP is among the world's highest – Denmark, 48 per cent; Sweden and Finland, 44 per cent; and Norway, 42 per cent (2014).[9] In the Nordic countries 30 per cent of the labour force works in the public sector, which is twice the average of the Organization for Economic Cooperation and Development countries. Their philosophy is combining open economics and public investment in human capital. They pride themselves as having the least economic inequality among all the nations of the world – the Gini coefficient being just around 0.25. The Nordic countries provide a conducive atmosphere to private enterprise and is home to some of the most prestigious corporates. Denmark is world leader in shipping (Maersk), toys (Lego), drink (Carlsberg) and windpower. Sweden boasts of world-class manufacturing companies such as Ikea, Volvo and Ericsson. Norway is world leader in oil services and fish farming.[10]

The Nordics ranked the highest on the metrics of real GDP per capita, healthy life expectancy, freedom to make life choices and freedom from corruption. Former Soviet president Mikhail Gorbachev's ideal was to move the USSR in a similar direction to the Nordic system, combining free markets with a social safety net – but while retaining public ownership of key sectors – ingredients that he believed would transform the USSR into a socialist beacon for all mankind.

Sweden is a world leader in quality of life, has one of the highest per capita incomes, practically has no unemployment and is one of the most competitive economies in the world. In Sweden,[11] the government expenditure as a percentage of GDP was over 60 per cent over the past several decades, and had touched a level of 70 per cent in 1983, but this has been brought down to the 52 to 55 per cent level in the last few years, to contain welfare spending and enhance competitiveness. The high public expenditure is sustained through high taxation – the personal income-tax rates are over 45 per cent, one of the highest among the advanced industrial economies – and had peaked to a marginal tax rate of 60 per cent for white-collar workers and 80 per cent for managers in 1983. Sweden combines generous welfare benefits with what one can term as free enterprise economy. Besides universal health care, old-age pension and unemployment cover, Sweden provides benefits such as free education up to higher secondary and paid maternity leave for two years after the birth of a child and has the highest percentage of women in the workforce among the Western countries.

Prof. Michael Newman[12] describes five components of Swedish socialism. The first component is 'integrative democracy', with democratic decision making as the ultimate standard of legitimacy. Workers participate on equal terms in the organization and governance of society. The second component is the concept of 'people's homes', whose goals are solidarity, togetherness and equality of treatment. The third component is socio-economic equality and economic efficiency as complementary rather than contradictory goals. The fourth component is socially controlled political economy, rather than nationalization. This means abandonment of preoccupation with ownership, giving primacy to the market forces and emphasis on bargains between industrialists and labour. The fifth component is proper expansion of the public sector, which helped enhance security for ordinary people. *The Economist* after doing a detailed survey of Nordic countries concluded:

> The main lesson to learn from the Nordics is not ideological but practical. The state is popular not because it is big but because it works. . . . You can inject market mechanisms into welfare state to sharpen its performance. You can put entitlement programmes on sound foundations to avoid beggaring future generations. But you must be willing to root out corruption and vested interests.

175

You must be willing to abandon tired orthodoxies of the left and right and forage for good ideas across the political spectrum.[13]

Relevance of socialism today

The global economic crisis of 2008, which seriously impacted the US and West European countries, has shown the hollowness of the capitalist model and has put the philosophy of socialism once again at centre stage. Studies by distinguished economists such as Nobel laureate Joseph Stiglitz and Jeffrey Sachs and many other eminent scholars have shown that unregulated free market system creates vast economic inequalities. Most recently, Thomas Piketty in his monumental study *Capital in Twenty-First Century* has established how inequality is embedded in the capitalist system itself, as the return on capital is much greater than the wages of toiling masses, generating extreme inequality that stirs discontent and undermines democratic values. It is now well established that from the 1980s onwards, particularly in the US and UK, inequality has been rapidly increasing. Similar trends are appearing in India, posteconomic liberalization – its most visible symbol being the emergence of a large number of dollar billionaires controlling a large chunk of the country's economy. All the benefits of economic growth are cornered by a miniscule upper 1 per cent of the population, while the income of majority of the people in the bottom of the economic ladder remains stagnant, with a huge army of unemployed who are unable to find work.

In an essay, on socialism, Albert Einstein had observed,

> This crippling of individuals I consider the worst evil of capitalism. I am convinced there is only *one* way to eliminate these grave evils, namely through the establishment of a socialist economy, accompanied by an educational system which would be oriented toward social goals.[14]

It is apparent that throughout the world, the life chances of the wealthy, in terms of health, life expectancy, educational opportunities, travel and job satisfaction, are vastly greater than those of the poor. As inequality is embedded in the social structure, legal guarantee of 'equality of opportunity' remains a hollow word. As a political commentator observed:

> Indeed equality of opportunity is an empty notion unless the social setting to which it refers is structured on the basis of inequality. Thus the very use of the term, in a sense, sanctifies and accepts as constant predicament what socialism is bent on annihilating.[15]

In order to create an egalitarian society, we have to work towards a system in which life chances are not allocated by structural inequalities in social, economic and political constructions of societies. This is the laudable aim which socialism, when understood correctly, aspires.

Notes

1 M. K. Gandhi, compiled by R. K. Prabhu, *India of My Dreams*, Ahmedabad: Navjivan Trust, 1947–reprint 2011, pp. 22, 24; (*Harijan*, 13–7–1947; 20–2–1937).

2 *Fabian Policy Report, Beveridge at 70, quote from Beatrice Webb, Minority Report*, 1909, available at http://www.fabians.org.uk/wp-content/uploads/2012/12/Beveridge-supplement_29.11_SPREADS.pdf (accessed 6 February 2015).

3 For a detailed discussion, see Michael Newman, *Socialism: A Very Short Introduction*, Oxford: Oxford University Press, 2005, pp. 1–4.

4 See *Socialism*, Encyclopaedia Britannica, available at http://www.britannica.com/EBchecked/topic/551569/socialism (accessed 6 February 2015).

5 Jayaprakash Narayan, 'Foreword', in Asoka Mehta (ed.), *Democratic Socialism*, Bombay: Bhartiya Vidya Bhawan, 1963, pp. ix, xi.

6 For details, see *Social Democracy*, Wikipedia, available at http://en.wikipedia.org/wiki/Social_democracy (accessed 7 February 2015).

7 *Fabian Policy Report, Beveridge at 70, Beatrice Webb, Minority Report*, 1909, available at http://www.fabians.org.uk/wp-content/uploads/2012/12/Beveridge-supplement_29.11_SPREADS.pdf (accessed 6 February 2015).

8 W. Arthur Lewis, *The Principle of Economic Planning*, London: Dennis Dobson-George Allen & Unwin, 1954, pp. 10–11.

9 '2015 Index of Economic Freedom', *Heritage Foundation/Wall Street Journal*, available at http://www.heritage.org/index/explore?view=by-variables (accessed 8 February 2015).

10 For a detailed discussion, see survey 'Special report, the Nordic countries', *The Economist*, 2–8 February 2013, pp. 9, 1–16.

11 Newman, *Socialism*, pp. 53–64.

12 Ibid., pp. 55–56.

13 *The Economist*, 2–8 February 2013, p. 9.

14 Albert Einstein, 'Why Socialism?', *Monthly Review*, May 1949, available at http://monthlyreview.org/2009/05/01/why-socialism (accessed 8 February 2015).

15 Zygmunt Bauman quoted by Newman, *Socialism*, pp. 141–142.

14

GOOD GOVERNANCE
Pre-requisite for development

In the happiness of his subjects lies the king's happiness;
in their welfare his welfare.
He shall not consider as good only that which pleases him,
but treat as beneficial to him whatever pleases his subjects.
                                        Kautilya: Arthashastra[1]

We can no longer afford to pay more for – and get less
from – our government. The answer to every problem cannot always be another programme or more money. It is
time to radically change the way the government operates –
to shift from top down bureaucracy to entrepreneurial
government that empowers citizens and communities to
change our country from bottom up. We must reward the
people and ideas that work and get rid of those that don't.
                            Bill Clinton and Al Gore, US National
                                        Performance Review[2]

Good governance is increasingly being realized as the primary reason
behind the success story of the West. It is widely perceived that India's
dismal record in economic and social development is largely due to poor
governance. Governance is the exercise of political, administrative and economic authority to manage a country's affairs. Governance in common
parlance is understood as 'state' or the 'government', though in broader
sense it encompasses the private sector and civil society as well. Government consists of three wings – parliamentary, judicial and executive –and it
is on effective functioning of all the three wings that good governance can
be secured. However, it is the executive which plays the most crucial role in
governance, as that is where people have an interface with the government
in their day-to-day affairs. In this chapter we discuss the 'public administration' or 'public services' component of the government.
    Good governance implies a high level of organizational effectiveness in
policy formulation and capacity to implement it. Unfortunately, in India,

178

the capacity to implement policy is sorely lacking due to malfunctioning of the administrative machinery. Policymakers are aware of the problem, but very little has been done to fix it. The Tenth Five-Year Plan had noted,

> While the functions of the State in India have steadily widened, capacity to deliver has steadily declined over the years due to administrative cynicism, rising indiscipline, and a growing perception that the political and bureaucratic elite views state as an area where public office is to be used for private ends.[3]

The 11th Five-Year Plan makes a candid admission, 'Corruption in public services has today assumed serious dimension . . . corruption is a major factor in the wastefulness, inefficiency and inequities we find in public administration today.'[4] The Second Administrative Reforms Commission (ARC), which made wide-ranging recommendations for improvement of public administration, noted that 'inefficiency, corruption and delays have become in public perception, the hallmark of public administration today' and observed, 'Often systematic rigidities, needless complexities and over-centralization make public servants ineffective and helpless in achieving positive outcomes. On the other hand, negative power of abuse of authority through flagrant violation of law, petty tyranny and nuisance value is virtually unchecked.'[5]

Reforming public services

> Here are the six characteristics of Bureaucracy. They are first, the disadvantages of excessive centralization, impersonality, departmentalism, rigidity, complexity, and finally incompetence. To find a remedy for this evil we must replace each of them by their opposite, thus introducing delegation, responsibility, coordination, flexibility, simplicity and effectiveness.
>
> C. Northcote Parkinson[6]

Reforming public services holds the key to good governance.[7] The biggest problem that we face today is our continuing adherence, seven decades after independence, to the Weberian model of bureaucracy, which we inherited from the British. The Weberian bureaucracy constitutes a career, with a system of promotion based on seniority, fixed remuneration for officials with a right of pension, organized as hierarchy and adhering to rigid rules. Experience has shown that these old-fashioned bureaucracies are unresponsive to people's need, as they are embroiled in red tape and formalism, love tradition, and stand for conservatism and status quo. Today's environment, where developments in the field of computers, electronics and avionics have crushed time and space, demands institutions which are extremely flexible and adaptable so that they are capable of delivering high-quality services to the people and meet multiple challenges in a complex globalized world. Advanced countries such as the UK, New Zealand, Australia, Canada, the US, Japan and Singapore have discarded the Weberian model of bureaucracy and embraced a new administrative philosophy, known as New Public Management (NPM), with dramatic increase in public service efficiency. The main component of NPM philosophy is performance and delivery of services, customer focus and devolution of authority.

In India, several high-level committees and commissions consisting of eminent men have come out with laudable recommendations to reform public management systems, but most of their recommendations have remained unimplemented. As a result, we are trapped in an outdated bureaucratic machine for which the people of this country are paying a heavy price. The main reasons for poor functioning of public services are absence of accountability; lack of professionalism; poor work culture; outdated laws, rules and procedures; highly centralized administrative system; and politicization of services. It is time we bring fundamental reforms in public administration and make them efficient so that they serve the needs of people.

Bringing accountability in public services

One of the main reasons for poor performance of public services is lack of accountability. Accountability can be brought about by: (a) linking promotion and career advancement of a public servant with actual performance on the job, (b) bringing competition and specialist knowledge in civil services and (c) enforcing strict disciplinary regime.

Emphasize performance

Today in public services there is hardly any emphasis on job performance and incentive for hard and meritorious work. Promotions are made on the basis of Annual Confidential Reports, which an employee's superior officer writes, and everyone gets his or her promotion when his or her turn comes. This encourages mediocrity and ignores meritorious and dedicated workers. The Second ARC[8] noted that the existing system of performance appraisal is unsatisfactory and has suggested that it should be transparent with a 360-degree feedback, there should be numerical rating on the pattern of the armed forces and an independent third party be associated with assessment. ARC's most important suggestion is a comprehensive in-depth assessment, at important milestones in an officer's career – first review be done on completion of 14 years of service and another on completion of 20 years. If he or she is found unfit after second review, the service may be terminated. A government servant's promotion, career advancement and continuance in service should be linked to his or her actual performance on the job and the dead wood should be weeded out.

Bring competition and specialist knowledge
for senior-level appointments

The task of policymaking in government is complex and needs specialist knowledge of the subject. Under the existing system most senior-level appointments in the Central Secretariat as well as top field-level posts are made from among the Indian Administrative Service (IAS) officers who are generalists. The First ARC, far back in 1969, had emphasized the need for specialization by civil servants as a prequalification for holding senior-level posts and had suggested that all the services should have an opportunity to enter middle-and senior-level management levels in the Central Secretariat and selection should be made by holding mid-career competitive examination, which should include interview, to be conducted by Union Public Service Commission (UPSC). The Surendra Nath Committee[9] (2003) and Hota Committee (2004),[10] set up by the government, had also emphasized domain knowledge and merit as the bases for appointment to the posts of joint secretary and above in the government.

The Second ARC has observed that the present process of empanelment of officers for the post of joint secretary and above is not fair, objective and transparent, and overlooks the real merit of the officer and his or her suitability for a particular job. It has identified 12 domains in which officers should specialize. It has recommended that domains should be assigned to all the officers of the All India Services and Central Civil Services on completion of 13 years of service and vacancies at the level of deputy secretary/director should be filled only after matching the domain competence of the officer for the job. The commission has suggested introduction of competition for senior positions in the senior administrative grade and above (joint secretary level) by opening these positions to all the services. For higher administrative-grade posts (additional secretary and above), recruitment for some of the posts could be done from the open market. It has further suggested constitution of a statutory Central Civil Services Authority which should deal with matters of assignment of domains, preparing panel for posting of officers at different levels, fixing tenures and determining which posts should be advertised for lateral entry.

It is imperative that the running of government be professionalized, and joint secretary and higher posts in the Central Secretariat, as well as all SAG/HAG (senior/higher administrative grade) posts in the field such as Commissioner Income Tax, Collector Central Excise, Accountant General, Chief Engineer and Director Health Services, should be thrown open for competition, to not only candidates within the civil services but also competent professionals such as corporate executives, academics, engineers, doctors, lawyers and chartered accountants, if we wish to bring real efficiency in the public services. (However, to prevent demoralization among services, only certain percentage of posts – e.g. 50 per cent – should be open for competition outside the government.) In order to keep objectivity, the selection for these posts should be made by UPSC. In the

UK, Australia, New Zealand and so on, all top posts in the civil services have been thrown open to competition, and selection is done by the Public Service Commission. The proposal, if implemented in true spirit, will meet several objectives: it will help in getting the best person for each job as recruitment will be job specific, it will introduce the much-needed specialization in services and it will take away power of appointment of top posts from the hands of politicians and depoliticize the services.

Enforce an effective disciplinary regime

Public employees are like headless nail, you can get them in, but can't get them out.

Anonymous

At present, the provisions of discipline rule are so cumbersome and tortuous that it becomes very difficult to take action against a delinquent employee for inefficiency, insubordination and misbehaviour. Thus, once appointed it is almost impossible to remove or demote an employee. This results in poor work culture and all-round inefficiency. The provisions of Civil Service Conduct and Discipline Rules are porous and complicated with numerous loopholes and weighted in favour of the delinquent. The Commission to Review the Working of the Constitution (2002),[11] headed by Justice Venkatachaliah, has noted that 'the constitutional safeguards have in practice acted to shield the guilty against swift and certain punishment for abuse of public office for private gain' and suggested revisiting the issue of constitutional safeguards under Article 311, to ensure that while the honest and efficient officials are given the requisite protection, the dishonest are not allowed to prosper in office. The Second ARC has expressed similar views and observed that legal protection given has created a climate of excessive security without fear of penalty for incompetence and wrong doing. There is a need to recast the disciplinary procedure so that quick and summary punishment could be given to delinquent employees, while keeping in view the principle of natural justice.

Transforming work culture

Both the central and state governments have a vast sprawling bureaucracy. Government offices are dominated by clerks, assistants, superintendents, section officers and inspectors, in what is nicknamed *babucracy* (clerk-oriented system, lacking decision making capacity). There is a hierarchical structure in offices with multiple levels of reporting before a decision is taken. Most of the subordinate staff are ill trained and lack commitment towards work. It is a common sight in a government office to find employees loitering, gossiping sipping cups of tea, with no urgency to dispose of work, and showing indifference, if not contempt, towards public.

While the government recruits bright young officers in senior positions through stiff tests conducted by UPSC, and most of them work sincerely, they are overwhelmed by the army of demotivated *babus* (clerks and junior functionaries) around them. Senior civil servants, belonging to 'Group A' Services, out of the total workforce, are just about 2 per cent. Out of 35 lakh central government employees, there are only 70,000 officers, who belong to Group A Services such as IAS, Indian Police Service, Indian Revenue Service, Railways, Engineering and Medical. This lop-sided structure leads to poor work culture and low productivity.

Several committees and commissions have given a vast array of measures for restructuring, reorganizing and downsizing various ministries and departments so that greater efficiency could be brought. (These include First and Second ARCs, Fifth and Sixth Pay Commissions and Expenditure Reforms Commission 2000–2001.) Some of the key recommendations are as follows: (a) the multi-level hierarchical structure should be reduced and an officer-oriented system with level jumping should be introduced, to speed up decision making; (b) in ministries which are policy-making bodies, section should be abolished and a desk officer system should be introduced from where noting of the file should begin; (c) the division of ministerial staff into numerous categories such as assistant, upper division clerk (UDC), lower division clerk (LDC) and personal assistant (PA) should be abolished and replaced by a multi-skilled position called executive assistant who should be computer savvy; (d) government offices should be modernized with provision of computer and other gadgets, and a conducive work environment should be created.

Today the working of the government with its highly diversified function has become very complex. There is need to recruit bright, technically qualified and dedicated personnel at all levels and transform the *babu culture* to officer-oriented system. There is also need to change the attitude of public servants through training and other modern management practices. Public employees are knowledge workers and are less likely to defer to authority and top-down command. They should be motivated and empowered by giving them more responsibility and decision-making authority and instil in them a feeling of pride that they are doing national service.

Outdated laws, rules and procedures – need for streamlining

A large number of rules and procedures relating to citizens' day-to-day interface with the government in matters such as registration of property, sanction for construction of dwelling units, licence for starting a business, inspection of factories, payment of taxes and licence fees are outdated and complicated and give opportunity to public servants to delay and harass citizens. These rules need to be updated and simplified, and discretionary power of public servants needs to be eliminated.

A good part of efficiency of a government office depends on sound personnel, financial and procurement systems. Many of these rules such as

Fundamental and Supplementary Rules, Conduct Rules, General Financial Rules and Delegation of Power Rules were framed during the British rule or during the 1950s and 1960s and bear a heavy imprint of 'control mindset', with emphasis on check and balance and lack of trust and suspicion. The existing rules relating to budgetary utilization lead to a huge waste of money, as it gives perverse incentives to rush expenditure and use up allotted funds, towards the end of fiscal year in March. Many advanced countries have shifted to multi-year budgeting. The UK now has a three-year budgeting cycle, with no lapse of money at the end of fiscal year. Ministries and departments have not been given adequate powers to transfer funds from one expenditure head to another; as a result, huge money lapses at the end of financial year. They need to be given greater flexibility to transfer funds between various heads and schemes as per their need and priority, within the overall budgetary allocation. The procurement rules require buying from the lowest bidder after floating a tender. This 'one-size-fits-all rule' often results in unreliable suppliers undercutting prices and supplying inferior products. The rule plays havoc when buying high-tech products or making procurement for large-value projects. There is need to give freedom to executing departments to buy best-value products, keeping in view the guiding principles of equity, integrity and efficiency.

At present, there are hundreds of statutes, some of them of 19th-century vintage passed by the British administration, which have become obsolete but exist on rule book. They create all-round confusion and give opportunity to public officials to harass citizens. A five-star hotel in Delhi was issued notice for prosecution by municipal authorities for not serving free drinking water to passers-by under the Sarais Act of 1867 – the real reason was the refusal of the hotel to pay bribes to municipal staff. Bibek Debroy in his book *In the Dock: Absurdities of Indian Law*[12] makes a forceful plea for junking old statutes and dysfunctional sections of laws. The Commission to Review Administrative Law (1998), the Law Commission and the Ramanujam Committee (September 2014) have identified a large number of statutes which have become obsolete and need to be repealed. Successive government's action has been slow and halting. However, the present NDA government has taken this work more seriously and brought two bills before Parliament and repealed 125 of these laws (2015). The government has also introduced two more bills, seeking to repeal 1,053 acts, and they are pending in Parliament (December 2015).[13] There cannot be greater indictment of government's indifference to reform and modernize administration than the fact that hundreds of old, outdated and dysfunctional laws still exist on statute book.

Highly centralized system

The administrative system is marked by a high degree of centralization, with all powers concentrated in the central ministries and directorates, with very little delegation to field outfits that execute projects, programmes and schemes and are at cutting edge of interface with people. The ARC and Pay Commissions have been advocating decentralization, but very little action has been taken. The Sixth Pay Commission had observed,

> There should be decentralization and delegation of powers with clear accountability at each level of delivery combined with flatter management structures so that responsibility is pushed down to the operational level and to the employees who are close to cutting edge.[14]

A centralized system is largely due to psychology of 'mistrust' and 'exercising control' over subordinate formations. Wide delegation of powers to operating agencies in the field is necessary for effective functioning of public services.

Create performance-based organization

> Individuals can form communities, but it is institutions alone that can create a nation.
>
> Benjamin Disraeli[15]

We need to create new institutions of governance to make public services efficient. Advanced countries such as Britain, New Zealand, Australia, Canada, Singapore and the US have revamped the bureaucratic system and migrated to professional management of the bulk of the government activity thorough creation of 'agency' or 'performance-based organizations'.[16] Operational freedom and flexibility have been given to individuals in the field who implement programme and schemes by placing trust in their ability to deliver results. In Britain, which took the lead in reforming public services, the chief executives of agency are selected through competition open to both public and private sectors and are hired on the basis of a contract. Each agency negotiates an annual performance agreement with its parent department that includes measurable targets of financial performance, efficiency and service quality. The creation of executive agencies has resulted in substantial gains in efficiency in the British public services. Reviews by the Treasury and Civil Service Committee of the House of Commons and other expert bodies have concluded that executive agencies have brought about 'overall transformation in government' and termed it as 'the single most successful reform programme in recent decades'.

Many scholars of management in India, including this author, support the philosophy of NPM and agencification model, which implies creation of performance-based organizations for revamping public administration.[17] Prof. Pradeep N. Khandwalla says,

> Agencification seems to represent the best hope of making the machinery of governments in India efficient, economical,

sensitive to citizens needs and staff needs, clean, objective and agile. This promises to do basically by transforming bureaucratic management into professional, stakeholders sensitive, performance oriented management.[18]

India should draw lessons from the experience of other countries and move towards creation of performance-based organizations for public service delivery. This will make the machinery of government efficient, economical and sensitive to citizens' needs and transform it into professional and performance-oriented management.

Politicalization of services

One of the most serious problems facing public administration is politicalization of higher civil services. The political masters often resort to arbitrary and questionable methods of appointments, promotions and transfers, which corrode their morals and independence. It gives rise to temptations to civil servants, with weak moral fibre, to work in collusion with politicians, do their bidding and gain advantage in terms of promotion, cushy postings and foreign assignments. To prevent unholy nexus between politicians and civil servants, several high-level committees have recommended constitution of Civil Services Authority to formulate norms and evaluate and recommend officers for senior positions in government. They have also recommended fixed tenure for senior civil servants, as frequent transfers prevent an officer from discharging his or her duty effectively. There is an imperative need to depoliticize appointment, transfer, promotion and other service matters of civil servants so that they can function objectively and efficiently.

The relationship between a minister, secretary and departmental head is most delicate in a democracy, as ministers due to their political and party interest sometimes try to influence and pressurize civil servants. The principle of good administration requires that civil servants function in a politically neutral and impartial manner. In the UK, the Ministerial Code of Conduct requires that ministers have a duty to uphold political impartiality of civil servants and not ask them to act in a manner that would conflict with the Civil Service Code. In India the relationship between civil servants and ministers is very fuzzy. It is necessary that the relationship be governed by rule of law and public interest. There is need for a suitable legislation to define the powers of political executives vis-à-vis civil services so that they are able to function independently and objectively.

The corruption challenge

Corruption is recognized as one of the major problems facing the country. It obstructs national development and has serious adverse effects on the society, corroding the moral fibre of people. According to Transparency International's Corruption Perception Index (2015), India's score is just 38 out of 100 and is ranked at the bottom half, at 76th place out of 168 countries for which the index has been prepared.

Corruption is a symbol of something that has gone wrong in the management of the state. It undermines the legitimacy of the government as people become cynical about it. Corruption is defined as misuse of public office for private gain. There are generally two types of corruption: *coercive* and *collaborative*. *Coercive corruption* is one where a person is forced to give bribe to get a job done to which he is otherwise entitled, such as getting a ration card, a driving licence, a passport, an electric connection or a sanction for constructing a building. Such corruption is endemic to how the government carries out its routine activities, such as issue of licence, permit, policing and revenue collection. *Collaborative corruption* is one involving high officials and ministers that often implicates multinationals and large domestic firms, in which both parties gain substantial pecuniary benefits, though the public is the ultimate loser. They mostly relate to mega projects, large-value contracts, concessions and other favours and difficult-to-prove nexus, as both bribe givers and bribe takers are beneficiaries. While both the coercive and collaborative corruptions are inter-related, and it is not easy to draw a dividing line, the countries which are rated as 'very corrupt' have a high incidence of coercive corruption, where corruption is institutionalized and citizens have to pay bribes for even basic services to which they are entitled, making day-to-day life difficult.

Some of the reasons for corruption in our country are as follows: (1) weak laws and regulations to punish the guilty due to which corruption has become a high-reward and low-risk activity; (2) the system of fighting elections in which money power plays a decisive role; (3) the economic policies and rules and procedures of conduct of the business of government; (4) the influence of big business, corporates and multi-nationals on government; and (5) the societal and cultural attitudes and values of society and its moral standards.

Corruption at high places was the hallmark of the political scene during the past three to four decades. This reached its zenith during UPA II regime, when corruption scandals such as 2G spectrum case, Coalgate and Commonwealth Games drew widespread media attention and public uproar. An anti-corruption crusade was launched under the leadership of veteran Gandhian Anna Hazare and other activists. This finally led to Parliament passing the Lokpal Act in December 2013 and creation of an institutional mechanism to deal with corruption cases against people holding high public office. People's anger against corruption was also one of the reasons for rout of Congress in the elections of May 2014, which resulted in NDA coming to power.

In India corruption thrives as 'it is a low-risk high-profit business'. There are many safeguards and protection built in the system that it is very difficult to take action against an official indulging in corruption. While there is a Prevention of Corruption Act, the judicial process is slow, with cushions of safety built, and majority of delinquent officials escape punishment. Even the institution of Lokpal, created after much public uproar, has remained non-functional, as appointment of its members is caught in bureaucratic rigmarole (April 2016). It takes a great deal of political will to tighten the law against corruption and enforce it.

While a good legal framework together with an effective implementation machinery is necessary to check corruption, this alone is not sufficient. The societal attitude and moral standards of people play an important part. Unfortunately, during the past few decades there has been a steep decline in values and character in society. The model of development, with materialist ideology and consumerism that we have embraced, is largely responsible for decline in values. Earning money and leading a life of luxury and opulence has become the primary goal of life for majority of people, without caring for the means to earn it. This is in contrast to India's cultural ethos, which stands for the virtue of 'simple living and high thinking'. From time immemorial, Indian culture has stood for high ideals of truth, honesty, self-discipline, controlling indulgence and service to society. We should use our great cultural heritage to inculcate noble values in society at every level – in children and youths in school and colleges, among public servants and among people in general. This is the most effective means to check the menace of corruption.

Inculcating values – an ethics code for public servants

Public managers can provide good governance only if they have moral and ethical commitment. Public administration is about caring for every citizen and transcends family, ethnicity, gender, racial and religious affiliation. Moral governance reflects basic values such as common good, democratic pluralism and controlling corruption. Morality instils public confidence and trust in government. Public administration scholar Gerald Caiden and O. P. Dwivedi observe,

> The objective of good governance is to create an environment in which public servants as well as politicians are able to respond to the challenges of good governance. The challenge of public officials involves a notion of duty, as well as acting morally and accountably. . . . Confidence and trust in democracy can be safeguarded only when the governing process exhibits a higher, credible and real ethical stand, deriving from justice, equity and morality.[19]

Considering the importance of moral values in management of public services, most advanced countries have prescribed a code of ethics for public servants and created a suitable infrastructure to enforce them.[20] In the UK, a Committee on Standards of Public Life headed by Lord Nolan laid down the following seven principles of public life: *integrity, objectivity, accountability, openness, selflessness, honesty and leadership*. The Nolan Committee report formed the basis of formulating a code of Civil Service Values which were issued in 1996 and further amplified in 2006. The code, which has now a statutory backing, enjoins that civil servants are expected to carry out their roles with dedication and a commitment to civil services values of integrity, honesty, objectivity and impartiality. *Integrity* is putting the obligations of public services above your own personal interests; *honesty* is being truthful and open; *objectivity* is basing your advice and decisions on rigorous analysis of the evidence; *impartiality* is acting solely according to the merits of the case and serving equally well governments of different political persuasions.

In the US, as part of an initiative to promote ethics and financial integrity in the government, the Congress has passed Ethics in Government Act of 1978, which among other things has established the Office of Government Ethics (OGE). The core principle enunciated by OGE is that employees hold their positions as a public trust. They will fulfil that trust by adhering to principles of ethical conduct, as well as specific ethical standards. Public trust implies that employees shall not use public office for private gain and employees shall act impartially and not give preferential treatment to any private organization or individual. OGE's ethics infrastructure includes prevention, investigation and prosecution.

Countries which are known for honest administration such as Australia, Canada and Singapore have all prescribed Code of Ethics, enjoining high standards of integrity and efficiency on the part of public servants. The United Nations has also adopted an International Code of Conduct for public officials.

India should learn from the experience of the countries which provide good, corruption-free administration. There is an imperative need to lay down a statutory code of values and ethics for public servants, together with suitable ethical infrastructure for enforcing it, so that integrity and probity of public services is maintained.

The challenge of public service reform – need for political will

Reforming public services poses a formidable challenge to the government. Since independence a large number of official committees and commissions, consisting of eminent men, have made recommendations for administrative reforms, but their key recommendations involving fundamental changes have not been acted upon. The political leaders, at both the centre and state, have very little interest, as they are obsessed with holding on to power and manipulating civil services for their narrow partisan end. They have failed to appreciate that larger social and economic reforms in the country cannot be brought about without reforming public services. The bureaucracy has deep-vested interest in maintaining the status quo and resists any reform, and thwarts any move to make it accountable and performance oriented. Veteran civil servant N. C. Saxena sums up:

> Governance reforms are intractable under a 'kleptocracy' that exploits national wealth for its own benefits and is, by definition, uninterested in transparency and accountability. A pliable and unskilled civil service is desirable from its point of view – public

employees dependent on the regime's discretionary largesse are forced to become corrupt, cannot quit jobs, and reluctantly become the regime's accomplice.[21]

Gunnar Myrdal, Noble Prize–winning sociologist, had observed, more than four decades ago, that Indian leaders are unwilling to govern vigorously and disinterestedly and take hard and unpopular decisions and described India as a 'soft state'.[22] There is need for political will at the highest level to bring meaningful reforms. Only a coalition of strong political will, with radical elements in bureaucracy devoted to public cause, can bring about the desired change. It is time political and administrative leadership make a sobering realization that without public service reform, the much-talked-about development of the country cannot take place.

Notes

1 L. N. Rangarajan, *Kautilya: The Arthashastra*, New Delhi: Penguin Books, 1992, p. 149.
2 Report of the National Performance Review – Vice President Al Gore, *Creating a Government That Works Better and Costs Less*, Washington: US Government Printing Office, 1993, p. i.
3 Government of India, Planning Commission, *Tenth Five Year Plan 2002–07*, Vol. I, New Delhi: Planning Commission, 2002, p. 22.
4 Government of India, Planning Commission, *Eleventh Five Year Plan, 2007–12*, Vol. I, New Delhi: Oxford University Press, 2008, pp. 236–237.
5 Government of India, Second Administrative Reforms Commission, *Refurbishing Personnel Administration: Scaling New Heights, 10th Report*, New Delhi: GOI, 2008, pp. 1–3.
6 C. Northcote Parkinson, 'Excessive Control and Bureaucracy', in P. K. Agarwal and N. Vittal (eds), *I Am Sorry: Indian Bureaucracy at Crossroads*, New Delhi: Manas Publication, 2005, p. 121.
7 For a detailed discussion regarding problems of public service and measures to reform them, see B. P. Mathur, *Ethics for Governance: Reinventing Public Services*, New Delhi: Routledge, 2014, Chapters 15–18, pp. 197–270; *Governance Reform for Vision India*, New Delhi: Macmillan, 2005, Chapters 4–8, pp. 55–185.
8 Government of India, Second Administrative Reforms Commission, *Refurbishing Personnel Administration*, pp. 172–212.
9 Department of Personnel, *Report of the Group Constituted to Review the System of Performance Appraisal, Empanelment and Placement for the All India Services and Other Group A Services*, July 2003, available at http://persmin.gov.in/DOPT/Publication/CommitteeReport/ACRReport/contents.htm (accessed 2 April 2016).
10 Department of Personnel, *Committee on Civil Services Reform (Hota Committee)*, July 2004, available at http://www.darpg.gov.in/sites/default/files/CivilServiceReforms2004.pdf (accessed 2 April 2016).
11 Government of India, *Commission to Review the Working of the Constitution*, March 2002, Vol. I, p. 186, Section 6.7.4.

12 Bibek Debroy, *In the Dock: Absurdities of Indian Law*, New Delhi: Konarak Publishers, 2000.
13 Bibek Debroy, 'Old but not gold', *The Indian Express*, 23 July 2015, p. 14, available at http://www.dnaindia.com/india/report-govt-s-plan-to-repeal-over-1000-obsolete-laws-remains-stuck-in-rajya-sabha-2159903 (accessed 31 March 2016).
14 Government of India, *Report of the Sixth Pay Commission*, 2008, Vol. I, p. 366, para 6.3.5.
15 Benjamin Disraeli, 'No more heroes', *Times*, 23–30 January 2006, p. 36.
16 For a detailed exposition about New Management Philosophy, see Mathur, *Ethics for Governance*, Chapters 17 and 18, pp. 233–270.
17 See Mathur, *Ethics for Governance*, pp. 258–265.
18 Pradeep Khandwalla, *Transforming Government through New Public Management*, Ahmedabad: Ahmedabad Management Association, 2010, p. 216.
19 Gerald E. Caiden and O. P. Dwivedi, 'Official Ethics and Corruption', in Gerald E. Caiden, O. P. Dwivedi and Joseph G. Jabbra (eds), *Where Corruption Lives*, Sterling, VA: Kumarian Press, 2001, pp. 254–255.
20 For a detailed discussion, see Mathur, *Ethics for Public Services*, Chapters 19–21, pp. 271–312.
21 N. C. Saxena, *Challenges of Good Governance*, New Delhi: India International Centre, Occasional Publication, 2014, No. 62, p. 37.
22 Gunnar Myrdal, *Asian Drama: An Enquiry into Poverty of Nations*, Vol. I, London: Allen Lane, 1968, pp. 273–277.

Part IV

CULTURE AS FOUNDATION
OF DEVELOPMENT

15

INDIAN CULTURE
A spiritual and humanistic approach to life

Today we are still living in this transitional chapter of world history, but it is already becoming clear that a chapter which had a Western beginning will have to have an Indian ending if it is not to end in self-destruction of human race. In the present age, the world has been united on the material plane by Western technology. But this Western skill has not only 'annihilated distance'; it has armed the peoples of the world with weapons of devastating power at a time when they have been brought to point-blank range of each other without yet having learnt to know and love each other. At this supremely dangerous moment of human history, the only way of salvation of mankind is the Indian way. The Emperor Asoka's and Mahatma Gandhi's principle of non-violence and Sri Ramarishna's testimony to the harmony of religions; here we have an attitude and spirit that can make it possible for human race to grow together in a single family – and, in the Atomic Age, this is the only alternative to destroying ourselves.

Arnold Toynbee[1]

[In] the 21st century we need a new ethic that transcends all religions. Far more crucial than religion is our elementary human spirituality. It is a predisposition towards love, kindness, and affection that we all have within us, whatever religion we belong to. . . . It (India) is a society that lives by secular ethics. . . . All in all Indian society is peaceful and harmonious. All religious persuasions uphold the ancient Indian principle of non-violence, ahimsa, with which Gandhi was so successful. It was the foundation of peaceful coexistence. That is practical secular ethic that transcends all religion. The present day world would do well to emulate it.

Dalai Lama (2015)[2]

India's ancient culture is embedded in humanistic values, as it aims at welfare and happiness of human beings. To appreciate this, we should understand the basic values of our ancient culture and civilization.

What is culture?

Human history is the history of civilizations. Civilization is basically a cultural entity. Culture basically means shared belief and values of a group of people or nation. According to Samuel P. Hutington,

> Civilization and culture both refer to the overall way of life of a peo-ple, and a civilization is a culture writ large. They both involve the val-ues, norms, institutions, and modes of thinking to which successive generations in a given society have attached primary importance.[3]

Civilizations' unique feature is their long historical continuity. Empires rise and fall, governments come and go, but civilization remains and sur-vives political, social, economic and ideological upheavals. While civiliza-tions endure, they also evolve. They are dynamic; they rise and fall; they merge and divide, and they also disappear and are buried in sands of time.

Historian Arnold Toynbee says that behind every civilization there is a spiritual vision which he defines as 'an endeavor to create a state of soci-ety in which whole of Mankind will be able to live together in harmony, as members of a single all inclusive family'.[4] Civilizations remain invis-ible, though there are some manifestations like art which are visible, but they are merely its outer expression and have to be analysed in terms of ideas and values. According to Toynbee, culture represents 'regularities in the behavior, internal and external, of the members of a society'.

According to Hutington,[5] religion is a central defining characteristic of civilization, and the great religions are the foundation on which great civilizations rest. He points out that out of five great religions, four – Christianity, Islam, Hinduism and Confucianism – are associated with major civilizations. The only exception is the fifth major religion, Bud-dhism, but in countries such as Japan, Korea, Vietnam and China, it was adapted and assimilated with the local culture.

Historian S. Abid Hussain defines 'culture' in the following words:

> Culture is a sense of ultimate values possessed by a particular society as expressed by its collective institutions, by its individual members in their dispositions, feelings, attitudes and manners as well as in significant forms which they give to material objects.

Abid Hussain further elaborates that religion in its wider sense coincides with, and goes beyond, culture, and in its narrower sense forms part of it.

> Where religion signifies the inner experience which reveals to the mind the real meaning and purpose of life, it is the very soul of

culture; but where it is used for the external form in which the inner experience has crystallized itself, it is only part of it.[6]

Distinguished litterateur and freedom fighter K. M. Munshi defines culture as follows:

It is the characteristic way of life inspired by fundamental values, in which people live. It is the sum total of the values expressed through art, religion, literature, social institutions and behavior, the overt acts of individuals and mass action inspired by collective urges.[7]

According to K. M. Munshi,[8] the first characteristic of culture is continuity. It comes from the past, adjusts itself to the present and moves forward to shape the future. Such continuity expresses itself in various ways: in common tradition and norms of conduct, in common institutions, in common memory of triumphs achieved, in common aesthetic outlook and in a capacity of common collective action. The most important characteristic of a vital culture is a common outlook among the people, which when faced with difficulty, resistance of adversity, can generate a collective will for action. The vitality of a culture is determined by the fact that there is a *central idea* which has the power to replenish itself. The vitality of the culture lasts only so long as the best of its men in the dominant minority of each generation find self-fulfilment by living up to its fundamental values afresh. These values of a culture are recaptured for each generation by a subtle process of re-interpretation, re-integration and adaptation.

Prof. G. D. Sharma[9] outlines the salient characteristics of culture as follows. (a) It is an acquired behaviour, learned from the elders in the family and in the society. It is not inborn and instinctive behaviour. The 'learned' behaviour is a gift of society, not of nature. (b) The 'learned behaviour' determines the 'Way of Life', of the group (society), and is expressed in the 'Way of Living'. (c) It is transmitted from generation to generation. In this transmission certain changes do take place, but the fundamentals remain unaffected. (d) Culture is internal to man, when distinguished from civilization. Prof. Sharma says that all cultures have human values, but the difference lies in hierarchy of these values.

For every culture the value it represents are the ultimate values. There can be no compromise on this point. If the values in a society are decaying or becoming weaker, it is clear sign of culture's decline. Similarly, on the other hand, the restoration of the values in a society is the rejuvenation of its culture.

Culture is internal to the man, whereas civilization is manifested in outward possession. 'Culture is the mental equipment of life, whereas civilization is the material equipment of life. The present day Indians subscribe to the Indian culture (to be more correct cultural values) and follow (ape) Western civilization.'

Distinctive feature of Indian culture

According to Prof. Radhakamal Mukerjee,[10] Indian civilization has three distinct features. First, it is its continuity for about 5,000 years, which shows its vitality with roots in humanistic spirit and distinctive system of values and social arrangement. Second, Indian civilization through several centuries established a unity of Asian civilization. Third, India's reflection on the problems of human life and society has produced and nurtured a mental pattern distinct from Western's. This pattern believes in peace and harmony. The state, politics and conquest are far less significant in India than metaphysics, religion, myth and art as factors of social integration.

The foundation of Indian culture rests on an ethico-spiritual view of life. While discussing the essential features of Indian culture, Swami Bodhananda[11] observes that Indian culture is essentially a culture of coexistence and a mindset of inclusion, as distinct from monotheism with its emphasis on coercion and conversion. This is reflected in the statement *Vasudhaiva kutumbakam*, that is the world is one family. The Indian world view is fundamentally pluralistic. Indian culture believes in the coexistence of different faiths. Indians regard the material world as an expression and an inalienable part of the spiritual reality. Hence, they have a healthy respect for nature and all living forms.

According to Swami Ranganathananda, universality and humanism are the two essential characteristics of Indian culture. 'Its concern is with the man as such and not man cut up into caste, creed, sect or race. The achievement of man of the highest glory and excellence what it seeks.'[12] The glory and excellence is achieved through the increasing manifestation of man's spiritual potential through education.

The salient features of Indian culture can be described as follows:

1 tolerance and accommodation of everyone;
2 oneness and solidarity of universe and all life;
3 essential divinity of human being;
4 family as basic unit of social system;
5 ashram culture – evolution through four stages of human life: *brahamcharya* (life of student and acquisition of knowledge), *grihastya* (house-holder), *vanaprastha* (retirement from worldly responsibilities), *sanyas* (total renunciation and freedom from dependence on people, money and objects);
6 *purusharth* – all human urges and aspirations as *artha* (wealth), *kama* (worldly pleasures), *dharma* (righteous living) and *moksha* (salvation).[13]

According to Indian philosophy, all human urges and aspirations, called *purusharthas*, can be placed in four categories. In actual life, a human being first seeks sensory satisfaction – not merely food, clothing and shelter but also love, sex and social appreciation. All these come in the category of *kama*. To satisfy this, one needs *artha* or wealth. The ancient wisdom says that it is a combination of *dharma, artha* and *kama* – the doctrine of *trivarga* (three goals of life) – which secures the welfare and happiness of people. *Trivarga* strikes a balance between the interest of the individual and the public. But there is a caveat. While the pursuit of *kama* and *artha* is a legitimate activity, it must be regulated by *dharma* and secondary to it. In Indian tradition, *dharma* has been the guiding principle for all human endeavours and needs to be practised by individuals as well the state.

Dharma sustains and ensures progress and welfare of the individual and society and embraces every type of righteous conduct, covering all aspects of life. *Dharma*, according to Justice M. Rama Jois, is

> Justice (*Nyaya*), what is right in a given circumstance, moral values of life, pious obligation of individuals, righteous conduct in every sphere of activity, being helpful to other living beings, giving charity to individuals in need of it or to a public cause or alms to the needy, natural qualities or characteristic or properties of living beings and things, duty and law as also constitutional law.[14]

A key feature of Indian culture is family as a basic unit of society. C. Rajagopalachari observes:

> The large joint family is a special pattern of ours. It is an institution which gives a distinctive feature to life in India. The institution is still alive, not quite wiped out by impact of the West and its cult of individuality. . . . The joint family is a socialist institution within itself and at the same time, the individual is a potentially free person. The joint family is perhaps the chief characteristic of Indian life differentiating it from Western way of living.[15]

Acharya Mahapragya and A. P. J. Kalam in their book *The Family and the Nation* plead strongly for preserving India's traditional family values to make us a strong and happy nation. 'The family is an institution of love, care, compassion and kindness. It brings progress, prosperity, peace and tranquility in society. It nurtures values and makes human being civilized.'[16]

The essence of Indian culture

Every culture and civilization has behind it the inspiration of a philosophy. While Indian culture has experimented with life in various ways, its most unique contribution is in the field of religion and philosophy. The origin of Indian culture, which is more than 5,000 years, can be traced back to the Vedas. In the Vedic philosophy and its quintessence Upanishad, the basic principle of the universe, the ultimate reality on which cosmos exists, is the principle of *ritam* (the word 'right' is derived from it). This implies that the right moral order is built into this universe. Hence, truth and right are linked: to penetrate through illusion and understand the ultimate truth of human existence is to understand what is right. According to Indian thought, the spirit pervades the whole universe and the material world is merely a manifestation of that spirit. There is an infinite knowledge, power, purity and bliss behind the body–mind complex. Swami Vivekananda said, 'Each soul is divine. The goal is to manifest this divinity within, by controlling nature, external and internal.'[17] *Brahman* is the ultimate all-pervading reality: the inner essence of everything. This is expressed in Vedic saying: *aham brahmasmi (Brihadaranyaka Upanishad* 1.4.10), that is existence is a field of infinite potentialities. One should boldly take up the worldly responsibilities and accept the challenges of life as it gives expression to one's inner potentialities. Vedanta teaches the technique of self-development. The ultimate destiny of an individual is to discover within himself or herself the true self as the changeless behind the changing, the eternal behind the ephemeral and the infinite behind the finite.

The essence of Indian wisdom is most succinctly expressed in the Bhagavad Gita. According to Aldous Huxley, 'Gita is one of the clearest and most comprehensive summaries of the perennial philosophy ever to have been made. Hence, its enduring value, not only for the Indians but for all mankind.'[18] Mahatma Gandhi described the Gita as his mother, 'When I am in difficulty or distress, I seek refuge in her bosom.'[19] While the Gita offers a complete philosophy of life, its key message for the modern individual is its doctrine of *karmayog*. This is expressed in two famous *shlokas* (verses): *karmanev adikarste ma phaleshu kadachan* (verse II.47) and *yoga karmesu kaushalam* (verse II.50), that is perform your duties diligently and piously, excel in it, but without any expectation of the results. The teachings of the Gita have the most telling appeal to leaders and shakers of society as well as to the common man, all those engaged in the pursuit of earning and righteous living, where they have to face battles of life, struggle, accept challenges and keep moving on.

According to Swami Ranganathananda, the essence of a culture is expressed in the type of man that finds his own highest excellence manifested:

A culture is worldly, if worldly success is what its most admired hero represents. If there is any truth in calling Indian culture spiritual, it derives from the fact that the most admired hero of the Indian people has been, and is a man of God.[20]

Expressing similar views, Dr S. Radhakrishnan says,

The ideal man lives always in the light of heaven, and his life embodies the great virtues of truth, purity, love and renunciation. Moral progress is judged not by man's power over the forces of nature, but his control over the passions of the heart. To speak the truth under the shower of the bullet, to refrain from reprisals even when you are on the Cross, to respect man and animals, to toil for others, and turn the other cheek, are the principal duties of man.[21]

Emphasizing that the Indian culture is basically spiritual, Sri Aurbindo observes:

> Spirituality is the master key to Indian mind; the sense of infinite is native to it. India saw from the beginning that life cannot be lived in the sole power of externalities. But she saw that the physical does not get its full sense until it stands in right relation to the supra-physical; she saw that the complexity of the universe could not be explained in the present terms of man or seen by his superficial sight, that there were other powers within man himself of which he is normally unaware, that he is conscious only of a small part of himself, that the invisible always surround the visible, the supersensible the sensible, even as infinity surround the finite.[22]

India's spirit of synthesis

Throughout its long history India has assimilated various religions and cultures with which it has come in contact. Its culture has become richer as a result of absorbing what is best of outside influences and integrating those influences to enrich its own identity. Dr K. M. Munshi sums it up:

> Indian culture is a living force. It absorbs alien elements when necessary but transmits them to a new pattern of homogenous richness. . . . Its vitality has been shaping attitudes, discipline and approaches to life to suit new conditions, age after age – as vigorously in the past as in the present.[23]

Prof. Radhakamal Mukerjee further elaborates:

> Even in midst of bitter struggles with foreign peoples establishing themselves on Indian soil, the genius of Indian culture was maintained: its spirit of assimilation, comprehension, and synthesis was able to meet the challenge of diversity and conflict. The great formative period of Indian history, the significant religious, artistic and philosophical movements through the ages, throw into sharp relief India's persistent efforts at reconciliation and concord amidst political and racial conflicts and struggles that would have overwhelmed any other culture. This distinctive cultural pattern, the outcome of accumulated forces of environment, tradition and race, has maintained a remarkable continuity for well nigh five millennium – a unique achievement in the history of the world. It has found articulate expression in India's basic metaphysical notions of unity and solidarity of life, and of the Real, Universal

Man (Visvatman); her religious doctrine of universality of creeds, sects and Dharma; her political conception of universal sovereignty (Sarva-bhauma), which upholds the universal Dharma; and her ethical conception of the commonality of the earth community.[24]

Although religious discord in the first half of the 20th century led to creation of Pakistan, and occasional conflicts arise between Hindus and Muslims even now, its root cause is political and vote bank politics, rather than cultural differences. There is a basic harmony between Hinduism and Islam. Historian Abid Hussain explains:

> But an unbiased study of contemporary history will show that it was not religious feeling itself but extraneous elements which had become associated with religion; vested interests which used the name of religion for their own purpose, started the separatist movement culminating in the partition of the country. As far as pure religion is concerned, there is a fundamental harmony in the inner spiritual experience of Hindus and Muslims. No doubt on the level of positive religion – dogma, ritual, religious law – there are considerable differences which could lead to perpetual conflict. But the heart of India which supplies life blood to Muslims as well as Hindus has been so nurtured on the breadth of mind and vision of mystic traditions, that religious antagonism leading to war, which was a common phenomenon in Europe in Middle ages, was rare in Indian history. Even in the last thousand years when two religions as different as Hinduism and Islam were brought together on the soil of India, her saints and Sufis created an atmosphere of not only toleration but of harmony, so that while Hindu and Muslim princes were struggling for power, the common people of both religion could live together in harmony.[25]

Hinduism, which has shaped the Indian culture, has never been rigid or stagnant. Dr Radhakrishnan says, 'Hinduism is a movement, not a position; a process, not a result; a growing tradition, not a fixed revelation.'[26] In the modern phase, Mahatma Gandhi was the best example of the capacity of Hinduism for synthesis, combining it with Western thought and rejecting the undesirable features of Hindu society. Prof. M. V. Nadkarni observes:

> The synthesis of Hinduism has two significant features. Firstly, it did not wipe out the culture, value system, customs and sometimes even the rituals or the method of religious practice of people with whom the synthesis was achieved. Secondly, the synthesis was achieved often by rediscovering and invoking its own earlier values in the scriptures and traditions of Hinduism, without having to lose Hinduism's own identity. Hinduism became more diversified at the same time. The synthesis represented change as well as continuity.[27]

Essential unity of all religions

Secularism does not mean irreligon or atheism or even stress on material comfort. It proclaims that it lays stress on the universality of spiritual values which may be attained by a variety of ways.

Dr S. Radhakrishnan[28]

Hinduism being the dominant religion of India, ancient scriptures such as the Vedas, the Ramayana and the Mahabharata have made a deep impact on the Indians' way of life. At the same time, the scriptures and teachings of other religions such as the Bible and the Quran have also profoundly influenced the Indian mind. Indians have always recognized scriptures of various religions and their teachings as a common heritage of the whole humanity. Islam has brought a spirit of brotherhood and social equality in Indian society. The Sufi tradition in Islam has much in common with the mysticism of Vedanta. Contact with Christianity during the period of British domination helped revival of Hinduism and reinstating the spirit of service to society. Buddha is considered an Indian deity and worshipped. His greatest disciple, Emperor Asoka, renounced violence and preached tolerance of other religions and brotherhood of man, an ideal which has made a deep impact on Indian thought. Indian music, art, architecture, poetry and literature is a rich amalgam of diverse cultures. India has thus developed a composite culture, in which various religious and cultural groups live in peace, harmony and brotherhood.

From ancient times India accommodated followers of all the religions of the world, as its people recognized that beyond differences in outward rituals and practices, the ideals of all the religions are the same. Bharat Ratna recipient Bhagwan Das in his classic study *Essential Unity of All Religions*[29] has graphically described harmony and concord among all the religions of the world. This rich tradition of equal respect for all belief systems is expressed in the saying *sarva dharma sambhava* (respect for all religions and belief systems). There are five immortal values preached by all the religions of the world: *satya* – truth, *dharma* – righteous conduct, *shanti* – peace, *prem* – love and *ahimsa* – non-violence.

- *Satya* not only means truth but also implies the maxim 'there is no religion higher than truth'.
- *Dharma* connotes righteousness, nobility, proper conduct and a philosophy of life for harmonious living.
- *Shanti* transcends peace – it implies a calm mind, serenity and inner peace.
- *Prem* is not simply love but encompasses compassion and brotherhood of mankind.
- *Ahimsa* is not only non-violence but a feeling of kinship and oneness with all life.

In order to inculcate the universal message of religions, a Parliamentary Standing Committee of the Ministry of Human Resource Development, headed by S. B. Chavan (1999), had reiterated these five core values, which can be the foundation of all educational programmes: Truth (*satya*), righteous conduct (*dharma*), peace (*shanti*), love (*prem*) and non-violence (*ahimsa*).[30] These are universal values and represent the five domains of human personality – intellectual, physical, emotional, psychological and spiritual. Ramakrishna Mission, which is doing pioneering work on value education, has found that comparative religion recognizes five common values – truthfulness, love, non-violence, righteousness and peace – and called for inculcating them in children in schools.[31] Satya Sai Institute of Human Values has also brought out several erudite publications, explaining that these five common values are preached by all the religions of the world and emphasized the fact that there is basic harmony among all the religions of the world.[32]

Religion should normally be a binding force that should enhance the solidarity of human society. Tragically, religions have often split humanity and have oppressed and terrified people, rather than freeing and inspiring them. Spiritual leaders who are misguided or unethical may play havoc with people who have blind faith in them. Religions are also potential centres of political power – the belief that the dominant national religion is the only true religion may be used to oppress those who follow other beliefs. It may also be a rallying point for war against other nations. Throughout history, large numbers of people have been killed in the name of eradicating 'false religions', replacing the latter with 'true religion'. Mankind at each period of its history cherishes the illusion of the finality of existing knowledge. This illusion causes intolerance and fanaticism, and the world suffers from dogmatism and conformity. For this reason, some of the great thinkers have denounced religion, pointing out that religion has been invented and is used to manipulate people. Sigmund Freud described religion as 'universal obsessional neurosis'.[33] Karl Marx said, 'Religion is the sigh of the oppressed creature, the sentiment of a heartless world, and the soul of soulless conditions. It is the opium of the people.'[34]

There is a need to correct the misunderstanding about religion. Faith without wisdom, without tolerance for and respect for others' ways of life is dangerous. Bharat Ratna recipient Bhagwan Das advises:

> In religion we must make the greatest efforts to maintain what is most indubitable, most in accord with the best science, and more than all else, is most approved and agreed by all concerned, and most likely to promote goodwill and active sympathy between human beings. It is imperative to sift elements of religion from non-essential forms and nourish the younger generation with only vital grains.[35]

The International Religious Foundation, which seeks to explore inter-religious unity and harmony, observes:

> Humankind need to rediscover the spiritual foundations of values in order to overcome the sterile materialist outlooks and philosophies

of our day. Despite both the common moral values and the traditional spiritual wisdom found in all religions, persistent squabbles among all religions have served to discredit them, making universal values appear to be relative and sectarian. The foundations of a pluralistic society – its cultural expressions, legal system, and public schools – require values that are grounded in universal experience of human kind, not in the doctrines of one particular faith.[36]

It goes to the credit of India's ancient culture that it has shown respect to and tolerance of other religions and faiths. This spirit is expressed in a great Vedic verse: *Ekam sad vipra bahudha vadanti* – the Truth is one, sages call it by different names (Rig Veda 1.164.46). It was this catholicity of outlook that led India to declare itself as a secular state and incorporate it in the preamble of the Constitution.

Indian culture – universally admired

Great scholars and philosophers in the West, such as Ralph Waldo Emerson, Henry David Thoreau, Arthur Schopenhauer and Will Durant, were full of admiration for Indian philosophy and culture and derived inspiration from it. The German indologist Max Muller paid a glowing tribute:

If I was asked under what sky the human mind has most fully developed some of its choicest gifts, has most deeply pondered on the greatest problems of life and has found solutions to some of them which well deserve attention of even those who have studied Plato and Kant, I should point to India.[37]

American historian and philosopher Will Durant observed:

India was the motherland of our race, and Sanskrit the mother of Europe's languages: she was the mother of our philosophy; mother, through the Arabs, of much of our mathematics; mother, through the Buddha, of the ideals embodied in Christianity; mother, through the village community, of self-government and democracy. Mother India is in many ways the mother of us all.

Perhaps in return for conquest, arrogance and spoliation, India will teach us the tolerance and gentleness of the mature mind, the quiet content of the unacquisitive soul, the calm of the understanding spirit, and a unifying, a pacifying love for all living things.[38]

Eminent jurist N. A. Palkhivala laments that Indians are unaware of their great cultural heritage.

It has been my long standing conviction that India is like a donkey carrying a sack of gold – the donkey does not know what it is carrying but is content to go along with the load on its back. The load of gold is the fantastic treasure – in arts, literature, culture, and some of the sciences like Ayurvedic medicine – which we have inherited from the days of the splendour that was India.[39]

Many people in the West are gradually embracing the essential features of Indian philosophy. An article by Lisa Miller in *The Newsweek* notes that conceptually Americans are slowly becoming more like Hindus in the ways they think about God, themselves, each other and eternity.[40] A study titled *American Veda* by Philip Goldberg[41] elaborates the influence of Vedantic philosophy and Yoga in America and profoundly affected the world view of millions of Americans and radically altered the religious landscape.

Indian and Western cultural values

Analysing the basic features of Indian and Western cultures, Indian management scholars say that Western culture is masculine, while Indian culture is feminine.[42] In a masculine-oriented culture 'win as much as you can' is the basic ethic and human actions are largely governed by the 'grabbing orientation'. In a feminine-oriented culture, cooperation and sharing are the basic ethics and human actions are largely governed by 'giving orientation'. Another distinguishing characteristic of the two cultures is that in the Western culture 'individual' is the primary unit, while in Indian culture, it is 'collectivist', with 'family' as the primary social unit of interaction. The 'individualistic' approach has given rise to the spirit of 'competition' and 'survival of the fittest', while 'collectivist' approach gives birth to 'cooperation' and *vasudhaiva kutumbakam* as a behavioural pattern.

Analysing Indian ethos, Prof. G.D. Sharma opines that what distinguishes Indian culture from the West is the approach towards life.[43] Indian culture is predominantly a 'spiritual culture', while the Western culture is predominantly a 'materialistic culture'. The Indian culture has a cosmic vision in which the orientation is towards 'welfare', 'social good' and the 'good of the greatest numbers'; on the other hand, the materialist culture is guided by 'economic orientation' and it is guided by 'bottom line' approach. Western society has certain values like independence, initiative, achievement, objectivity and impartiality. These values have grown in an environment in which adults shun family protection and fend for themselves. On the other hand, in Indian society even adults are attached to the joint family and have developed values like interdependence, cooperation and personalized relationship.

Simple living and high thinking is a characteristic feature of Indian culture. Because of the influence of religion and spirituality, hankering after material possessions has never been our goal. Self-abnegation and self-sacrifice have been our values. For this reason Mahatma Gandhi, who believed in the virtue of simple living, became a national hero and enjoyed a countrywide following, which eventually led to our freedom from

British rule. Swami Vivekananda said, 'In the West they are trying to solve problem how much can a man possess and we are trying here to solve the problem on how little a man can live.' The Indian philosophy leads to seeking of *sattvik gunas* that requires control over one's passions and senses and focuses on the development of qualities of sympathy, empathy, comradeship and brotherhood. On the other hand, in the West *rajas gunas* are adorned. This leads to an approach of manipulating physical and social environments for human development and mastering nature.

India cannot progress imitating the West

The idea of analysing distinguishing cultural traits of India and the West is not to pass value judgement about superiority or inferiority of the two cultures. As the world is today getting integrated as a result of technological progress and annihilation of time and distance, certain common and universal values cherished by the whole of humanity have emerged. Nevertheless, there are strong differences in values between different nations and culture. Any development model has to be culture specific to be successful. For this reason, our leaders had warned against blind imitation of the West. Swami Vivekananda cautioned:

> Imitation is not civilization. . . . Imitation, cowardly imitation, never makes for progress. It is the very sign of degradation in a man. . . . Learn everything that is good from others, but bring it in, and in your own way absorb it; do not become others. . . . Look back, therefore, as far as you can, drink deep of the eternal fountain that are behind, and after that, look forward, march forward and make India brighter, greater and much higher than she ever was.[44]

Sri Aurbindo says,

> India can at best develop herself and serve humanity by being herself and following the law of nature. This does not mean, as some narrowly and blindly suppose, the rejection of everything new that comes to us in the stream of Time or happens to have been first developed or powerfully expressed by the West. . . . It means simply to keep our centre, our essential way of being, our inborn nature and assimilate to it all we receive, and evolve out of it all we do and create.[45]

Mahatma Gandhi was not enamoured of Western civilization with its materialistic orientation, self-indulgence, exploitation and domination over others and cautioned:

> European civilization is no doubt suited for the Europeans but it will mean ruin for India, if we endeavor to copy it. This is not to

say that we may not adopt and assimilate whatever may be good and capable of assimilation by us, as it does not also mean that even the Europeans will have to part with whatever evil might have crept into it. The incessant search for material comfort and their multiplication is such an evil, and I make bold to say that Europeans themselves will have to remodel their outlook, if they are not to perish under the weight of comforts to which they are becoming slaves. It may be that my reading is wrong, but I know that for India to run after the Golden Fleece is to court certain death. Let us engrave in our heart the motto of a Western philosopher, 'plain living and high thinking'.[46]

There are fundamental differences between Indian and Western outlooks about life and its purpose. Therefore, a model of economic development which has been successful in the West may not succeed here. *It is important we appreciate our great civilizational heritage; do not blindly imitate Western ideas, values and economic ideology; and devise a model of development which is in synergy with our cultural and spiritual ethos.*

Notes

1 Arnold Toynbee, 'Foreword', in Swami Lokeshwarananda (ed.), *World Thinkers on Ramakrishna Vivekananda*, Calcutta: Sri Ramakrishna Institute of Culture, 1983, p. 5.
2 Dalai Lama, 'Ethics Is More Important Than Religion', *Reader's Digest*, July 2015, pp. 110–116, interview by Franz Alt.
3 Samuel P. Hutington, *The Clash of Civilizations and the Remaking of the World Order*, New Delhi: Penguin Books, 1996, p. 41.
4 Arnold Toynbee, *A Study of History*, London: Oxford University Press and Thames and Hudson, 1972, pp. 43–46.
5 Hutington, *Clash of Civilizations*, p. 47.
6 S. Abid Hussain, *National Culture of India*, New Delhi: National Book Trust, 1978, p. 3.
7 K. M. Munshi, *Foundations of Indian Culture*, Mumbai: Bhartiya Vidya Bhawan, 2012, p. 4.
8 Ibid., pp. 5–11.
9 G. D. Sharma, *Management and Indian Ethos*, New Delhi: Rupa & Co., 2001, pp. 4–6.
10 Radhakamal Mukerjee, *The Culture and Art of India*, London: George Allen and Unwin, 1959, p. 9.
11 Swami Bodhananda, *Indian Management and Leadership*, New Delhi: Bluejay Books and Srishti Publishers, 2007, pp. 211–226.
12 Swami Ranganathananda, *The Essence of Indian Culture*, Kolkata: Advaita Ashram, 2011, pp. 31–32.
13 For a detailed discussion, see Sharma, *Management and Indian Ethos*, pp. 9–28.
14 M. Rama Jois, *Dharma: A Global Ethic*, Mumbai: Bhartiya Vidya Bhawan, 1997, pp. 1–2.

15 C. Rajagopalachari, *Our Culture*, Mumbai: Bhartiya Vidya Bhawan, 2005, pp. 16–17.
16 Acharya Mahapragnya and A. P. J. Abdul Kalam, *The Family and the Nation*, New Delhi: Harper Collins, 2008, p. 133.
17 Swami Vivekananda, *His Call to the Nation*, Calcutta: Advaita Ashram, 1969, p. 47.
18 Aldous Huxley, 'Introduction', in Swami Prabhavananda and Christopher Isherwood (transl.), *Bhagvad-Gita: The Song of God*, Madras: Sri Ramakrishna Math, 2000, p. 10.
19 M. K. Gandhi, *Gita the Mother*, Jag Parvesh Chander (ed.), Lahore: India Printing Works, 1946–47, p. 5.
20 Swami Ranganathananda, *Essence of Indian Culture*, p. 27.
21 S. Radhakrishnan, *Indian Religions*, New Delhi: Orient Paperbacks, 1999, p. 63.
22 Sri Aurbindo, *The Foundations of Indian Culture*, Pondicherry: Sri Aurbindo Ashram, 1998, pp. 398–399.
23 K. M. Munshi, *Pilgrimage to Freedom*; quoted by N. A. Palkhivala, *Essential Unity of All Religions*, Mumbai: Bhartiya Vidya Bhawan, 2003, p. 2.
24 Mukerjee, *Culture and Art of India*, p. 383.
25 Abid Hussain, *National Culture of India*, pp. 7–8.
26 Dr Radhakrishnan quoted in M. V. Nadkarni, *Hinduism: A Gandhian Perspective*, New Delhi: Anne Books, 2008, p. 149.
27 Ibid., p. 153.
28 S. Radhakrishnan, 'Foreword', in S. Abid Hussain (ed.), *National Culture of India*, New Delhi: National Book Trust, 1978, p. vii.
29 Bhagwan Das, *Essential Unity of All Religions*, Bombay: Bhartiya Vidya Bhawan, 1990.
30 Parliamentary Standing Committee, Ministry of Human Resource Development, *81st Report on Value Education, 1999*, extract reproduced in *Value Education*, New Delhi: Sri Satya Sai International Centre for Human Values, 2009, pp. 87–89.
31 Ramakrishna Mission, *Value Education: Proceedings of a Seminar on Value Education, March 2002*, New Delhi: Ramakrishna Mission, 2002, pp. vi and 10–20.
32 *Value Education*, New Delhi: Sri Satya Sai International Centre for Human Values, 2009.
33 Sigmund Freud quoted by Mary Pat Fisher and Robert Luyster, *Living Religions*, New Jersey: Prentice Hall, 1994, pp. 10–11.
34 Marx quoted by Fisher and Luyster, *Living Religions*, New Jersey: Prentice Hall, 1994, p. 11.
35 Das, *Essential Unity of All Religions*, p. 38.
36 International Religious Foundation, *World Scripture: A Comparative Anthology of Sacred Texts*, New Delhi: Motilal Banarsidass, 1993, p. 3.
37 Friedrich Max Muller, *India: What Can It Teach Us?* New Delhi: Penguin Books India, 2000, p. 6, quoted from lecture delivered in 1886.
38 Will Durant, quotes about India, available at http://hinduism.about.com/od/history/a/indiaquotes.htm; http://indyas.hpage.co.in/quotes-about-india_28580324.html (accessed 2 March 2015).
39 N. A. Palkhivala, *India's Priceless Heritage*, Bombay: Bhartiya Vidya Bhawan, 1994, p. 29.

40 Lisa Miller, 'We are all Hindus now', *The Newsweek*, 15 August 2009.
41 Philip Goldberg, *American Vedas: How Indian Spirituality Changed the West*, New York: Harmony Books, 2010.
42 Sharma, *Management and Indian Ethos*, pp. 30–43.
43 Ibid., p. 33.
44 Swami Vivekananda, *Rebuild India*, Howrah: Ramakrishna Math, 1993, pp. 25–26; *Collected Works*, Vol. III, Calcutta: Advaita Ashram, 1973, p. 302, Vol. II, pp 381–382, 386.
45 Sri Aurbindo, *Foundations of Indian Culture*, Pondicherry: Sri Aurbindo Ashram, 1998, p. 430.
46 M. K. Gandhi, *India of My Dreams*, compiled by R. K. Prabhu, Ahmedabad: Navjivan Publishing House, 2011, pp. 5–6; *Young India*, 30 April 1931.

16

INDIAN CULTURE AND MONEY
Challenge of a materialist world

> Great civilization in the East as well as in the West have flourished in the past because they produced food for the spirit of man for all time; they tried to build their life upon the faith in ideals, the faith which is creative. These great civilizations were at last run to death by men of the type of our precocious schoolboys of modern times, smart superficially critical, worshippers of the self, shrewd bargainers in the market for profit and power, efficient in their handling of the ephemeral, who presume to buy human souls with their money and throw them into their dustbins when they have been sucked dry, and who, eventually, driven by suicidal forces of passion, set their neighbour's houses on fire and are themselves engulfed by the flame. . . . It is some great ideals which creates great societies of men, it is some blind passion which breaks them into pieces. They thrive so long as they produce food for life; they perish when they burn up life in insatiate gratification. We have been taught by our sages that it is truth and not things which saves man from annihilation.
>
> Rabindranath Tagore[1]

> I ask you to ensure that humanity is served by wealth and not ruled by it.
>
> Pope Francis, message to business and political leaders, Devos, January 2014[2]

In the modern world, should money making be the primary aim of human beings, as normal life cannot be lived without it? The Western culture, with its materialistic orientation, considers money making and wealth creation as the summum bonum of life. It is felt that without money the comfort and pleasures which the modern world offers cannot be enjoyed. What does Indian culture say about the importance of money and wealth in human affairs?

Part I

Wealth and its importance in India's cultural tradition

India's ancient philosophy (Hindu philosophy) has deeply reflected on human beings' purpose on planet earth and recognized four goals of life called *pursharth* – *artha* (wealth), *kama* (worldly pleasures), *dharma* (righteous living) and *moksha* (salvation). These goals reconcile worldly pursuits with spiritual goals. The doctrine recognizes that every human being has multiple goals and to pursue them gives meaning and purpose to life. While *moksha* falls in the realm of metaphysics, a normal human being is to pursue the other three goals – *artha*, *kama* and *dharma* – in what is known as *trivarga*. The doctrine of trivarga says that while it is perfectly legitimate to make money, engage in livelihood and enjoy pleasures of life and recreational activities, they must be within the bond of dharma. Dharma is that which sustains progress and welfare of the world and embraces every type of righteous conduct on the part of the individual as well as the state.

Western philosophers such as Max Weber and Albert Schweitzer have expressed a view that Hinduism as well as eastern philosophies are life negating, take mundane world as an illusion and feel that the purpose of human life is to seek liberation from the world and unite with Supreme Reality. Due to this philosophical outlook, they have neglected life in this world, which is responsible for their lack of economic development and backwardness. Weber has developed a theory of cultural roots of capitalism and emphasized that Protestant ethics, more particularly its Calvinist version, has been responsible for developing a work culture and attitude towards life which is responsible for the success and prosperity of Western societies. The conclusion that Indian philosophy is life negating is unfair and an incorrect understanding of it. Historian A. L. Basham in his *Wonder That Was India* observes:

> In ancient India, her people enjoyed life, passionately delighting both in the things of the senses and the things of the spirit. . . . The average Indian, though he might pay lip service to the ascetic and respect his ideals, did not find life a vale of tears from which to escape at all costs; rather he was willing to accept world as he found it, and to extract what happiness he could from it. . . . India was a cheerful land, whose people, each finding a niche in a complex and slowly evolving system, reached a higher level of kindliness and gentleness in their mutual relationships than any other nation of the antiquity.[3]

Mahabharata and material prosperity

It would be instructive to look at some of our ancient scriptures and literature to understand Indian culture's outlook towards money.

Mahabharata discusses two general attitudes to *artha* (wealth), radically opposed to each other. On the one hand, wealth is regarded as the first condition not only of a happy and dignified family life but also of a stable social order. On the other hand, wealth when accumulated gives rise to further desire for it, and therefore lack of happiness and peace, and is destructive of spiritual life. Mahabharata balances these two opposite viewpoints. After the great war, with enormous destruction and bloodshed, Yudhishthira is overcome with remorse, does not want to rule and renounces everything. He is dissuaded by his brothers and given a long sermon on statecraft by Bhishma lying on his death bed (*Shanti-parva*).[4] Arjuna argued for material prosperity, as evident from the following stanzas:

- From increased wealth flow all the good works, as do the rivers from the mountains (8.16 *Shanti-parva*).
- On wealth depends the rise of a family, and on wealth depends the rise of dharma; for him who has no wealth, there is happiness neither in this world nor in the next (8.22 *Shanti-parva*).

To a question from Yudhishthira about what should be the attitude towards money, Bhisma takes a very balanced position and explains that there are contexts in which it is legitimate to regard wealth as a primary factor in life and material prosperity as of great importance in life. However, there are contexts in which craving for wealth would lead to misery and unhappiness.

- Given money a person masters this world as well as the next, and gains access to truth and dharma. With no money, his life is no life at all (*Shanti-parva* 130.43).
- The loss of money and property is for a man a great misfortune, greater than even death; for they, money and wealth, are also the means to his fulfilling his desires and dharma as well (*Udyog* 72.27).

Commenting on the evil effects of money, Bhisma says, 'Striving for money is certainly not conducive to happiness. When obtained one is overcome with desire to protect it' (*Shanti-parva* 177.26) and 'greed for money is suffering' (*Shanti-parva* 177.37).

- The ways of making money are the ways that produce mental obsession, miserliness, arrogance, pride, fear anxiety. For human beings these are money related pain and suffering (*Vana* 2.42).
- Accumulated wealth like beauty, youth, health, and company of dear ones is transitory (*Vana* 2.47).

Mahabharata aims at self-control by individuals. The aim is to prevent the necessity of wealth turning into greed and greed into lawlessness. Wealth should be earned through *dharma*.

- Only that wealth is truly wealth that has been earned in the ways of *dharma*. What has been collected through *adharma* to others is a

213

wealth damned. One should not, in one's greed for money, abandon what is universally right and good (*Shanti-parva* 292.19).

State and money

Mahabharata makes a distinction between individual and the state regarding money. While an individual should have a balanced approach towards money, the state's (king's) coffers should be full, for a kingdom to be powerful and strong. In fact, it is the *dharma* of the king to have an overflowing treasury.

- The strength of a king is based on treasury; army is based on treasury; the social order is based on army; and the people are based on *dharma* (*Shanti-parva* 130.35).
- The king whose treasury is empty is treated by indifference even by the common man; no body is satisfied with the little he gives, and none is eager to work for him (*Shanti-parva* 133.6).
- Let the king fill the treasury: having filled protect it: protecting it, increase it; for in all ages that is the dharma of the king (*Shanti-parva* 133.1–2).

Kautilya, wealth and statecraft[5]

Kautilya, also known as Chanakya, was the brain behind the Maurya dynasty coming to power and Chandragupta ascending the throne of Magadha around 300 BC and ruling a vast empire. He was the first philosopher to recognize the importance of wealth in both personal life and statecraft. The following stanza illustrates,

> *Sukhasya mulam dharma*
> *Dharmsya mulamartha,*
> *Arthasya mulam rajyam*
> Dharma (righteousness) is the root of happiness
> Wealth is the root of dharma,
> The State is the root of wealth.
>
> *Chanakya Sutra*[6]

Kautilya elaborates in great detail the importance of wealth in leading a comfortable and satisfied life:

- All virtues are ever dependent on wealth, wealth captures pleasures, everything is dependent on wealth. Wealth enriches and enhances life.[7]
- The rich are ever happy, the poor ever sad, happiness and sorrow are divided among the rich and poor.[8]

Kautilya was the first political theorist to realize that the accumulation of wealth is key to the power and authority exercised by the state.

- All State activities depend first on the Treasury. Therefore a King should devote its best attention to it[9] (*Arthashastra* 2.8.1.2).
- A king with depleted Treasury eats into the very vitality of the citizens and the country (*Arthashastra* 2.1.16).[10]
- From *kosa* (wealth) comes the power of the *danda* (Government). With the treasury and the army (*kosa–danda*) the earth is acquired with the treasury as the ornament (*Arthashastra* 2.12.37).[11]

Kautilya advocates an activist state taking part in manufacturing and trading and thus augmenting economic prosperity. While emphasizing the need for wealth collection, Kautilya underlines the principle of equity in taxation:

- As the gardener plucks each flower in the garden, without destroying the roots, so should the ruler collect revenue without destroying the source.[12]
- As the bee collects honey gradually from the flowers, so should the ruler fill up the treasury, collecting revenue gradually.[13]

Kautilya is often accused of advocating unscrupulous methods in statecraft and ruthless means to acquire power. This view is not correct. An expert on Kautilya, N. Rangarajan,[14] says that he always added qualification while advocating policies which appeared unjust. Kautilya made a difference between 'individual morality' of a ruler, a minister and high officials and ethics which should govern statecraft. He was a strong advocate of character, discipline and self-control on the part of the king and high public officials. His practical advice is rooted in *dharma*. Eminent scholar R. P. Kangle observes: 'It is not realised that the preservation of the State at all costs is the foremost duty of the ruler and that the interest of the State have to take precedence over all other considerations.'[15]

Religion and money

All the religions of the world have certain common views about life and its relation to the physical world. There is a certain ultimate mystery behind the whole universe, which can be understood only in terms of mind, spirit and consciousness. All religions recognize that virtue and merit is rewarded, vice and sin is punished, some day, somewhere, sooner or later, here or hereafter. This is the principle behind the law of *Karma* (destiny; results of one's past actions) in Hinduism, *zannat* (Islamic concept of heaven) in Islam and paradise or heaven in Christianity. Every religion professes that greed for money and wealth exercise corrupting influence on the human being and plead for a simple, pious and truthful living.

Jesus Christ said, 'It is easier for a camel to go through the eye of a needle, than for a rich man to enter the kingdom of heaven.' The Bible pleads for economic justice, ecological conservation and ethical life in the family, polity and society at large. A significant tenet of Christianity is to earn bread by exertion of one's labour and advocates fair distribution of income and vehemently opposes interpersonal exploitation. Charity, mercy, generosity and magnanimity are considered to be spiritual and meritorious qualities which a Muslim should imbibe. The concept of ownership of wealth in Islam is that all wealth, after necessary personal and family expenses, belongs to Allah and the excess wealth should be given back.

The Hinduism perspective on wealth is conveyed in following famous verse of *Isavasya Upanishad – tena tyaktena bhunjeethaah maa gridhah kasya chit dhanam*[16] – enjoy wealth but in a detached manner and do not covet it. Bhagawad Gita eulogizes wealth for a happy life in its famous *shloka*,

Yatra yog'esvarah Krasno yatra Partho dhanur-dharah,
tatra srir vijayo bhutir dhruv nitir matir mama.

Wherever, there is Krishna, the Lord of Yoga, and Arjuna, the man
of action,
there is wealth, success, steady growth and justice (XVIII.78).

Great philosophers from time immemorial have pleaded that needs and wants be limited and cautioned against pursuing money as the main mission of life. Epictetus said, 'Wealth consists not in having great possessions, but in having few wants.'[17] Swami Vivekananda said that national ideals of India are renunciation and service. Mahatma Gandhi was against multiplying wants and declared, 'There is enough in the world for every one's need but not for their greed.'[18]

Eastern philosophy's influence on contemporary great men of science and arts is reflected in Boxes 16.1 and 16.2.

Box 16.1   Eastern – Japanese – attitude to money

Shinya Yamanaka, 45, cracked one of scientist's toughest challenges: creating the equivalent of human stem cells with a technique that does not require destroying an embryo, making him a national celebrity. But Yamanaka is bored with the fuss and resents spending time away from his work to explain his discovery to laymen; he would like to be back in his lab, turning his discovery into practical medical technology that can help people suffering from a myriad of ailments, from spinal injury to heart disease. He has no interest in becoming rich and famous and is only interested in what the discovery can do for patients. This fits with how Japanese expect their scientists to behave: humble and disdainful of wealth. They want them to be like neuroscientist Ryuta Kawashima, who turned his ideas on how to stave off senility into huge industry. He has not taken any of the millions in royalties he is entitled, nor any vacation, preferring to devote all his time to help the elderly.

In Japan those who have gone for recognition and reward risk ostracism. Shuji Nakamura invented blue light emitting diode in 1993, which opened the way for massive energy saving, but his company gave him a peanut bonus of $180. He left Japan in 1999, for a position in the University of California, Santa Barbara, and filed a lawsuit against his former employer. The Japanese were appalled by what they saw as unseemly grasp for wealth. A prolific inventor, Yoshiru Nakamatsu said, 'He chose the American way, not the Japanese. The purpose of science and invention is love, not making money.'[19] (Nakamura who became a naturalized US citizen won the Nobel Prize for Physics in 2014, along with two others.)

Box 16.2   M. F. Hussain on money – an Indian approach

M. F. Hussain was the first Indian to sell a painting for Rs 1 lakh; his name again splashed headlines when the octogenarian painter sold a painting for Rs 2 crore. But he warns, 'Don't hang on to every paisa you earn, you won't be able to enjoy life.' Hussain said in an interview, 'I don't keep a purse. I just stash some money in my pocket and set out. Nor do I keep a bank account.' Asked about investment in property, Hussain said, 'My museums are my property, and my best investment is buying paints. I don't believe in investing money in something in order to get more out of it.' Once a fire broke into the chawl he was living – he just picked up his favourite painting and walked off with his wife. Hussain says that money is good as long as it does not come with a sense of possession. When there is an urge to hoard, you become its slave and cannot enjoy life. '*Na ane ki khushi na jane ka gham* – like a *faquir*, I am not jubilant when money comes nor dejected when it goes.'[20]

Indian culture has an ethico-spiritual view of life and views wealth as playing a subordinate role to other human values. This is in marked contrast to the ideology of secular societies of the West.

Part II

Secularism and money

Secular doctrine arose in the West in the context of conflict between the Church and the State, a separation of power and jurisdiction between the two. Secular is defined by *Encarta* dictionary as 'not concerning religion; not religious or spiritual in nature'. According to *Webster* dictionary, secular means 'relating to worldly or temporal concerns; not overtly or specific religious; not ecclesiastical or clerical; not bound by monastic vows or rules'.

The Enlightenment movement in Europe and the scientific progress from the 17th century onwards led to the rise of secular ideologies. The ideas concerning God, reason, nature and man were transformed and that instigated revolutionary developments in art, philosophy and politics. Central to Enlightenment thought were the use and the celebration of reason, the power by which an individual understands the universe and improves his or her own condition. The goals of a rational individual were considered to be knowledge, freedom and happiness. The intellectual and political edifice of Christianity, seemingly impregnable in the Middle Ages, fell in turn to the assaults made on it by humanism, the Renaissance and the Protestant Reformation. The Reformation challenged the monolithic authority of the Roman Catholic Church. The idea of the universe as a mechanism governed by a few simple and discoverable laws had a subversive effect on the concepts of a personal God and individual salvation that were central to Christianity.

Simultaneously with development of secular doctrines, there emerged a strong socialist movement in Europe. The Industrial Revolution exposed the dark side of economic development; while the labour was exploited and toiled under subhuman conditions, the owners of capital made great fortunes. Socialist philosophy's main concern is creation of an egalitarian society. However, under the influence of Karl Marx, who believed in economic determinism, it took the shape of social control of means of production and distribution. The Soviet Union was the first country in the world to experiment with a completely socialized economy, and when Lenin took power, after the revolution of 1917, all the means of production and distribution were nationalized in one stroke. Events in the past century show that a completely socialized economy does not deliver the promised manna. The economies of the Soviet Union and other satellite Eastern European countries collapsed around the 1990s. The vast power placed in a highly centralized monolithic structure made it authoritarian and totalitarian, suppressing individual freedom and liberty. The socialist economies lagged behind in economic growth and could not provide the same standard of living to their people, as the capitalist market economies of the West Europe and the US.

With the collapse of the Soviet Union and its satellites, it was thought that socialism is doomed and capitalism has triumphed. Francis Fukuyama wrote a well-known book *The End of History and the Last Man* (1992), lauding free market as the only economic system to create a prosperous society. Later events have proved the absurdity of such a viewpoint. From the 1980s onwards, the neoliberal model of economic development with its belief in free and unregulated markets became the ruling mantra. The severe recession which afflicted the US and Western European countries from 2008 onwards has shown the hollowness of this ideology. Several years after the economic downturn, the US and Western European countries are unable to launch their economies in the sustained growth path. They are saddled with problems of massive public debt, unemployment and stagnant economy.

The economists and politicians plead in one voice acceleration of economic growth as a solution of their economic woes. In practice, it means more and more production and consumption of goods and services. It is not realized that economic growth at any cost has a huge cost to society and the future of the planet. It causes ecological devastation, encourages consumerism and creates vast inequalities in society, causing social unrest. The fetish with growth is largely due to Western countries' psychology of economism under which life is understood, valued and measured in terms of economic calculation, ignoring other life concerns. People are primarily regarded as economic individuals, driven by wants for material goods, and factors such as equity and justice become irrelevant. Societal development is given an economistic interpretation and measured by gross domestic product/gross national product. The psychological and spiritual dimensions of human personality are ignored.

Economism and materialism which dominates US thinking influences the government's policies. Take the case of rising inequality in the US, which is root cause of many of the problems that the country is facing today (see Chapter 8). In the current capitalist system, labour is losing out and millions who created wealth are being pushed into poverty, while billions in profits are being transferred to the upper rich class. The rich with their economic clout can influence policy decisions. Harvard professor Michael Sandel in his classic study *What Money Can't Buy* deliberates on the increasing hold of market mechanism on the economy and says, 'The logic of buying and selling no longer applies to material goods alone, but increasingly governing the whole life.'[21] Today everything is on sale – health, education, art, citizenship, sports, family life and friendship. Market triumphalism has destroyed the meaning and purpose of life and empties it of spiritual and moral substance. Distinguished economist and social worker Jeffrey Sachs points out that America is facing a crisis of values, which was responsible for the recession of 2008. He says that a healthy society cannot be organized around the single-minded pursuit of wealth and has led to deprivation of the benefits of social trust, honesty and compassion.[22]

Part III

Restoring values

Tragically under the influence of the West and acceptance of free market economy model, India is losing its cherished values and people are becoming 'worshipers of material wealth'. There is a steep decline in values in society today. The sole aim of the well-to-do class is to attain personal and material success, in terms of acquisition of money, power and prestige. A culture has been created in the society which encourages the single-minded pursuit of career growth and economic success. This psychology encourages corruption, which has permeated every walk of life, as people want to make money by hook or by crook, shaking the very foundation of society. In Western countries, the focus on individualism is leading to deterioration of the family life, with increasing divorce, children born out of wedlock and neglect of parents and the elderly. The psychology of enhancing social status through vulgar display of material wealth is a never-ending game, often leading to nervous breakdowns and psychopathic ailments.

We need to question the values that underpin a consumer and individualistic culture and ask whether material values have overtaken life values, such as love, sharing, community spirit and service. The deadening of social consciousness has reduced our sensitivity to social evils, such as poverty, injustice, exploitation and caste and gender inequalities, and other such evils. Thus, in spite of physical well-being and high intellectual growth, we find that human beings have become inwardly poor and unstable. Mankind is constantly burdened with stress, and there has been a phenomenal increase in psychosomatic diseases. This results in people feeling a sense of unhappiness and lack of inner fulfilment, despite huge material progress and every means of comfort at their disposal.

Swami Chinmayananda advises:

> The sacred and the secular can be blended. They must be integrated if man is to be saved, if the world is to be redeemed from its self-destruction.[23]

The tragedy of modern world is that the material benefits of the scientific and technological age have overwhelmed the moral values, which should have been the guiding principles of life. Philosopher Bertrand Russell gives a word of caution, 'Unless men increase in wisdom as much in knowledge, increase in knowledge will be increase of sorrow.'[24] Nobel Prize winner, philosopher and medical missionary Albert Schweitzer warns that modern civilization, while it has developed materially, has not developed spiritually, thereby disturbing its balance. He calls for reverence for life through spiritual progress of the individual and mankind:

> Through the discoveries which now place the forces of Nature at our disposal in such an unprecedented way, the relations with each other of individuals, of social groups, and of States have undergone a revolutionary change . . . we value too highly its material achievements, and no longer keep in mind vividly as necessary the importance of spiritual element in life. . . . The essential nature of civilization does not lie in its material achievements, but in the fact that individuals keep in mind the ideals of

the perfecting man, and the improvement of the social and political conditions of peoples, and of mankind as a whole, and their habit of thought is determined in living and in constant fashion by such ideals.[25]

The Indian culture, which is ethico-spiritual, provides an answer to the predicament of the modern materialist world. Swami Ranganathananda says, 'It is only spiritual growth that makes for fearlessness, character-strength, independence, human love and concern, and the inward qualitative richness of the individual and the health and strength and integrity of the nation.'[26] Our cultural values contain profound wisdom, which can provide the guiding light for a good human being and a good society. It seeks meaning and purpose of life in the world beyond the physical and material, as we have discussed in the previous chapter (Chapter 15).

Dharma as guiding principle

It would be a misunderstanding of the Indian culture if it is understood as one against economic betterment and prosperity of human beings. Indian world view is that earning money (*arth*) and enjoying pleasures of life (*kama*) are desirable activities, but they must be regulated by *dharma*. This moral guideline is not only for the individual but also for the state in what is known as *rajdharma*. *Rajdharma* would therefore require the creation of an egalitarian society and public policies so framed that it prevents few individuals becoming millionaires and billionaires, while majority do not have even the bare necessities of life. Similarly, the noble professions of education and medicine are not allowed to become a means of minting money by unscrupulous individuals and exploitation of poor and needy. *Rajdharma* enjoins that educational institutions impart true knowledge and build character of students and medical services ameliorate sufferings of individuals and serve society.

India's great mystic Sri Aurbindo expresses an ideal attitude towards wealth:

> Money is a visible sign of a universal force, and this force in its manifestation on earth works on the vital and physical plane and is indispensable to the fullness of the outer life. . . . The seekers or keepers of wealth are more often possessed rather than its possessor. . . . For this reason most spiritual disciplines insist on a complete self-control, detachment and renunciation of all bondage to wealth and all personal and egoistic desire for wealth. . . . But this is an error. . . . You must neither turn with an ascetic shrinking from the money power, the means it gives and the object it brings, nor cherish a *rajsic* attachment to them or a spirit of enslaving self-indulgence in their gratification. . . . All wealth belongs to the Divine and those who hold it are trustees, not possessors.[27]

221

Pope John Paul II in his encyclical (1991) observed that it is fine to have free market but it must be placed at the service of humanity and expressed himself against consumerism, 'It is fine to want to live better, but bad to make it important.'[28] Pope Francis in his exhortation (2013) called for establishment of a new world order based on equity and justice. He questioned free market ideology and trickle-down capitalism. 'Money must serve, not rule!' 'A theory that makes profit the exclusive norm and ultimate aim of economic activity is morally unacceptable' and called for return of economics and finance to an ethical approach which favours human beings.[29]

It is time we reinstitute spiritual and cultural values in society and synthesize them with modern democratic values and scientific temper, so that an egalitarian, just and prosperous society is created.

Notes

1 Rabindranath Tagore, 'The Education Mission of Vishwa Bharati', 1930, in Rakesh Batabyal (ed.), *The Penguin Book of Modern Indian Speeches*, New Delhi: Penguin Books, 2007, pp. 742–743.
2 Pope Francis, message to business and political leaders who gathered at Devos in January 2014, *Time*, 3 February 2014, p. 3.
3 A. L. Basham, *The Wonder That Was India*, New Delhi: Rupa & Co., 2003, p. 9.
4 Chaturvedi Badrinath, *The Mahabharata*, Hyderabad: Orient Longman, 2007, Chapter 10, pp. 272–293. All the *shlokas* and quotes are from this book.
5 For a detailed discussion, see B. P. Mathur, *Ethics in Governance*, New Delhi: Routledge, 2014, Chapter 8.
6 V. K. Subramaniam, *Maxim of Chanakya*, New Delhi: Abhinav Publications, 2000, p. 21.
7 Ibid., p. 97.
8 Ibid., p. 98.
9 L. N. Rangarajan, *Kautilya Arthashastra*, New Delhi: Penguin Books, 1992, p. 253.
10 Ibid.
11 Ibid.
12 Subramaniam, *Maxim of Chanakya*, p. 99.
13 Ibid., p. 100.
14 Rangarajan, *Kautilya Arthashastra*, p. 523.
15 R. P. Kangle, *The Arthashastra*, Vol. III, New Delhi: Motilal Banarsidass, 1997, p. 282.
16 *Isavasya Upanishad*, Verse 1; Swami Gambhirananda (transl.), *Eight Upanishads*, Vol. 1, Calcutta: Advaita Ashrama, 1995, p. 4.
17 Brainy Quote: Epictetus Quotes, available at http://www.brainyquote.com/quotes/quotes/e/epictetus384225.html.
18 Wisdom quote: Mohan Das K. Gandhi quotes, available at http://www.wisdomquotes.com/quote/mohandas-k-gandhi-54.html (accessed 25 March 2016).

19 'No nonsense Science', *The Indian Express*, 17 February 2008, reporting Bruce Wallace: *Los Angeles Times*.

20 'I sold my horses and slept peacefully', *Sunday Times of India*, New Delhi, 18 May 2003, p. 5, interview by Ratnottama Sengupta.

21 Michael Sandel, *What Money Can't Buy: The Moral Limits of Market*, London: Penguin Books, 2012.

22 Jeffrey Sachs, *The Price of Civilization – Economics and Ethics after the Fall*, London: The Bodley Head, 2011.

23 Swami Chinmayananda, *The Pursuit of Happiness*, Mumbai: Central Chinmaya Mission Trust, 2008, p. 9.

24 Bertrand Russel, *Impact of Science on Society*, quoted in Swami Kamalananda *et al.*, *Education: Total Development of Personality*, Mysore: Ramakrishna Institute of Moral and Spiritual Education, 2003, p. 8.

25 Albert Schweitzer, *Civilization and Ethics*, London: Unwin Books, 1961, p. 20.

26 Swami Ranganathananda, *Democratic Administration in the Light of Practical Vedanta*, Chennai: Sri Ramakrishna Math, 2006, p. 91.

27 Sri Aurbindo, *The Mother*, Pondicherry: Sri Aurbindo Ashram, 1984, pp. 11–12.

28 'Pope Paul II's encyclical of May 1991, God's visible hand', *The Economist*, 4 May 1991, p. 46.

29 Ambrose Pinto, 'The Economics of Pope Francis', *Mainstream*, 28 December 2013, Vol. LII, No. 1, pp. 45–50.

17

QUEST FOR HAPPINESS

Public policies and national happiness

The ultimate goal of humankind is to experience uncondi-
tional happiness, a happiness that does not change but is
always new and is not born out of indulgence.

Swami Bodhananda[1]

We have now clearly distinguished the 'happiness' in GNH
(Gross National Happiness) from the fleeting, pleasurable
'feel good' moods so often associated with that term. We
know that true abiding happiness cannot exist while others
suffer, and comes only from serving others, living in harmony with nature, and realizing our innate wisdom and the
true and brilliant nature of our own minds.

Lyonchhen Jigmi Y. Thinley, Former
Prime Minister of Bhutan[2]

Every human being on this planet wants to be happy. But happiness is a
very elusive concept, and people often misunderstand it for short-term
thrill. A person who drinks heavily, a gambler, a womanizer all seek
happiness according to their own concept of happiness. So are also a
moneyed man wanting to own a Rolls-Royce and a palatial villa in a
posh colony and an upcoming socialite spending a fortune on buying
a diamond necklace. But the thrill that one gets momentarily is not true
happiness. Happiness is a state of inner fulfilment, not the gratification of
inexhaustible desires for outward things.

People confuse pleasure with happiness, 'Pleasure is simply a shadow of
happiness.'[3] It is the result of a pleasurable sensual or intellectual stimuli.
Most of the time pleasure is a fleeting experience and depends on circumstances, on specific location or on moment of time. It is unstable by nature,
and the sensation it evokes soon becomes neutral or even unpleasant.
When repeated it may grow boring or even lead to disgust. Eating a sump-
tuous meal in a five-star hotel may be a genuine pleasure, but once we have
our fill, we do not get any pleasure in continuing eating and may fall ill if

we overeat. Pleasure is exhausted by usage, like a candle consuming itself. An individual pampering desire and fulfilling it all the time gets only transient pleasure, which is called *bhogsukha* according to Indian terminology.

Materialists who idolize pleasures preach the doctrine of 'eat, drink and be merry'. In the world of today, people are all the time busy satisfying wants of material existence. There is a mad rush of competition among individuals, families, societies and nations to beat others in furthering material comforts and luxuries. But while doing this, they are restless and unhappy. The religious leaders of the world have preached different methods of gaining happiness and conquering pain according to varying conditions of different ages. Great sages, yogis, prophets and thinkers have left us a heritage of culture, philosophy, morality and scriptures, which are worthy of adherence, if we want to be happy.

According to our ancient wisdom true happiness is *sat chit anand* – a state of inner bliss.[4] It is also called *yogsukha*, which is a state of lasting happiness when a person gains freedom from the pull of objects and desires. The mind becomes quiet, detached, serene and self-abiding. According to Vedanta philosophy, happiness is a state of consciousness, when a person abides in *brahman* (God consciousness). Great saints and swamis abide in *brahman* and are known as *brahm-gyani*. They have a perfectly balanced mind; they go around giving and sharing joy and bliss, and for them life is a continuous process of thanksgiving.

True happiness (*anand*) can come only through mastery over oneself. Mahabharata[5] says that conquest of the self is the greatest *dharma*. The conquest of the self leads to truth, control over one's physical senses, gentleness, modesty, generosity, freedom from anger, forgiveness, patience, non-violence, pleasant speech, not seeking fault in others and a feeling of contentment.

True happiness can be achieved only by individual effort and understanding the meaning and purpose of life, irrespective of external circumstances. Our saints and yogis achieved it by doing years of *tapas* (penance) in the Himalayas. Great leaders like Mahatma Gandhi, Jawaharlal Nehru and Nelson Mandela, who spent years in prison, at great physical suffering, were at peace with themselves and radiated joy and bliss, as they were inspired by the noble purpose of serving humanity. There are stories of Jews in Nazi ghettos and Tibetan monks in Chinese concentration camps who survived years of torture and brutality because of positive attitude towards life, but bore no ill will towards their tormentors.

Achieving true happiness (*anand*) is the ideal of life that saints and great thinkers have set before us. It is difficult for an individual to achieve it, but by grasping its meaning he or she can understand the ultimate purpose of life and strive towards it. An ancient proverb says, 'Ideals are like stars, we may not achieve them, but like mariners on the sea we can set our course by them.'

Life satisfaction and well-being

In common parlance people equate life satisfaction and well-being with happiness. This is perfectly legitimate, as it is within the grasp of an individual by making personal effort and for society and public policy to create those conditions which help achieve it. We will use the words 'happiness', 'life satisfaction' and 'well-being' interchangeably in the following discussion. A number of factors determine an individual's well-being: income, job, education, health, family and community support, religious belief and outlook towards life. However, in the West, happiness is largely equated with money and material prosperity. This is best reflected in the obsession with gross domestic product (GDP) growth or per capita income, as a measure of the country's prosperity or development. When translated into public policy, it can create disastrous outcomes for people.

Income divide and consumerism

Post-economic liberation, India has adopted the neoliberal model of economic development, blindly imitating Western free market economic ideology. This implies continuous GDP growth and for all practical purposes means more and more production and consumption of goods and services, irrespective of its social and economic utility. This model creates vast inequalities in society, leads to a culture of consumerism and results in environmental degradation.

In the US and other Western countries, the existing economic development model has led to a vast increase in economic inequality and is threatening to break the social fabric. Corporate owners and executives appropriate most of the profit to themselves, sharing very little with workers who are equal partners in wealth creation. Experts say that this was responsible for the recession of 2008 and the current slow growth of the economy. Similar trends of vast inequalities in society are evident in India (see Chapter 8). The disparity in wealth, with a large part of it being cornered by a privileged section of society, is leading to conspicuous consumption in India as well. The springing up of luxury villas all over the country, the rising sale of expensive cars and the culture of shopping malls and five-star hotels are obvious symbols of fast-spreading consumerism. Top cricketers command crores of rupees as fees, thanks to the advertisement industry which lures them to advertise products of dubious value, promoting consumerism.

Consumerism is a cultural pattern that leads people to find meaning, contentment and acceptance primarily through the consumption of goods and services. Consumerism leads people everywhere to associate high consumption levels with well-being and success. Today consumerism has become a transactional way of life. Excess consumption is fuelled by social pressures, and advertising causes confusion between needs and wants in a consumer society. This growth outstrips eco-efficiency, causing rapid ecological deterioration. The cost of consumerism includes stressful inducement to consume more even if the quality of life declines.

No correlation between high income and life satisfaction

Various studies of rich societies show that an increase in income is not leading to a happier and fulfilling life. Affluence has created its own set of afflictions and addictions. Obesity, tobacco-related illnesses, eating disorders, depression, mental disorder and addictions to shopping, television and gambling are all examples of disorders of development. So too are the loss of community, the decline of social trust and the rising anxiety levels associated with the vagaries of the modern globalized economy, including the threats of unemployment and chronic diseases. The US has a very high rate of suicide, which has risen from 11 per 100,000 people in 2005 to 13 per 100,000, seven years later.[6] Over 40,000 Americans took their lives in 2012 – more than the number of persons who died in car crashes.

Professor Richard Easterlin[7] points out that US gross national product per capita has risen by a factor of three since 1960, while measures of average happiness have remained essentially unchanged over the half century. Easterlin noted a paradox in the US that while at any particular time richer individuals are happier than poorer ones, over time the society did not become happier as it became richer. The first reason is that individuals compare themselves to others. They are happier when they are higher on the social (or income) ladder. Yet when everybody rises together, relative status remains unchanged. A second reason is that the gains have not been evenly shared but have gone disproportionately to those at the top of the income and education distribution. A third one is that other societal factors – insecurity, loss of social trust, a declining confidence in government – have counteracted any benefits felt from the higher incomes. A fourth reason is adaptation: individuals may experience an initial jump in happiness when their income rises but then at least partly return to earlier levels as they adapt to their new higher income. The increased US output has caused massive environmental damage, notably through greenhouse gas concentrations and human-induced climate change, without doing much at all to raise the well-being of Americans.

Studies based on the data of World Value Survey have found that in rich countries above certain average incomes, there is virtually no co-relationship between increased income and life satisfaction.[8] In the US and Japan, there has been little change in life satisfaction over several decades. In the UK, the percentage reporting themselves as very happy dropped 15 percentage points in five decades from the 1950s to 2010s. This is for the reason that a whole range of non-monetary factors such as family, friendship, health, peer approval, community and purpose determine people's life satisfaction and happiness. Unequal societies systematically report higher levels of 'distress' than more equal ones.

Researchers from the University of Warwickshire gathering data from British Household Panel Survey found out that money can buy out happiness, only when an individual has a lot more than neighbours.[9] The envy of being lower in the social pecking order tarnishes the satisfaction of being well off. Psychologist Christopher Boyce observed that when it comes to chasing money for money's sake, only a limited amount of happiness can be obtained from that. It is a no-win game; you can easily get locked into this race for status. A better way to increase well-being and happiness is focusing away from income, as chasing money is a kind of zero-sum game, and overall, no one can become more satisfied. Another study by Prof. Eugenio Proto and Aldo Rustichini found that life satisfaction dips in rich countries beyond a certain level of income.[10] Once you reach an income level of $36,000 per year, adjusted to purchasing power parity, increase in happiness is less obvious, and the link between life satisfaction and GDP is flat (November 2013).

Two British epidemiologists Richard Wilkinson and Kate Pickett[11] in their book *The Spirit Level: Why Greater Equality Makes Societies Stronger* argue that greater inequality tears at the human psyche, creating anxiety, distrust and an array of mental and physical ailments. Supported by copious amounts of data, they say that the toll of inequality is not just economic but melancholy of the soul. Inequality undermines social trust and community life and causes stress. The upshot appears to be increasing crime rates, high narcotics use, high teenage birth rates and an exponential rise in heart diseases. There is a strong correlation between a country's level of economic inequality and its social outcomes. Japan and the Scandinavian countries have better social outcomes than the UK and the US, where inequality levels are higher. Around a quarter of British people, and more than a quarter of Americans, experience mental problems in any given year, compared with fewer than 10 per cent in Japan, Germany, Sweden and Italy. The authors call for stiffer taxes on the rich and more cooperative ownership of the companies.

Philosopher Alain de Boton has shown how an unequal society leads to high levels of 'status anxiety' among its citizens.[12] Striving for self-esteem through material wealth appears to be a kind of zero-sum game in which constant need for betterment and approval only serves to entrench people in an almost neurotic spiral of consumption.

It is well established that a household's income counts for happiness or life satisfaction but only in a limited way. Other things matter more: steady job, education, community trust, mental and physical health and the quality of governance – law and order, security and rule of law. It is, of course, one thing to identify the correlates of happiness and quite another to use public policies to bring about a society-wide rise in happiness (or life satisfaction).

Measuring happiness

While happiness and life satisfaction is a subjective experience, experts in the West feel that happiness can be objectively measured and correlated with observable brain functions, and related to the characteristics of an individual and the society. Asking people whether they are happy, or satisfied with their lives, offers important information about the society. A group of academics from Earth Institute Columbia University supported by the Sustainable Development Solutions Network have been bringing out the *World Happiness Report* since 2012. The report offers evidence of how the systematic measurement and analysis of happiness can teach us much about ways to improve the world's well-being and sustainable development. The report observes:

> GNP is a valuable goal, but should not be pursued to the point where economic stability is jeopardized, community cohesion is destroyed, the vulnerable are not supported, ethical standards are sacrificed, or the world's climate is put at risk. While basic living standards are essential for happiness, after the baseline has been met, happiness varies more with quality of human relationships than income. Other policy goals should include high employment and high-quality work; a strong community with high levels of trust and respect, which government can influence through inclusive participatory policies; improved physical and mental health; support of family life; and a decent education for all.[13]

In July 2011 the UN General Assembly passed a resolution inviting member countries to measure the happiness of their people and to use this to help guide their public policies. The World Happiness Report outlines four steps to improve policymaking: the measurement of happiness, explanation of happiness, putting happiness at the centre of analysis and translation of well-being research into design and delivery of services.

The *World Happiness Report 2016* gives a table in which happiness across countries has been graded (2013–15). India occupies a very low position at 118 out of 157 countries graded.[14] There are severe limitations in such measurements as they are based on self-reported surveys which are subjective. There are vast differences in cultural values, outlook towards life and religious orientation among people in different countries, and therefore, cross-country comparison of happiness becomes meaningless and misleading. Economists have obsession with numbers, but they should realize that 'subjective well-being' is very difficult to measure in precise numbers.

Bhutan – happiness as goal of public policy

Bhutan is the first country in the world to make happiness as a goal of public policy. Bhutan computes the Gross National Happiness Index (GNHI), which is a multidimensional development approach that seeks to achieve a harmonious balance between material well-being and the spiritual, emotional and cultural needs of society. Founded on the belief that happiness can be achieved by balancing the needs of the body with those of the mind within a peaceful and secure environment, it requires that the purpose of development must be to create enabling conditions through public policy.

Unlike the other development models, GNHI is a more comprehensive and holistic approach to development by having incorporated innovative dimensions like psychological well-being, community vitality, time use and cultural diversity and resilience, otherwise undermined in the other policy-making frameworks. This makes GNHI a more realistic measure of progress, which ensures a consistent alignment between what an individual aspires from development and what the government does. GNHI has four pillars and nine domains.[15] The four pillars are (1) sustainable and equitable development, (2) preservation and promotion of culture, (3) conservation of environment and (4) good governance. The nine domains are (1) living standards, (2) education, (3) health, (4) cultural diversity and resilience, (5) community vitality, (6) time use, (7) psychological well-being, (8) ecological diversity and (9) good governance. A very interesting aspect of Bhutan's happiness survey (for 2010) shows that good health, community, ecology and psychological well-being contributed 50 per cent to GNH of happy people, while living standard (income wealth) contributed only about 10 per cent to happiness.

I visited Bhutan sometime back and am a witness to life there. Bhutan is slowly modernizing, keeping its culture intact. All the modern amenities of life are available in its capital Thimphu and major towns Punakha and Paro. People lead a life which is stress-free, peaceful, tranquil and full of smiles. The environment is pure; there are pristine forests, unpolluted air and rivers, which give the people their genteel character despite harsh mountains and tough winter. Who would not want to live a life like theirs? It is one of the few Shangri-Las left on planet earth.

Virtue ethics

The economists consider higher GDP as the most important goal of national policy. But this viewpoint is completely at variance with the teachings of the sages, the research of psychologists and sociologists and the survey conducted by various agencies concerned with people's well-being. The US Founding Fathers recognized the inalienable right to the pursuit of happiness, which is written in the US Constitution. British philosophers like Jeremy Bentham talked about the greatest good for the greatest number. Moral sensibility is a value people cherish from ages and fundamental principle of progress in the world. Aristotle said moderation in all aspects is key to eudemonia, or human fulfilment.

The essence of every religion and spiritual practice is to attain happiness and bliss. Buddha advocated the 'Middle Path' which would keep humanity balanced between the false allures of asceticism on the one side and pleasure seeking on the other. Each of us is thrust into a world of temptation, desire and allusion, and we must find a lifelong path in the midst of these obstacles and traps. We must balance consumption and savings, work and leisure, individualism and members of a society. Economist Jeffrey Sachs,[16] who is a leading scholar of 'happiness', pleads for observing Buddha's teaching of *mindfulness* for securing happiness. The Indian wisdom has been telling, from time immemorial, the limitation of money to buy happiness and pleads for selfless work and service to society for peace and harmony. People do not feel happy when they find their brethren suffering and living in poverty. This has been the idea behind legal protection of basic human rights and the creation of a welfare state.

India: government's policies exacerbating unhappiness

In India, during the past two decades, government is relentlessly pursuing a policy of boosting economic growth and considers it as a success of its economic policies. This is a fallacious approach. Due to distributional imbalance, growth that is taking place in the country is giving rise to vast economic inequality and a culture of consumerism. India's experience is similar to free market economies of the West, except that in the West everyone has the basics of life and there are hardly any poor. Inevitably, this is giving rise to huge social unrest and violence and people feeling dissatisfied with life in general. The current model of economic development has favoured better educated, urban middle- and higher-income group and completely bypassed majority of the population. It is a matter of great shame that a tiny minority lives in opulence with lifestyles comparable to the maharajas and nabobs of yesteryears, while 30 per cent of Indians live in abject poverty and another 50 per cent barely eke out a living.

Government policies are completely geared to pander the wants of urban middle class and higher-income groups. The policy of free import of luxury goods, massive production of cars, construction of palatial houses and huge public investment in building airports in metropolitan cities to facilitate air travel are symptoms of public policy promoting unabashed consumerism. Low personal taxation rates and numerous incentives given for production and consumption of luxury goods, which have no social utility, are indicative of government pampering this privileged class.

If India is to become a happy society, the first priority should be complete elimination of poverty and hunger. Swami Vivekananda had said, 'To the hungry, religion comes in the form of bread,' and Mahatma Gandhi reiterated the same, 'To a hungry man a piece of bread is the face of God.' Poverty can be eliminated only by increasing the capability of people by providing high-quality education and health services, which can give them gainful employment and make them dignified members of society.

To create a happy society, the government needs to promote egalitarian policies. This means a system in which life chances are not allocated by structural inequalities in social, economic and political power. This, in effect, implies a commitment to the philosophy of socialism, if understood in its true sense (see Chapter 13). True socialism has to be practised within the democratic framework and involves reorganizing the economic and social life of society, so as to abolish exploitation, inequality and injustice and preserve individual freedom and efficiency. Post–Second World War Britain, France and Scandinavian countries became welfare states by embracing the philosophy of socialism and provided unemployment benefits, medical cover, old-age pension and other social benefits to its citizens. Today countries such as Denmark, Norway and Sweden are models of social democracy, which India should emulate. In these countries economic and social policies combine a market economy with a welfare state, with maximum emphasis on labour force participation in production process, gender equality and income redistribution.

Our precious heritage

All the great religions of the world have socialist underpinnings. They are deeply concerned with problems of poverty, economic inequality and social injustice, and have been preaching from time immemorial that earning money and accumulating wealth should not be the primary goal of life. Bhagawad Gita's main message is detached engagement – one should do one's duty, earn money and enjoy worldly comforts but in a detached manner. You may enjoy what the world offers you, but restrain and control your indulgence. Wealth and possession of worldly goods and property should not overpower one's vision of higher purpose of life which can be achieved through *loksanghraha* (service to society and humanity). Buddhism's key message is that suffering and happiness are mainly determined by psychology, by one's state of mind, rather than by the relative presence or absence of material goods. Happiness can be gained by compassion towards others and following Four Noble Truths and the Noble Eightfold Path. Jesus Christ's key message is, 'Love your neighbor, as thyself' and serve the society.

In India people are contended and satisfied, if only bare necessities of life are met, largely due to its spiritual and cultural heritage, which is embedded deeply in their psyche. That makes India a peaceful and non-violent place to live despite majority of people lacking material riches.

It is greed and lust for money that is responsible for many ills of society such as corruption, exploitation of labour and environmental degradation. The problem is accentuated when the state blindly pursues a policy of economic growth, which leads to consumerism and economic inequality, propped by an influential section of elite, who want to lead a life of luxury and indulgence. This results in a great deal of dissatisfaction and unhappiness among a majority of population who are left out of the economic race for betterment. *It is unfortunate that India despite its great heritage is imitating the West and following its materialist model of development. The West itself is getting tired of a model of development where money and wealth plays a dominant role and is searching for more meaningful goals which make life satisfying. In its quest for development, India must not give up its ancient philosophy, which provides guidance to lead a life, which is peaceful and self-fulfilling. Our public policy should be designed to create an egalitarian society, where everyone has the minimum necessities of life, and nobody is in want of the bare essentials. This is possible when we redefine our national goal as well-being and happiness of the entire population which lives in our land.*

Notes

1 Swami Bodhananda, *Self-Unfoldment in an Interactive World*, New Delhi: Sambodh Foundation, 2001, p. 21.
2 Quoted in Centre for Bhutanese Studies, *A Short Guide to Gross National Happiness Index*, Thimpu, 2012, p. 7, available at http://www.grossnational happiness.com/wp-content/uploads/2012/04/Short-GNH-Index-edited.pdf (accessed 4 December 2014).
3 For a detailed discussion on happiness, read French scientist turned Buddhist monk: Matthieu Richard, *Happiness: A Guide to Developing Life's Most Important Skill*, London: Atlantic Books, 2006.
4 For understanding Hinduism point of view regarding true happiness, see Swami Bodhananda, *Self-Unfoldment*; and Swami Chinmayananda, *The Pursuit of Happiness*, Mumbai: Central Chinmaya Trust, 2008.
5 Chaturvedi Badrinath, *The Mahabharata: An Enquiry into the Human Conditions*, Hyderabad: Orient Longman, 2007, p. 108 (*Shanti-parva* 160.15.16).
6 'An awful hole: Why more Americans are killing themselves', *The Economist*, 31 January–6 February 2015, p. 27.
7 Cited in John Helliwell, Richard Layard and Jeffrey Sachs, *World Happiness Report*, The Earth Institute, Columbia University, pp. 1–9, available at http://www.earth.columbia.edu/sitefiles/file/Sachs%20Writing/2012/World%20 Happiness%20Report.pdf (accessed 4 December 2014).
8 Cited by Tim Jackson, 'The Challenge of Sustainable Lifestyles', in *World Watch Institute: State of the World 2008*, New York: W. W. Norton & Co., 2008, pp. 45–60.
9 'Money really can't buy happiness, study finds', *CBC News*, 24 March 2010, available at http://www.cbc.ca/news/money-really-can-t-buy-happiness-study-finds-1.974466 (accessed 4 December 2014); 'Money buys happiness only if you earn more than others', *Times of India*, 24 March 2010, p. 21.
10 Eugenio Proto and Aldo Rustichini, 'Money can buy happiness, only if you earn $ 36K a year', *Times of India*, 29 November2013, p. 21.
11 'The rise and rise of the cognitive elite, the few, a special report on global leaders', *The Economist*, 22–28 January 2011.
12 Cited by Jackson, 'The Challenge of Sustainable Lifestyles', p. 50.
13 John Helliwell, Richard Layard and Jeffrey Sachs (eds), *World Happiness Report, 2013*, Sustainable Development Solution Network and Earth Institute, Columbia University, p. 9, available at http://unsdsn.org/wp-content/ uploads/2014/02/WorldHappinessReport2013_online.pdf (accessed 4 December 2014).
14 John Helliwell, Richard Layard and Jeffrey Sachs (Eds.), *World Happiness Report 2016*, available at http://worldhappiness.report/wp-content/uploads/ sites/2/2016/03/HR-V1_web.pdf (accessed 3 May 2016).
15 Centre for Bhutanese Studies, *A Short Guide to Gross National Happiness Index*.
16 Jeffrey Sachs, *The Price of Civilisation: Economics and Ethics after the Fall*, London: Bodley Head, 2011, pp. 162–166; and Jeffrey Sachs, 'Restoring Virtue Ethics in the Quest of Happiness', in John F. Helliwell, Richard Layard and Jeffrey Sachs (eds), *World Happiness Report 2013*, Chapter 5, pp. 81–94, available at http://unsdsn.org/wp-content/uploads/2014/02/WorldHappiness Report2013_online.pdf (accessed 4 December 2014).

18

SYNERGIZING DEVELOPMENT WITH CULTURAL ETHOS

Sarve bhavantu sukhina, sarvesantu niramayah,
Sarve bhadrani pashyantu, makashchiddukhabhagbhavet!
May all beings be happy, may all be healthy.
May people have the well-being of all in mind.
May no body suffer in any way.

Ancient Indian Prayer[1]

True development is development and flowering of the personality of human beings. This implies that we create an environment in which people can lead a satisfied, fulfilling and happy life. All the great religions of the world – Hinduism, Christianity, Islam and Buddhism – have been preaching philosophies which are focused around growth of human beings and how they can face ups and downs of daily life and lead a peaceful, harmonious and happy life. The secular ideologies of the West, which arose as a result of the Enlightenment movement, have also been giving the highest priority to humanistic values such as equality, liberty, freedom and justice. In course of time, these values have been incorporated in the national constitution of every country as an ideal to be achieved. The preamble to the Indian Constitution declares that we as a nation shall try to secure justice, liberty, equality and fraternity for all its citizens. The Universal Declaration of Human Rights, embraced by all the countries of the world, recognizes that everyone has a right to live with dignity, which can be secured through guarantee of liberty, freedom and security of life.

Unfortunately, under materialist ideology and philosophy of economism, 'development' has come to be interpreted in narrow terms as 'economic development', and growth of GDP (gross domestic product) is considered a litmus test of progress of a society. Nothing could be more misleading. GDP growth in practical terms means more and more production and consumption of goods and services, irrespective of its social and economic utilities. As discussed in this study, this ideology creates serious socio-economic problems. UNDP's Human Development reports have been repeatedly pointing out that high growth rates do not automatically get translated into higher levels of human development. In fact, it is just the opposite – it is only through human development that higher

234

economic growth can be achieved. UNDP defines human development as 'expansion of people's freedom to live long, healthy and creative lives', and its core principles are equity, sustainability and empowerment.[2] It is necessary that we redefine our national goal.

India's development goal should be creation of a happy, healthy and prosperous society

Happiness

Happiness is not mere pleasure; it is a state of one's consciousness. Happiness, at least for those who are above basic wants, depends on one's attitude towards life. Happiness also depends on cultural attitudes of a society in which an individual lives. Indian culture has done a great deal of reflection on the goals of life called *purshartha* and advanced the doctrine of *trivarga* – *artha* (wealth), *kama* (pleasure) and *dharma* (righteous living) – which strikes a balance between the interest of an individual and the public. While the pursuit of earning money (*arth*) and pleasure (*kama*) is a legitimate goal, it must be within the bond of *dharma* and regulated by it. The Western cultural attitude towards life is in marked contrast to Indian cultural attitude. In the West earning money and material comforts has become the summum bonum of life, and earning tonnes of money is considered an ideal one should strive for. However, studies of rich societies have shown that an increase in income and wealth is not leading to a happier life. Affluence creates its afflictions, such as health-related diseases like obesity, heart trouble, anxiety, depression, mental illness and even suicides. Thinkers and philosophers in these countries are now preaching virtue ethics to enable people to lead a more joyful and fulfilling life.

In common parlance, people equate life satisfaction and well-being with happiness. This is a reasonable approach as it is within the grasp of everyone to make personal effort and improve the material conditions under which he or she lives. A number of factors determine an individual's well-being, such as income, job, education, health, family and community support. However, it is necessary that the state create conditions under which an individual can achieve his or her economic and social well-being. This is where the role of public policy comes.

Creating a prosperous society

A prosperous society is one in which there is no poverty and everyone is above basic want, and not the one in which some people live in great luxury and opulence and the vast majority do not have even the basics of life.

To create a prosperous society in India, the first task is to completely eliminate poverty and hunger. This is possible only when there is dignified employment for every citizen.

Unemployment is the biggest curse of modern society and most demeaning to the person who has no work, whether he or she is educated, semi-educated or illiterate. Unemployment is built into the structure of modern urban-centric, industrialized, market-oriented society. Work is a medium of self-sustenance and self-expression. It is by working and earning his or her bread and livelihood that he or she earns dignity. For Mahatma Gandhi, individual dignity and the welfare of the poorest of the poor was the core of economic development philosophy. There is need for social and economic systems to be so organized as to give work to everyone.

Dignified employment for everyone is possible only when highest priority is given to

- agriculture and rural development and
- micro, small and medium industries (MSMEs).

From the time of independence, agriculture and rural development has been neglected in the country's planning process. This is evident from the fact that today while almost 70 per cent of people live in rural areas and closer to 60 per cent are employed in agriculture and allied activities and depend on them for their livelihood, their contribution to GDP has come down to only 15 per cent, despite rising agriculture productivity. The main reason is low prices of food grains and agricultural products. Through political means, policymakers have created an indentured agriculture to serve the interests of a vociferous urban population. One of the most disquieting features of the rural economy is declining public investment. During the post-independent 60-year period from 1950 to 2011, the central and state government's expenditure on rural development has been only 9.5 to 12 per cent of their total combined public expenditure, despite 70 to 80 per cent of population living in rural areas (see Chapter 4). There has been complete neglect of irrigation, crucial to farming – its share in public expenditure which was around 7 to 8 per cent during the 1950s and 1960s has fallen to less than 1 per cent from the 1990s onwards. There is need for massive public investment in agricultural infrastructure such as irrigation, farm machinery and equipment, seeds, post-harvesting handling and processing, warehouses and research and development to make agriculture a remunerative occupation and mainstay of the economy. The PURA model (providing urban amenities in rural areas) advanced by the former president Dr A. P. J. Abdul Kalam offers solutions to some of the challenges of rejuvenating rural India.

Industrial development is route to prosperity, and it is through industrialization that the Western countries have achieved the present level of prosperity. Indian planners had forgotten this lesson of economic history and relegated industry to secondary position, particularly after the economic liberalization of 1991, in naïve belief that 'services' sector will leapfrog the country to a developed economy stage. Worldwide small and medium enterprises (SMEs) are at the core of the industrial development strategy and are the main providers of employment. In rich countries (Organization for Economic Cooperation and Development), SMEs account for 60 to 70 per cent employment. Smaller firms are increasingly present in technology-intensive industries such as information and communication and biotechnology. We need to give massive support to micro, small and medium enterprises (MSMEs) by way of provision of cheap credit and finance, technology upgradation and skill development. MSMEs should get 24 hours' supply of electricity and be protected from unfair competition from abroad, particularly China. MSMEs, if given strong support, can act as engines of growth and hold potential of employing our vast manpower, particularly educated youth.

For every individual to be employed and secure a dignified job, it is necessary that the workforce is educated and healthy and possesses the requisite capability.

India's education system is in complete disarray. Periodic surveys conducted by Pratham, a non-governmental organization, known as Annual Status of Education Report, present an alarming picture of the state of primary education. In most government schools, even after several years of schooling, a large section of children cannot read simple textbooks and do basic arithmetical sums. The secondary education system hardly gives any emphasis on vocational education and skill development, with the result that there is a complete mismatch between the manpower that educational institutions produce and what the market needs. Due to privatization policy, higher education has become a commodity available to the highest bidder. There is hardly any emphasis on learning and search for knowledge, without which universities cannot become organs of civilization. There is a complete misdirection of higher education. The aim of education should be building character of young boys and girls, developing in them a spirit of enquiry and a consciousness to serve the society.

Good health is most important for human beings. Everything depends on health: efficiency and productivity, the inner peace and happiness. As a matter of fact, life itself depends on health. India's public health system is in a pathetic state; as a result, members of the public bypass government medical services and go to private doctors and hospitals, who charge exorbitant fees which only the rich can afford. There is need for publicly funded universal health coverage so that every citizen can have access to primary and secondary health care, an essential component of social security in the modern world.

Most of the problems that we face today in agriculture, industry, education and health are due to two reasons: poor governance and wrong economic policies. They must be fixed if India is to become a prosperous society. If we look deeply at history, we will find that the Western countries have achieved their economic prosperity by focusing on the development and growth of human beings. They provide high-quality education to children and youths and health care to everyone and take responsibility of employment of every citizen (the unemployment insurance cover reflects this policy). They have been able to achieve this by embracing a political system of social democracy, whose core values are embedded in economic equality and social justice and creation of an egalitarian society.

Post-1980s and 1990s, the US, which dominates the global economic policy, embraced a neoliberal model of economic development, under the influence of materialist ideology. This model is beset with numerous problems. While it generates a great amount of wealth, the same is cornered by a small upper crust of the population, while the standard of living of the vast majority stagnates. The model promotes a culture of consumerism and vulgar display of wealth. It is based on continuous growth of the economy, for which the earth's natural resources have to be mercilessly exploited, causing ecological devastation. With profit as motive, there is constant search for technology to save on labour cost, causing unemployment and hardship to people. Over the years the free market model has slid into hyper-commercialism, bordering on greed, untethered by moral and ethical considerations. Life itself has become a commodity available to the highest bidder. Unfortunately, Indian policymakers are blindly imitating the economic ideology of the West, whose adverse impact we are witnessing all round. The benefit of economic growth has been cornered by a microscopic minority who roll in fabulous wealth and live a life of luxury, while the vast majority do not have even the bare necessities of life.

Choosing the best path

In today's globalized world, India cannot remain isolated. We should embrace progressive ideas from the West, without giving up our cherished values. The Enlightenment movement brought an age of reason and knowledge in the European societies. This also led to the development of democratic institutions and the noble ideals of freedom, liberty and equality. Today the defining features of Western societies are scientific temper, rule of law, social equality, opportunity for everyone to climb up the economic ladder, dignity of labour, high work ethics, universal education and health care for everyone. India should inculcate these values but reject the recent Western fetish, with economism and money occupying a dominating place in all human relationships.

Celebrated poet and litterateur Ramdhari Singh Dinkar in his classic book *Sanskriti ke Char Adhyay* comments, 'By fulfillment of material necessities, India's inner personality will not flower and if to fulfill material necessities, it is considered necessary to suppress her inner personality, the Indian public will never support such a programme.'[3] Outlining an ideal path, he elaborates:

From Rammohan Roy to Gandhi, Vinoba, Radhakrishnan and Jawaharlal Nehru all our leaders and thinkers have been stressing one point, that India's success lies when she can explore and synthesize old with the new. The kernel of Western knowledge should be synthesized with our ancient wisdom. India can fulfill its cherished goal, if it can hold the lotus of dharma in one hand and flame of science in another. And it is this aspiration towards which the whole world is looking towards India with mystic hope. What West has lost by embracing science, if India can find it by befriending science, then it will be a boon not only for India, but the whole world.[4]

It is therefore necessary that India choose those values and ideas of the West which suit its needs and genius and synergize them with its wisdom and tradition.

The golden means - the Middle Path

Eastern religions have expounded a philosophy of life which can provide valuable guidelines to deal with problems that humanity is facing today. Gautama Buddha had advocated the Middle Path, in which he spoke of the concept of a harmonious, balanced life, steering between two extremes of self-indulgence and total abstinence. The Noble Path transcends the two extremes. It consists of Noble Eightfold Path: right view, right thought, right speech, right behaviour, right livelihood, right effort, right mindfulness and right concentration. The Middle Way transcends the duality of suffering and happiness and merges into Oneness. The Bhagavad Gita extols the virtue of moderation and balance in all our activities: 'To him who is temperate in eating and recreation, in his effort for work, and in sleep and in wakefulness, wins Yoga, balance, peace and joy' (shloka 6.17).

Our development philosophy also should follow the Middle Path. Our economic policy should be a healthy and judicious mix of free market and socialist ideology, the market and the state working in harmony and in tandem to deliver people-centric services. We should synthesize our ancient heritage and wisdom with modern scientific temper to create a prosperous society.

India's priceless heritage

Most of the problems that we face today in India, as well as in the global arena, are due to worship of a materialist ideology, which is devoid of human values. If India is to become a happy and prosperous society, our national policies should be focused on 'higher philosophy' of life. Our cultural and spiritual heritage offers solution to the problems with which the modern world is afflicted. According to Indian thought, the spirit pervades the whole universe and the material world is merely a manifestation of that spirit. The foundation of Indian culture rests on the ethico-spiritual view of life. Human beings have not only physical and biological dimensions but also psychological and spiritual dimensions. It is the spiritual dimension of human beings which gives rise to noble values such as truth, honesty, love, compassion, sharing, community spirit and service. On the other hand, materialistic values give rise to baser motives such as selfishness, greed and corruption. This results in deadening of social consciousness and insensitiveness to social evils such as poverty, injustice, exploitation, caste and gender inequalities and other evils.

Thus, in spite of physical well-being and high intellectual growth, mankind has become inwardly poor and unstable. Swami Gokulananda of Ramakrishna Mission laments, 'Never in history, the man been so rich in material possessions and technological achievements; but never has he felt such an inner poverty, a spiritual emptiness, as that he feels today.'[5] According to renowned historian Arnold Toynbee,

> [While] mankind has made phenomenon economic progress due to advances of technology which has vastly increased Man's wealth and power, but, the 'morality gap' between Man's physical power of doing evil and his spiritual capacity for coping with this power has yawned wide open as the mythical jaws of Hell. During the last 5,000 years, the 'widening gap' has caused mankind to inflict on itself grievous disaster.[6]

The core of Indian philosophy is *dharma* (righteous living), which embraces all aspects of human values such as truth, *ahimsa*, compassion, service before self and universal brotherhood. Our national policy should promote these values so that we produce young men and women of character and discipline, who have the courage to fight poverty, corruption, injustice and other evils with which the society is afflicted. Swami Vivekananda said that 'the national ideals of India are *tyag* (renunciation) and *sewa* (service). Intensify her in those channels, and the rest will take care of itself.'[7] Surveying ancient Indian culture, eminent lawyer N. A. Palkhivala observed that in the past, India had been a moral leader of the world and India's ancient wisdom is necessary not only for the rebirth of the Indian nation but also for the re-education of the human race. Ancient India was great because of its sense of values:

> Our old sages judged the greatness of a State not by the extent of its empire or the size of its wealth, but by the degree of righteousness and justice which marked the public administration and the private life of the citizens. Their timeless teachings were that man's true progress is to be judged by the moral and spiritual standards, and not by material and physical standards. Sacrifice was far more important than success; and renunciation was regarded as a crowning achievement. The citizens ranked in society, not according to wealth or power, but according to standard of learning, virtue and character which he had attained.[8]

Gurudev Rabindranath Tagore had expressed the vision of an ideal India in his famous poem,

Where the mind is without fear and the head is held high;
Where knowledge is free;
Where world is not broken into fragments into narrow domestic walls;
Where words come from the depth of truth;
Where tireless striving stretches its arms towards perfection;
Where the clear stream of reason has not lost its way into dreary desert sand of dead habits;
Where the mind is led forward by thee into ever widening thought and action-
Into that heaven of freedom, my Father, let my country awake.[9]

Today, the country needs a new awakening, for which we should reinstate our cultural and spiritual values in society, as well as in public policy, to create a happy, healthy and prosperous India.

Notes

1 *Invaluable Gems*, compiled by Balgopal, Thane: Sri Tara Mataji Trust, 1999, p. S3.
2 UNDP, *Human Development Report 2010*, New York: UNDP, 2010, pp. 11–24.
3 Ramdhari Singh Dinkar, *Sanskriti ke Char Adhyay* (*Four Volumes of Culture*), Allahabad: Lokbharti Prakashan, 2011, p. 678, in Hindi – translation by author.
4 Ibid., pp. 679–680.
5 Swami Gokulananda, *Goodbye to Negativity*, Kolkata: Advaita Ashram, 2014, p. 88.
6 Arnold Toynbee, *Mankind and Mother Earth*, London: Book Club Associates, 1976, pp. 591–592.
7 Swami Vivekananda, *His Call to Nation*, Calcutta: Advaita Ashram, 1969, p. 79.
8 N. A. Palkhivala, *India's Priceless Heritage*, Bombay: Bhartiya Vidya Bhawan, 1994, p. 38.
9 Rabindranath Tagore, *Collected Poems and Plays*, London: Macmillan, 1985; *Gitanjali*, No. XXXV, p. 16.

INDEX

For Product Safety Concerns and Information please contact our EU
representative GPSR@taylorandfrancis.com Taylor & Francis Verlag GmbH,
Kaufingerstraße 24, 80331 München, Germany

Printed and bound by CPI Group (UK) Ltd, Croydon, CR0 4YY
01/05/2025
01858426-0002